For the celebration of Mass
and the Liturgy of the Hours
during the liturgical year
2012/2013

VERITAS

The Liturgical Calendar for Ireland 2013
is an adaptation for use in the dioceses of Ireland
of the *Universal Norms for the Liturgical Year* and
the *General Roman Calendar*

Published 2012 by
Veritas Publications
7–8 Lower Abbey Street
Dublin 1
for the National Secretariat for Liturgy

Email publications@veritas.ie
Website www.veritas.ie

Edited by Patrick Jones

Copyright © Irish Episcopal Commission for Liturgy, 2012

ISBN 978 1 84730 398 1

Pastoral and homiletic notes
with ecclesiastical permission according to Canon 830:3
✠ Diarmuid Martin
Archbishop of Dublin

1 October 2012

Design and typesetting by Colette Dower, Veritas Publications
Cover image: *Ego sum Pastor Bonus* (I am the Good Shepherd)
mosaic in apse of the chapel of the Pontifical Irish College, Rome
by Fr Marko Ivan Rupnik SJ.
© Pontificio Collegio Irlandese, Via dei Santi Quattro, 1 – 00184 Roma

Printed in the Republic of Ireland by Hudson Killeen Ltd, Dublin

INTERNATIONAL EUCHARISTIC CONGRESS

The images on the front and back cover of this year's Liturgical Calendar are a reminder of the International Eucharistic Congress, held in Dublin, 10–17 June 2012.

In his message at the conclusion of the Congress, Pope Benedict XVI reminded us of its theme: 'The theme of the Congress "Communion with Christ and with One Another", leads us to reflect upon the Church as a mystery of fellowship with the Lord and with all the members of his body. From the earliest times the notion of *koinonia* or *communio* has been at the core of the Church's understanding of herself, her relationship to Christ her founder, and the sacraments she celebrates, above all the Eucharist. Through our Baptism, we are incorporated into Christ's death, reborn into the great family of the brothers and sisters of Jesus Christ; through Confirmation we receive the seal of the Holy Spirit; and by our sharing in the Eucharist, we come into communion with Christ and each other visibly here on earth. We also receive the pledge of eternal life to come.'

This understanding of the Church and its sacramental life resonates with the phrase of St Augustine, frequently heard and used at the Congress: Become what you receive.

With memories of the week that will last a lifetime, all who took part saw the Congress not as an end but a beginning. The Year of Faith, what it recalls and what it points to, marks that beginning.

THE YEAR OF FAITH

In his Apostolic Letter, *Porta Fidei* (11 October 2011), Pope Benedict XVI announced a Year of Faith, beginning on 11 October 2012, on the 50th anniversary of the opening of the Second Vatican Council, and concluding on 24 November 2013, the solemnity of Our Lord Jesus Christ, Universal King.

The Year of Faith is intended to contribute to a renewed conversion to the Lord Jesus, for our faith is an encounter with an 'event, a person, which gives life a new horizon and a decisive direction' (*Deus Caritas Est* 1). The Year of Faith is also intended to contribute to the rediscovery of faith, so that we may be credible and joy-filled witnesses to the Risen Lord in the world of today – capable of leading those many people who are seeking it to the 'door of faith'. This 'door' opens wide our gaze to Jesus Christ, present among us 'always, until the end of the age' (*Mt* 28:20). Pope Benedict, addressing the Pontifical Council for the Promotion of the New Evangelisation (25 October 2011), said that Jesus Christ shows us how 'the art of living' is learned 'in an intense relationship with him'. He has written: 'Through his love, Jesus Christ attracts to himself the people of every generation: in every age he convokes the Church, entrusting her with the proclamation of the Gospel by a mandate that is ever new. Today too, there is a need for stronger ecclesial commitment to new evangelisation in order to rediscover the joy of believing and the enthusiasm for communicating the faith' (*Porta Fidei* 11).

From the beginning of his pontificate, Pope Benedict XVI has insisted that this situation needs to be addressed. At that time he said: 'The Church as a whole and all her Pastors, like Christ, must set out to lead people out of the desert, towards the place of life, towards friendship with the Son of God, towards the One who gives us life, and life in abundance.' The Church feels the responsibility to devise new tools and new expressions to ensure that the word of faith, which has begotten the true life of God in us, be heard more and be better understood, even in the new deserts of this world.

The idea of renewing the Church's evangelising activity was also the inspiration of the Second Vatican Council as it is that of the XIII Ordinary General Assembly of the Synod of Bishops on 'the new evangelisation for the transmission of the Christian faith' (7–28 October 2012).

Pope Benedict writes, 'It seemed to me that timing the launch of the Year of Faith to coincide with the fiftieth anniversary of the opening of the Second Vatican Council would provide a good opportunity to help people understand that the texts bequeathed by the Council Fathers, in the words of Blessed John Paul II, "*have lost nothing of their value or brilliance.* They need to be read correctly, to be widely known and taken to heart as important and normative texts of the Magisterium, within the Church's Tradition ... I feel more than ever in duty bound to point to the Council as *the great grace bestowed on the Church in the twentieth century:* there we find a sure compass by which to take our bearings in the century now beginning" (*Novo Millennio Ineunte 57*)' (*Porta Fidei* 5).

The Year of Faith also marks the twentieth anniversary of the publication of the *Catechism of the Catholic Church*, promulgated by Pope John Paul II, with a view to illustrating for all the faithful the power and beauty of the faith. The *Catechism* is an authentic fruit of the Second Vatican Council, requested by the Extraordinary Synod of Bishops in 1985 as an instrument at the service of catechesis.

LITURGICAL CALENDAR 2012–2013

In this *Liturgical Calendar for 2012–2013* the general format is that the left-hand page or calendar page sets out the day to be observed in the celebration of Mass and the Liturgy of the Hours. Often on weekdays, this will be a combination of the season weekday or weekday in Ordinary Time with the commemoration of a saint. The right-hand page notes the readings for Mass.

The Mass texts for the National Proper are included in the sequence of the Proper of Saints in the new edition of the *Missal*. Short biographical notes for the National Proper are given on the monthly notes of this Liturgical Calendar, placed in sequence through the year. Many of the notes cite traditional material where historical data is lacking.

In the Lectionary, the Sunday readings are from Cycle C and the weekday readings are Cycle I.

There are five weeks of Ordinary Time from Monday after the Feast of the Baptism of the Lord (14 January 2013) until Tuesday, 12 February 2013, before the beginning of the season of Lent. After the season of Easter, Ordinary Time, begins Monday, 20 May 2013, with Week 7.

SOLEMNITY OF ST PATRICK 2013

The Fifth Sunday of Lent is 17 March 2013, and by an indult granted by the Holy See in 1974, the Mass of St Patrick may be celebrated. This concurrence of the solemnity and a Sunday of Lent has happened in 1974, 1985, 1991, 1996 and 2002. The rescript asks that some aspects of the Sunday celebration be retained and this is catered for through the use of the Sunday readings (Year C of the Lectionary, though Year A may be used as alternative readings). Reference to the great themes of Lent, such as conversion and baptism, for example, in the homily and Prayer of the Faithful, is also appropriate.

MOVABLE FEASTS OF THE LITURGICAL YEAR

	2012–2013	**2013–2014**
First Sunday of Advent	2 December 2012	1 December 2013
The Holy Family	30 December 2012	29 December 2013
The Baptism of Our Lord	13 January 2013	12 January 2014
Ash Wednesday	13 February 2013	5 March 2014
Easter Sunday	31 March 2013	20 April 2014
The Ascension of the Lord	12 May 2013	1 June 2014
Pentecost Sunday	19 May 2013	8 June 2014
The Holy Trinity	26 May 2013	15 June 2014
The Body and Blood of Christ	2 June 2013	22 June 2014
The Sacred Heart of Jesus	7 June 2013	27 June 2014
Christ the King	24 November 2013	23 November 2014

HOLYDAYS OF OBLIGATION IN IRELAND
(Noted in the Calendar by ✠)

	2012–2013	**2013–2014**
	All Sundays of the Year	All Sundays of the Year
The Immaculate Conception	Sat, 8 December 2012	*
The Nativity of the Lord	Tues, 25 December 2012	Wed, 25 December 2014
The Epiphany of the Lord	Sun, 6 January 2013	Mon, 6 January 2014
St Patrick	Sun, 17 March 2013	Mon, 17 March 2014
The Assumption of the BVM	Thurs, 15 August 2013	Fri, 15 August 2014
All Saints	Fri, 1 November 2013	Sat, 1 November 2014

*Transferred to Monday, 9 December 2013, not holyday of obligation

Future Dates	**Ash Wednesday**	**Easter Sunday**	**Pentecost**
2014	5 March	20 April	8 June
2015	18 February	5 April	24 May
2016	10 February	27 March	15 May
2017	1 March	16 April	4 June
2018	14 February	1 April	20 May
2019	6 March	21 April	9 June
2020	26 February	12 April	31 May
2021	17 February	4 April	23 May
2022	2 March	17 April	5 June
2023	22 February	9 April	28 May
2024	14 February	31 March	19 May
2025	5 March	20 April	8 June

ABBREVIATIONS

RM Roman Missal (third edition, 2011)
Lect Lectionary (second edition, 1981)
GIRM General Instruction of the Roman Missal
GILH General Instruction of the Liturgy of the Hours
ILect Introduction to the Lectionary
UNLYC Universal Norms for the Liturgical Year and the Calendar

✠ indicates Sundays and holydays of obligation.

Excerpts from the *Ceremonial of Bishops*, by permission of ICEL © 1989.
Catechism of the Catholic Church (= *CCC*) English translation for Ireland copyright © 1994 Veritas Publications – Libreria Editrice Vaticana. All rights reserved. Veritas also publish the Irish language version, *Caithiciosma na hEaslaise Caitlicí*.

LITURGICAL NOTES

LITURGICAL NOTE 1
Table of Liturgical Days
according to their order of preference

I

1. The Paschal Triduum of the Passion and Resurrection of the Lord.
2. The Nativity of the Lord, the Epiphany, the Ascension and Pentecost.
   Sundays of Advent, Lent and Easter.
   Ash Wednesday.
   Weekdays of Holy Week from Monday up to and including Thursday.
   Days within the Octave of Easter.
3. Solemnities inscribed in the General Calendar, whether of the Lord, of the Blessed Virgin Mary or of Saints.
   The Commemoration of All the Faithful Departed.
4. Proper Solemnities, namely:
   a) The Solemnity of the principal Patron of the place, city or state
   b) The Solemnity of the dedication and of the anniversary of the dedication of one's own church
   c) The Solemnity of the Title of one's own church
   d) The Solemnity either of the Title or of the Founder or of the principal Patron of an Order or Congregation.

II

5. Feasts of the Lord inscribed in the General Calendar.
6. Sundays of Christmas Time and the Sundays in Ordinary Time.
7. Feasts of the Blessed Virgin Mary and of the Saints in the General Calendar.
8. Proper Feasts, namely:
   a) The Feast of the principal Patron of the diocese
   b) The Feast of the anniversary of the dedication of the cathedral church
   c) The Feast of the principal Patron of a region or province, or a country, or of a wider territory
   d) The Feast of the Title, Founder, or principal Patron of an Order or Congregation and of a religious province, without prejudice to the prescriptions given under no. 4
   e) Other Feasts proper to an individual church
   f) Other Feasts inscribed in the Calendar of each diocese or Order or Congregation.
9. Weekdays of Advent from 17 December up to and including 24 December.
   Days within the Octave of Christmas.
   Weekdays of Lent.

III

10. Obligatory Memorials in the General Calendar.
11. Proper Obligatory Memorials, namely:
    a) The Memorial of a secondary Patron of the place, diocese, region, or religious province
    b) Other Obligatory Memorials inscribed in the Calendar of each diocese, or Order or Congregation.
12. Optional Memorials, which, however, may be celebrated, in the special manner described in the *General Instruction of the Roman Missal* and of the Liturgy of the Hours, even on the days listed in no. 9.
    In the same manner Obligatory Memorials may be celebrated as Optional Memorials if they happen to fall on Lenten weekdays.

13. Weekdays of Advent up to and including 16 December.
    Weekdays of Christmas Time from 2 January until the Saturday after the Epiphany.
    Weekdays of the Easter Time from Monday after the Octave of Easter up to and including the Saturday before Pentecost.
    Weekdays in Ordinary Time.

LITURGICAL NOTE 2
The Liturgical Day

UNLYC 3–14
The Liturgical Day in General
3. Each and every day is sanctified by the liturgical celebrations of the People of God, especially by the Eucharistic Sacrifice and the Divine Office.
   The liturgical day runs from midnight to midnight. However, the celebration of Sunday and of Solemnities begins already on the evening of the previous day.

Sunday
4. On the first day of each week, which is known as the Day of the Lord or the Lord's Day, the Church, by an apostolic tradition that draws its origin from the very day of the Resurrection of Christ, celebrates the Paschal Mystery. Hence, Sunday must be considered the primordial feast day.
5. Because of its special importance, the celebration of Sunday gives way only to Solemnities and Feasts of the Lord; indeed, the Sundays of Advent, Lent and Easter have precedence over all Feasts of the Lord and over all Solemnities. In fact, Solemnities occurring on these Sundays are transferred to the following Monday unless they occur on Palm Sunday or on Sunday of the Lord's Resurrection.

Solemnities, Feasts and Memorials
8. In the cycle of the year, as she celebrates the mystery of Christ, the Church also venerates with a particular love the Blessed Mother of God, Mary, and proposes to the devotion of the faithful the Memorials of the Martyrs and other Saints.
9. The Saints who have universal importance are celebrated in an obligatory way throughout the whole Church; other Saints are either inscribed in the calendar, but for optional celebration, or are left to be honoured by a particular Church, or nation, or religious family.
10. Celebrations, according to the importance assigned to them, are hence distinguished one from another and termed: Solemnity, Feast, Memorial.
11. *Solemnities* are counted among the most important days, whose celebration begins with First Vespers (Evening Prayer I) on the preceding day. Some Solemnities are also endowed with their own Vigil Mass, which is to be used on the evening of the preceding day, if an evening Mass is celebrated.
12. The celebration of the two greatest Solemnities, Easter and the Nativity, is extended over eight days. Each Octave is governed by its own rules.
13. *Feasts* are celebrated within the limits of the natural day; accordingly they have no First Vespers (Evening Prayer I), except in the case of Feasts of the Lord that fall on a Sunday in Ordinary Time or in Christmas Time and which replace the Sunday Office.
14. *Memorials* are either obligatory or optional; their observance is integrated into the celebration of the occurring weekday in accordance with the norms set forth in the *General Instruction of the Roman Missal* and of the Liturgy of the Hours.

Obligatory Memorials which fall on weekdays of Lent may only be celebrated as Optional Memorials.

If several Optional Memorials are inscribed in the Calendar on the same day, only one may be celebrated, the others being omitted.
15. On *Saturdays* in Ordinary Time when no Obligatory Memorial occurs, an Optional Memorial of the Blessed Virgin Mary may be celebrated.
16. The days of the week that follow Sunday are called *weekdays*; however, they are celebrated differently according to the importance of each.

LITURGICAL NOTE 3
The Choice of the Mass and its Parts

GIRM

352. The pastoral effectiveness of a celebration will be greatly increased if the texts of the readings, the prayers and the liturgical chants correspond as aptly as possible to the needs, the preparation and the culture of the participants. This will be achieved by appropriate use of the many possibilities of choice described below.

Hence in arranging the celebration of Mass, the Priest should be attentive rather to the common spiritual good of the People of God than to his own inclinations. He should also remember that choices of this kind are to be made in harmony with those who exercise some part in the celebration, including the faithful, as regards the parts that more directly pertain to them.

Since, indeed, many possibilities are provided for choosing the different parts of the Mass, it is necessary for the Deacon, the readers, the psalmist, the cantor, the commentator and the choir to know properly before the celebration the texts that concern each and that are to be used, and it is necessary that nothing be in any sense improvised. For harmonious ordering and carrying out of the rites will greatly help in disposing the faithful for participation in the Eucharist.

I. The Choice of Mass

353. On Solemnities, the Priest is obliged to follow the Calendar of the church where he is celebrating.
354. On Sundays, on the weekdays during Advent, Christmas Time, Lent, and Easter Time, on Feasts, and on Obligatory Memorials:
    a) If Mass is celebrated with the people, the Priest should follow the Calendar of the church where he is celebrating
    b) If Mass is celebrated with the participation of one minister only, the Priest may choose either the Calendar of the church or his proper Calendar.
355. On Optional Memorials,
    a) On the weekdays of Advent from 17 December to 24 December, on days within the Octave of the Nativity of the Lord, and on the weekdays of Lent, except Ash Wednesday and during Holy Week, the Mass texts for the current liturgical day are used; but the Collect may be taken from a Memorial which happens to be inscribed in the General Calendar for that day, except on Ash Wednesday and during Holy Week. On weekdays of Easter Time, Memorials of Saints may rightly be celebrated in full.
    b) On weekdays of Advent before 17 December, on weekdays of Christmas Time from 2 January, and on weekdays of Easter Time, one of the following may be chosen: either the Mass of the weekday, or the Mass of the Saint or of one of the Saints whose Memorial is observed, or the Mass of any Saint inscribed in the Martyrology for that day.
    c) On weekdays in Ordinary Time, there may be chosen either the Mass of the weekday, or the Mass of an Optional Memorial which happens to

occur on that day, or the Mass of any Saint inscribed in the Martyrology for that day, or a Mass for Various Needs, or a Votive Mass.

If he celebrates with the people, the Priest will take care not to omit too frequently and without sufficient reason the readings assigned each day in the Lectionary to the weekdays, for the Church desires that a richer portion at the table of God's Word should be spread before the people (cf. *SC* 51).

For the same reason he should choose Masses for the Dead in moderation, for every Mass is offered for both the living and the dead, and there is a commemoration of the dead in the Eucharistic Prayer.

Where, however, the Optional Memorials of the Blessed Virgin Mary or of the Saints are dear to the faithful, the legitimate devotion of the latter should be satisfied.

Moreover, as regards the option of choosing between a Memorial inscribed in the General Calendar and one inserted in a diocesan or religious Calendar, preference should be given, all else being equal and in keeping with tradition, to the Memorial in the particular Calendar.

II. The Choice of Texts for the Mass

356. In choosing texts for the different parts of the Mass, whether for the time of the year or for Saints, the norms that follow should be observed.

The Readings

357. Sundays and Solemnities have assigned to them three readings, that is, from a Prophet, an Apostle and a Gospel, by which the Christian people are instructed in the continuity of the work of salvation according to God's wonderful design. These readings should be followed strictly. In Easter Time, according to the tradition of the Church, instead of being from the Old Testament, the reading is taken from the Acts of the Apostles.

For Feasts, two readings are assigned. If, however, according to the norms a Feast is raised to the rank of a Solemnity, a third reading is added, and this is taken from the Common.

For Memorials of Saints, unless proper readings are given, the readings assigned for the weekday are normally used. In certain cases, particularised readings are provided, that is to say, readings which highlight some particular aspect of the spiritual life or activity of the Saint. The use of such readings is not to be insisted upon, unless a pastoral reason truly suggests it.

358. In the Lectionary for weekdays, readings are provided for each day of every week throughout the entire course of the year; hence, these readings will in general be used on the days to which they are assigned, unless there occurs a Solemnity, a Feast, or Memorial that has its own New Testament readings, that is to say, readings in which mention is made of the Saint being celebrated.

Should, however, the continuous reading during the week from time to time be interrupted, on account of some Solemnity or Feast, or some particular celebration, then the Priest shall be permitted, bearing in mind the scheme of readings for the entire week, either to combine parts omitted with other readings or to decide which readings are to be given preference over others.

In Masses for special groups, the Priest shall be allowed to choose texts more particularly suited to the particular celebration, provided they are taken from the texts of an approved Lectionary.

359. In addition, in the Lectionary a special selection of texts from Sacred Scripture is given for Ritual Masses into which certain Sacraments or Sacramentals are incorporated, or for Masses that are celebrated for certain needs.

Sets of readings of this kind have been so prescribed so that through a more apt hearing of the Word of God the faithful may be led to a fuller understanding of the mystery in which they are participating, and may be educated to a more ardent love of the Word of God.

Therefore, the texts proclaimed in the celebration are to be chosen keeping in mind both an appropriate pastoral reason and the options allowed in this matter.

360. At times, a longer and shorter form of the same text is given. In choosing between these two forms, a pastoral criterion should be kept in mind. On such an occasion, attention should be paid to the capacity of the faithful to listen with fruit to a reading of greater or lesser length, and to their capacity to hear a more complete text, which is then explained in the homily (*GILH* 80).

361. When a possibility is given of choosing between one or other text laid down, or suggested as optional, attention shall be paid to the good of participants, whether, that is to say, it is a matter of using an easier text or one more appropriate for a given gathering, or of repeating or setting aside a text that is assigned as proper to some particular celebration while being optional for another (*GILH* 81), just as pastoral advantage may suggest.

Such a situation may arise either when the same text would have to be read again within a few days, as, for example, on a Sunday and on a subsequent weekday, or when it is feared that a certain text might give rise to some difficulties for a particular group of the Christian faithful. However, care should be taken that, when choosing scriptural passages, parts of Sacred Scripture are not permanently excluded.

362. In addition to the options noted above for choosing certain more suitable texts, the Conference of Bishops has the faculty, in particular circumstances, to indicate some adaptations as regards readings, provided that the texts are chosen from a duly approved Lectionary.

The Orations

363. In any Mass the orations proper to that Mass are used, unless otherwise noted.

On Memorials of Saints, the proper Collect is said or, if this is lacking, one from an appropriate Common. As to the Prayer over the Offerings and the Prayer after Communion, unless these are proper, they may be taken either from the Common or from the weekday of the current time of year.

On the weekdays in Ordinary Time, however, besides the orations from the previous Sunday, orations from another Sunday in Ordinary Time may be used, or one of the Prayers for Various Needs provided in the *Missal*. However, it shall always be permissible to use from these Masses the Collect alone.

In this way a richer collection of texts is provided, by which the prayer life of the faithful is more abundantly nourished.

However, during the more important times of the year, provision has already been made for this by means of the orations proper to these times of the year that exist for each weekday in the *Missal*.

LITURGICAL NOTE 4
The Eucharistic Prayers of the *Roman Missal*

Eucharistic Prayers I–IV

GIRM

364. The numerous Prefaces with which the *Roman Missal* is endowed have as their purpose to bring out more fully the motives for thanksgiving within the Eucharistic Prayer and to set out more clearly the different facets of the mystery of salvation.

365. The choice between the Eucharistic Prayers found in the Order of Mass is suitably guided by the following norms:

a) Eucharistic Prayer I, or the Roman Canon, which may always be used, is especially suited for use on days to which a proper text for the *Communicantes (In communion with those whose memory we venerate)* is assigned or in Masses endowed with a proper form of the *Hanc igitur (Therefore, Lord, we pray)* and also in the celebrations of the Apostles and of the Saints mentioned in the Prayer itself; likewise it is especially suited for use on Sundays, unless for pastoral reasons Eucharistic Prayer III is preferred;

b) Eucharistic Prayer II, on account of its particular features, is more appropriately used on weekdays or in special circumstances. Although it is provided with its own Preface, it may also be used with other Prefaces, especially those that sum up the mystery of salvation, for example, the Common Prefaces. When Mass is celebrated for a particular deceased person, the special formula given may be used at the proper point, namely, before the part *Remember also our brothers and sisters;*

c) Eucharistic Prayer III may be said with any Preface. Its use should be preferred on Sundays and festive days. If, however, this Eucharistic Prayer is used in Masses for the Dead, the special formula for a deceased person may be used, to be included at the proper place, namely after the words: *in your compassion, O merciful Father, gather to yourself all your children scattered throughout the earth;*

d) Eucharistic Prayer IV has an invariable Preface and gives a fuller summary of salvation history. It may be used when a Mass has no Preface of its own and on Sundays in Ordinary Time. On account of its structure, no special formula for a deceased person may be inserted into this prayer.

Eucharistic Prayers for Reconciliation I–II

RM p. 641

The Eucharistic Prayers for Reconciliation may be used in Masses in which the mystery of reconciliation is conveyed to the faithful in a special way, as, for example, in the Masses for Promoting Harmony, For Reconciliation, For the Preservation of Peace and Justice, In Time of War or Civil Disturbance, For the Forgiveness of Sins, For Charity, of the Mystery of the Holy Cross, of the Most Holy Eucharist, of the Most Precious Blood of our Lord Jesus Christ, as well as in Masses during Lent. Although these Eucharistic Prayers have been provided with a proper Preface, they may also be used with other Prefaces that refer to penance and conversion, as, for example, the Prefaces of Lent.

Eucharistic Prayer for use in Masses for Various Needs (Forms I–IV)

RM pp. 657–84

I – The Church on the Path of Unity … is appropriately used with Mass formularies such as, For the Church, For the Pope, For the Bishop, For the Election of a Pope or a Bishop, For a Council or Synod, For Priests, For the Priest Himself, For Ministers of the Church, and For a Spiritual or Pastoral Gathering.

II – God Guides His Church along the Way of Salvation … is appropriately used with Mass formularies such as, For the Church, For Vocations to Holy Orders, For the Laity, For the Family, For Religious, For Vocations to Religious Life, For Charity, For Relatives and Friends, and For Giving Thanks to God.

III – Jesus, the Way to the Father … is appropriately used with Mass formularies such as, For the Evangelisation of Peoples, For Persecuted Christians, For the Nation or State, For Those in Public Office, For a Governing Assembly, At the Beginning of the Civil Year, and For the Progress of Peoples.

IV – Jesus, Who Went about Doing Good … is appropriately used with Mass formularies such as, For Refugees and Exiles, In Time of Famine or For Those Suffering Hunger, For Our Oppressors, For Those Held in Captivity, For Those in Prison, For the Sick, For the Dying, For the Grace of a Happy Death, and In Any Need.

LITURGICAL NOTE 5
Anticipating the Sunday and holyday Masses on the previous evening

The obligation of assisting at Mass is satisfied wherever Mass is celebrated in a Catholic rite, either on a holyday itself or on the evening of the previous day (*Can.* 1248).

In Ireland this First Mass of a Sunday or holyday must not be celebrated before 6 p.m. No other Saturday Masses are permitted in the evening. Wedding Masses particularly should be held early in the afternoon or in the morning.

The Mass celebrated is that of the Obligation, and the homily and universal prayer or prayer of the faithful are not to be omitted. The general principle is to be followed in choosing the Mass texts of giving precedence to the celebration which is of obligation, regardless of the liturgical grade of the two occurring celebrations (*Notitiae* 20 (1984) 603).

LITURGICAL NOTE 6
Holydays of Obligation

At the October 1996 meeting of the Episcopal Conference, the bishops announced the removal of the obligation on the feasts of the Ascension of the Lord and the Most Holy Body and Blood of Christ (Corpus Christi), and the consequent transfer of these two feasts to the following Sundays in accordance with the universal liturgical law. This decision has been confirmed by the Congregation for Divine Worship (Prot. 1355/96, 9 October 1996).

LITURGICAL NOTE 7
Explanation of some rubrics

Funeral Mass. In this liturgical note, the term Funeral Mass means a Mass when the prayer texts and biblical readings are from Masses for the Dead.

No other celebrations, even/except funeral Masses, are permitted today. This rubric respects the order of precedence in the table of liturgical days (Lit. Note 1) and in the table of rules concerning Ritual and Votive Masses, Masses for Various Needs and Occasions and Masses for the Dead (see Lit. Note 12). The celebration of the day where this rubric appears uses the readings and prayer texts of the day. Other readings and prayer texts, except when Funeral Masses are permitted, are not used. Thus, at a Marriage celebrated during the Octave of Easter, the readings and prayers are taken from those of the day.

No Masses for the dead, except funeral Masses, are permitted today. This rubric follows the table of rules for Votive Masses, in this case, the daily Mass for the Dead (see Lit. Note 12). Thus, at a funeral on a Feast or Memorial, the texts used may be those for the dead.

No Masses for the dead, except funeral Masses and first anniversary, are permitted today. This rubric applies to the days after Christmas.

Memorial may be made of St N. This rubric appears in the last week of Advent, during the Octave of Christmas and during Lent indicating that the Mass of the day is celebrated but the Collect may be taken from the memorial (*GIRM* 355a).

HOURS Proper of the memorial. Some memorials have proper antiphons with psalms of Sunday I at Morning Prayer and psalms of the Commons at Evening Prayer.

MASS of the memorial. The Collect and other prayers that are proper to the memorial or taken from the Commons are used. The readings are of the weekday, except when proper readings are given (or accommodated readings are used. See Lit. Note 15).

Preface: Common or of the Saint(s). This note appears on the Mass of a memorial and indicates that the Preface may be from the Common Prefaces I–VI (*RM* pp. 478–89) or Saints I–II, Martyrs I–II, Pastors, Virgins & Religious (*RM* pp. 466–77) as appropriate.

LITURGICAL NOTE 8
Nuptial Mass

When marriage is celebrated within the Mass, the Mass for the celebration of Marriage, *RM* pp. 1082–100, is said, and white vestments are used. On Sundays of Advent, Lent and Easter, on holydays of obligation, where the celebration of Marriage is permitted, however, the Mass of the day is said, but the nuptial blessing is given, and the special final blessing may be used. On the Sundays of the Christmas season and on Sundays in Ordinary Time, where the celebration of Marriage is permitted, in Masses which are not parish Masses, the Ritual Mass may be said without change.

LITURGICAL NOTE 9
Order of Christian Funerals

The *Order of Christian Funerals* (© Irish Conference of Bishops 1991) has been the approved text in the dioceses of Ireland since Easter 1992. The pastoral notes give a comprehensive guide to the carrying out of the rites by which the Church manifests its care for the dead, and takes into consideration the spiritual and psychological needs of the family and friends of the deceased.
The responsibility for the ministry of consolation rests with the believing community. Each Christian shares in this ministry according to the various gifts and offices in the Church.
Among the priest's responsibilities are: (1) to be at the side of the sick and dying; (2) to impart catechesis on the meaning of Christian death; (3) to comfort the family of the deceased, to sustain them amid the anguish of their grief, and to prepare them for a funeral celebration that has meaning for them; (4) to fit the liturgy for the dead into the total setting of the liturgical life of the parish and his own pastoral ministry.
The *Order of Christian Funerals* makes provision for the minister, in consultation with the family, to choose those rites and texts that are most suitable to the situation; those that most closely apply to the needs of the mourners, the circumstances of death, and the customs of the local Christian community.
The celebration of the funeral liturgy is especially entrusted to parish priests. When no priest is available, deacons preside at funeral rites, except for the Mass. When there is no priest or deacon, it is recommended that lay persons carry out the stations at the home and cemetery and all vigils for the dead. The vigil services indeed should usually be entrusted to lay people who have been suitably prepared for this service.
Funeral Rites and Readings (Veritas) is a helpful aid for all who wish to assist at the funeral rites. The readings in Irish are available in *Léachtaí do Dheasghnátha na Marbh* (An Sagart).
A brief homily based on the readings should always be given at the funeral liturgy, but never any kind of eulogy.

Masses for the Dead

1. The Funeral Mass has first place among the Masses for the Dead and may be celebrated on any day except solemnities that are days of obligation, Holy Thursday, the Easter Triduum, and the Sundays of Lent and Easter. It may be celebrated during the Octaves of Christmas and Easter. On Holy Thursday, Good

Friday and Holy Saturday a Celebration of the Word takes place with the Rite of Final Commendation and Farewell, but Holy Communion may not be distributed.
2. On the occasion of the news of a death, final burial, or the first anniversary, Mass for the Dead may be celebrated even on days within the Christmas Octave, on obligatory memorials, and on weekdays, except Ash Wednesday and during Holy Week.
3. Daily Masses for the Dead may be celebrated on weekdays in Ordinary Time even when there is an optional memorial or the office of the weekday is used, provided such Masses are actually offered for the dead.
4. Masses for the Dead are in the Missal, *RM* pp. 1277–1318, with Prefaces, *RM* pp. 490–9. Funeral Masses are *RM* pp. 1277–86.

LITURGICAL NOTE 10
Saturday Mass of the Blessed Virgin Mary

On Saturdays in Ordinary Time when no obligatory memorial is to be celebrated, an optional memorial of Mary may be observed. This is celebrated as a memorial. Green or white vestments may be worn.

The texts may be chosen from the *Roman Missal* (*RM* pp. 954–66, pp. 1252–8) or the *Collection of Masses of the Blessed Virgin Mary* (Veritas, 1987). Irish language texts are available in *An Leabhar Aifrinn* and *Díolaim d'Aifrinn na Maighdine Beannaithe Muire* (An Sagart, 2000).

The ferial readings are to be preferred, but common texts may be selected from the *Lectionary* or the lectionary from the *Collection of Masses of the Blessed Virgin Mary*, *An Leiceanáir* or *Díolaim d'Aifrinn na Maighdine Beannaithe Muire* (see also Lit. Note 15). A homily should be given and general intercessions prepared. This Mass is permitted only in Ordinary Time, and never during the seasons of Advent, Christmas, Lent or Easter.

LITURGICAL NOTE 11
Diocesan celebrations

a) Proper celebration of the principal patron
The feast of the principal patron of the diocese does not have precedence over any Sunday.

However, for pastoral reasons, the feast of the principal patron of the diocese may be celebrated as a solemnity. As such, it would then have precedence over other feasts in the general calendar, and over Sundays in Ordinary Time. When it falls on other Sundays or solemnities it should be transferred to the closest day which is not a day listed in Nos. 1–8 in the table of precedence (Lit. Note 1).

The *General Instruction of the Roman Missal*, 374, also provides for the situation: When a serious need or pastoral advantage is present, at the direction of the diocesan Bishop or with his permission, an appropriate Mass may be celebrated on any day except solemnities, the Sundays of Advent, Lent and the Easter Season, Ash Wednesday, Holy Week. The Octave of Easter and the Commemoration of All the Faithful Departed (see also *Instructio Calendaria particularia*, II. 9, 24 June 1970).

b) Celebration of the anniversary of the dedication of the cathedral
In order that the importance and dignity of the local church may stand out with greater clarity, the anniversary of the dedication of its cathedral is to be celebrated, with the rank of a solemnity in the cathedral itself, and with the rank of a feast in the other churches of the diocese, on the date on which the dedication recurs.

It is desirable that the faithful of the entire diocese come together on the day of the celebration to celebrate the Eucharist with the bishop.

If the date is always impeded, the celebration is assigned to the nearest date open (see *Notitiae*, 8:103 [1972]).

The dedication anniversary in the cathedral itself ranks as a solemnity and thus takes precedence over Sundays in Ordinary Time and in the Christmas season. When it falls on other Sundays or solemnities it should be transferred to the closest day which is not a day listed in Nos. 1–8 in the table of precedence (*Lit. Note* 1).

But the celebration throughout the diocese ranks as a feast, proper to the diocese, and therefore does not have precedence over Sundays in Ordinary Time and in the Christmas season. The bishop may, however, use the power granted him in *GIRM* 374 noted above.

LITURGICAL NOTE 12
Ritual and Votive Masses, Masses for Various Needs and Occasions, Masses for the Dead: A Table of the Rules

- V1 = Ritual Masses (*GIRM* 372): Masses at the direction of the local ordinary or with his permission when a serious need or pastoral advantage is present (*GIRM* 374)
- V2 = Masses at the discretion of the rector of the church or the celebrant when some genuine need or pastoral advantage requires it (*GIRM* 376)
- V3 = Masses for various needs and votive Masses in accord with the piety of the faithful and chosen by the celebrant (*GIRM* 373)
- D1 = Funeral Masses (*GIRM* 380)
- D2 = Masses on learning of a death, on final burial, and first anniversary (*GIRM* 381)
- D3 = Daily Masses applied for the dead. When D1 and D2 are not permitted, so also are D3 (*GIRM* 381)
- + = Permitted
- − = Not permitted

1.	Solemnities that are holydays of obligation	V1−	
		D1−	
2.	Sundays of Advent, Lent and Easter	V1−	
		D1−	
3.	Holy Thursday, Paschal Triduum	V1−	
		D1−	
4.	Solemnities other than holydays of obligation, All Souls' Day	V1−	
		D1+	
5.	Ash Wednesday, weekdays of Holy Week	V1−	
		D1+	
6.	Days within the Easter Octave	V1−	
		D1+	
7.	Sundays of Christmas and Sundays of Ordinary Time	V1+	V2−
		D1+	D2−

8.	Feasts	V1+	V2–	
		D1+	D2–	
9.	Weekdays 17–24 December	V1+	V2–	
		D1+	D2+	D3–
10.	Weekdays within the Octave of Christmas	V1+	V2–	
		D1+	D2+	D3–
11.	Weekdays of Lent	V1+	V2–	
		D1+	D2+	D3–
12.	Obligatory Memorials	V1+	V2–	V3–
		D1+	D2+	D3–
13.	Weekdays of Advent until 16 December	V1+	V2+	V3–
		D1+	D2+	D3–
14.	Weekdays of Christmas from 2 January	V1+	V2+	V3–
		D1+	D2+	D3–
15.	Weekdays of Easter Time	V1+	V2+	V3–
		D1+	D2+	D3–
16.	Weekdays in Ordinary Time	V1+	V2+	V3+
		D1+	D2+	D3+

LITURGICAL NOTE 13
Lectionary Year C – Year of Luke

Luke's Gospel represents Jesus' journey from Galilee to Jerusalem – a journey which is completed in the Acts of the Apostles by the journey of the Church from Jerusalem 'to the end of the earth'. The Lectionary in the Year of Luke represents faithfully his 'Travel Narrative' (chapters 9–19) – Jesus' journey to death, to resurrection and his return to the Father (see Sundays 13–31). Luke's vision of the journey is not geographical or chronological. Rather it is seen as a journey for the whole Church and for the individual Christian, a journey towards suffering and glory. Each Gospel passage should mean a great deal more to a preacher and reader when it is seen in the context of the whole programme of readings for Year C.

Unit I	The figure of Jesus the Messiah	Sundays 1–2
Unit II	Luke's programme for Jesus' ministry	Sundays 3–4
Unit III	The Galilean Ministry	Sundays 5–12
Unit IV	The first part of the 'Travel Narrative': the qualities Jesus demands of those who follow him	Sundays 13–23
Unit V	The 'Gospel within the Gospel': the message of pardon and reconciliation the parables of God's mercy	Sunday 24
Unit VI	The second part of the 'Travel Narrative': the obstacles facing those who follow Jesus	Sundays 25–31
Unit VII	The ministry in Jerusalem	Sundays 32–33
Unit VIII	Christ the King: reconciliation	Sunday 34

(See *Introduction to the Lectionary*, vol. I, pp. lii-liii.)

LITURGICAL NOTE 14
Certain readings

In response to a request of the Irish Episcopal Conference, the Congregation for Divine Worship and the Discipline of the Sacraments (Prot. N.2410/93/L) has given permission (23 March 1994) for the inclusion of two alternative readings of Scripture in the *Lectionary*:
i. *Colossians* 3:12-17 as an alternative reading to *Colossians* 3:12-21. This occurs on the Feast of the Holy Family, Year A and in the Wedding Lectionary.
ii *Ephesians* 5:25-33 as an alternative reading to *Ephesians* 5:21-33. This occurs on the 21st Sunday in Ordinary Time, Year B, on Tuesday of the 30th Week in Ordinary Time, Year 2 and in the Wedding Lectionary.

LITURGICAL NOTE 15
Use of the Lectionary on celebration of saints

Three readings are assigned for solemnities. Feasts and memorials of saints have only two readings: the first can be chosen from either the Old Testament or from an apostle; the second is from the gospels. Following the Church's traditional practice, however, the first reading during the Easter season is to be taken from an apostle, the second, as far as possible, from the Gospel of St John (*ILect*, 83-4).
Proper readings: when they exist, biblical passages about the saint are given, and these must take the place of the weekday readings even on memorials. These are clearly noted in the *Lectionary* on the day.
Accommodated readings: passages from the Commons are suggested to bring out some particular aspect of a saint's life or apostolate; use of such does not seem binding, except for compelling pastoral reasons. The first concern of a priest celebrating with a congregation is the spiritual benefit of the faithful and he will be careful not to impose his personal preference on them. Above all he will make sure not to omit too often or needlessly the readings assigned for each day in the weekday Lectionary: the Church's desire is to provide the faithful with a richer share of the table of God's word (*ILect*, 83).

LITURGICAL NOTE 16
The celebration of the Divine Office

Sundays (*GILH* 204-7)
a) Everything is done as in the Ordinary, in the Psalter and in the Proper, according to the varying seasons.
b) Both First Evening Prayer and Second Evening Prayer are said.
c) At the Office of readings, after the second reading and responsory, the *Te Deum* is said, except in Lent.

Solemnities (*GILH* 225-30)
a) At First Evening Prayer everything is taken from the Proper or the Common.
b) Night Prayer following First Evening Prayer is the First Night Prayer of Sunday.
c) At the Office of Readings, everything is taken from the Proper or the Common and the *Te Deum* is said.
d) At Morning Prayer everything is taken from the Proper or the Common, using the psalms of Sunday Week 1.
e) At the Day Hour: (1) the hymn is taken from the Ordinary; (2) the antiphons, short reading, versicle and response and the prayer are taken from the Proper or the Common; (3) the psalms: if particular psalms are given they are said. If no particular psalms are given for a solemnity which occurs on a Sunday, the psalms are those of Sunday Week 1. In all other cases, the psalms are the complementary psalms.
f) At Second Evening Prayer everything is taken form the Proper or the Common.
g) Night Prayer following Second Evening Prayer is the Second Night Prayer of Sunday.

Feasts (*GILH* 231–3)
a) First Evening Prayer is said only on Feasts of the Lord which fall on a Sunday.
b) At the Office of Readings, everything is taken from the Proper or the Common and the *Te Deum* is said.
c) At Morning Prayer everything is taken from the Proper or the Common, using the psalms of Sunday Week 1.
d) At the Day Hour: (1) the hymn is taken from the Ordinary; (2) the short reading, versicle and response and the prayer are taken from the Proper or the Common; (3) the antiphons (unless there are proper ones) and psalms are taken from the current day of the week.
e) At Second Evening Prayer everything is taken from the Proper or the Common.
f) Night Prayer is that of the particular day of the week.

Memorials (*GILH* 220, 234–6)
a) At Morning Prayer, Evening Prayer and the Office of Readings: (1) the psalms and their antiphons are those of the weekday. (If there are proper antiphons for Morning Prayer, they are used with the psalms of Sunday Week 1; if there are proper antiphons for Evening Prayer, they are used with the psalms from the Common); (2) hymns, short readings with their versicle and response, the *Benedictus* and *Magnificat* antiphons and intercessions – if there are proper texts, these are used, otherwise they may be from the Common or the particular weekday; (3) the prayer is that of the memorial.
b) At the Office of Readings, the biblical reading is from the present season, the second reading is of the saint or in the absence of a proper reading for the saint, the reading is taken from the weekday.
c) The Day Hour and Night Prayer is that of the weekday.

Weekdays
a) Everything is taken from the Ordinary, from the Psalter and from the Proper, according to the season.
b) The prayer at the Office of Readings is taken from the Proper, at other Hours in Ordinary Time from the Psalter, and in the seasons from the Proper.

LITURGICAL NOTE 17
On the reception of Holy Communion

Can. 917 One who has received the blessed Eucharist may receive it again on the same day only within a eucharistic celebration in which that person participates, without prejudice to the provision of *Can.* 921. 2.

Can. 921.1. Christ's faithful who are in danger of death, from whatever cause, are to be strengthened by Holy Communion as Viaticum.

Can. 921.2. Even if they have already received Holy Communion that same day, it is nevertheless strongly suggested that in danger of death they should communicate again.

Can. 921.3. While the danger of death persists, it is recommended that Holy Communion be administered a number of times, but on separate days.

Holy Communion under both kinds

'Holy Communion has a fuller form as a sign when it is distributed under both kinds. For in this form the sign of the Eucharistic banquet is more clearly evident and clear expression is given to the divine will by which the new and eternal Covenant is ratified in the Blood of the Lord, as also the relationship between the Eucharistic banquet and the eschatological banquet in the Father's Kingdom.

Sacred pastors should take care to ensure that the faithful who participate in the rite or are present at it are as fully aware as possible of the Catholic teaching on the form of Holy Communion as set forth by the Ecumenical Council of Trent. Above all, they should instruct the Christian faithful that the Catholic faith teaches that Christ, whole and entire, and the true Sacrament, is received even under only one species, and consequently that as far as the effects are concerned, those who receive under only one species are not deprived of any of the grace that is necessary for salvation.

They are to teach, furthermore, that the Church, in her stewardship of the Sacraments, has the power to set forth or alter whatever provisions, apart from the substance of the Sacraments, that she judges to be most conducive to the veneration of the Sacraments and the wellbeing of the recipients, in view of changing conditions, times, and places. At the same time, the faithful should be encouraged to seek to participate more eagerly in this sacred rite, by which the sign of the Eucharistic banquet is made more fully evident' (*GIRM* 281–2).

In response to a request of the Irish Episcopal Conference, the Congregation for Divine Worship and the Discipline of the Sacraments (Prot. N/CD 653/91) has given permission (26 October 1991) for Holy Communion to be distributed under both kinds to the faithful at Masses on Sundays and holydays of obligation and on weekdays, if, in the judgement of the ordinary, Communion can be given in an orderly and reverent way. Each local bishop in Ireland can implement this permission in accordance with the norms that apply.

These norms are recalled in the letter of permission.

1. Adequate catechetical instruction must be given to the faithful concerning the doctrine of the Church on the form of Holy Communion.
2. The decision to receive or not to receive from the chalice is left to the individual communicant.
3. The directives already given in the various instructions are to be observed:
   (a) The consecrated wine must be consumed after the distribution (except in the case of someone who is ill and cannot receive solid food). Only the necessary amount of wine should be consecrated;
   (b) The proper ministers are to be provided;
   (c) The form and material of the sacred vessels must follow the norms. Rules for the purification are to be observed.

Reverent and careful celebration and reception of Holy Communion under both kinds is to be observed.

The letter of permission states that Communion should not be distributed under both kinds in the following situations:
   (a) At Masses celebrated in the open with a great number of communicants;
   (b) At other Masses where the number of communicants is so great as to make it difficult for Communion under both kinds to be given in an orderly and reverent way;
   (c) At Masses where the assembled congregation is of such a diverse nature that it is difficult to ascertain whether those present have been sufficiently instructed about receiving Communion under both kinds;
   (d) When circumstances do not permit the assurance that due reverence towards the consecrated wine can be maintained during and after the celebration (see *Inaestimabile donum*, 13–14).

LITURGICAL NOTE 18
Days of Prayer

The following Days of Prayer have been approved by the Episcopal Conference:

World Day of Peace	Tuesday, 1 January 2013
World Day of Migrants and Refugees	Sunday, 20 January 2013
Week of Prayer for Christian Unity	begins Friday, 18 January 2013
Catholic Schools Week	begins Sunday, 27 January 2013
World Day for Consecrated Life	Saturday, 2 February 2013
Day of Prayer for Temperance	Sunday, 10 February 2013
World Day of the Sick	Monday, 11 February 2013

Day of Prayer for Vocations	Sunday, 21 April 2013
World Communications Day	Sunday, 12 May 2013
Day for Life	Sunday, 6 October 2013
Mission Sunday	Sunday, 20 October 2013
Restorative Justice Week	begins Monday, 11 November 2013

St Patrick's Day (Sunday, 17 March 2013) is a Special Day of Prayer for Emigrants.

LITURGICAL NOTE 19
Exposition of the Holy Eucharist

Exposition of the Holy Eucharist, either in the ciborium or in the monstrance, is intended to acknowledge Christ's marvellous presence in the sacrament. Exposition invites us to the spiritual union with him that culminates in sacramental communion. Thus it fosters very well the worship which is due to Christ in spirit and in truth.

Full texts and rubrics for this exposition are to be found in *Exposition and Benediction of the Blessed Sacrament/Taispeáint agus Beannacht na Naomh-Shacraiminte*, published by the Irish Institute of Pastoral Liturgy (now National Centre for Liturgy, Maynooth), 1982.

LITURGICAL NOTE 20
Friday penance
Statement from the Irish Bishops on Canons 1249–53
November 1983

Following the example of Christ
The new Code of Canon Law reminds us that all of Christ's faithful are obliged to do penance. The obligation arises in imitation of Christ himself and in response to his call. During his life on earth, not least at the beginning of his public ministry, our Lord undertook voluntary penance. He invited his followers to do the same. The penance he invited would be a participation in his own suffering, an expression of inner conversion and a form of reparation for sin. It would be a personal sacrifice made out of love for God and our neighbour. It follows, that if we are to be true, as Christians, to the spirit of Christ, we must practise some form of penance.

Special penitential days
So that all may be united with Christ and with one another in a common practice of penance, the Church sets aside certain penitential days. On those days the faithful are to devote themselves in a special way to prayer, self-denial and works of charity. Such days are not designed to confine or isolate penance but to intensify it in the life of the Christian throughout the year.

Lent: a time of fast and abstinence
Lent is the traditional season of renewal and penance in the Church. The new Code reaffirms this. It also prescribes that Ash Wednesday and Good Friday are to be observed as days of fast and abstinence. Fasting means that the amount of food we eat is considerably reduced. Abstinence means that we give up a particular kind of food or drink or form of amusement.

The subjects of penitential observance
Those over eighteen are bound by the law of fasting until the beginning of their sixtieth year, while all over fourteen are bound by the law of abstinence. Priests and parents are urged to foster the spirit and practice of penance among those too young to be the subjects of either law.

Friday: a special penitential day
Because Friday recalls the crucifixion of our Lord, it too is set aside as a special penitential day. The Church does not prescribe, however, that fish must be eaten on Fridays. It never did. Abstinence always meant the giving up of meat rather than the

eating of fish as a substitute. What the Church does require, according to the new Code, is that its members abstain from meat or some other food or that they perform some alternative work of penance laid down by the Bishops' Conference.

The style of Friday abstinence
In accordance with the mind of the universal Church, the Irish bishops remind their people of the obligation of Friday penance, and instruct them that it may be fulfilled in one or more of the following ways:
(i) By abstaining from meat or some other food;
(ii) By abstaining from alcoholic drink, smoking or some form of amusement;
(iii) By making the special effort involved in family prayer, taking part in the Mass, visiting the Blessed Sacrament or praying the Stations of the Cross;
(iv) By fasting from all food for a longer period than usual and perhaps by giving what is saved in this way to the needy at home and abroad;
(v) By going out of our way to help somebody who is poor, sick, old or lonely.

Friday penance is a serious obligation
While the form of penance is an option and doesn't have to take the same form every Friday, the obligation to do penance is not. There is a serious obligation to observe Friday as a penitential day. We are confident that the Irish people as a whole will take this obligation to heart. We recommend that each person should choose some form of penance for Fridays, in memory, as was Friday abstinence, of the passion and death of our Lord.

LITURGICAL NOTE 21
Liturgical commissions

In changes to the structures of the Episcopal Conference in March 2010, the Irish Episcopal Commission for Liturgy and the Irish Commission for Liturgy became the Council for Liturgy. The Episcopal members of the Council are: Most Rev. Martin Drennan (Chairman), Most Rev. John McAreavey and Most Rev. Brendan Kelly. Reverend Patrick Jones is secretary of the Council, working from the National Secretariat for Liturgy, St Patrick's College, Maynooth, Co. Kildare.

There are three advisory committees: Sacred Art and Architecture (chairperson: Mr Alexander M. White; secretary: Rev. Patrick Jones); Church Music (chairperson: Prof. Gerard Gillen; secretary: Sr Moira Bergin): Liotúirge i nGaeilge – (Cathaoirleach: An Dr Marie Whelton; rúnaí: An Canónach Seán Terry).

The National Secretariat was established in 1973 and serves the Church in the work of liturgical renewal. It is responsible for the National Centre for Liturgy at St Patrick's College, Maynooth. The Centre offers a programme of liturgical formation, including a one-year course in pastoral liturgy and, through the Pontifical University of St Patrick's College and its Faculty of Theology, the Diploma and Higher Diploma in Pastoral Liturgy and the M.Th degree specialising in liturgy. It also works with the Department of Music, NUIM on a part-time Diploma in Arts (Church Music) course.

LITURGICAL NOTE 22
Copyright

In order to reprint copyright material for liturgies, permission should be obtained beforehand from the publisher/agent/composer, as appropriate.

Most of the texts in our liturgical books are owned by the International Commission on English in the Liturgy (ICEL), a joint commission of Catholic Bishops' Conferences. ICEL's address is 1100 Connecticut Avenue, NW, Suite 710, Washington, D.C. 20036-4101, USA. Tel. 001 202 347 0800. Fax 001 202 347 1839, email ICEL@eliturgy.org, www.icelweb.org.

The copyright of some rites in Ireland, such as the Marriage Rite, and of liturgical texts in Irish is held by the Irish Episcopal Conference. The contact address is the National Secretariat for Liturgy, St Patrick's College, Maynooth, Co. Kildare.

The copyright of scripture texts is held by the publishers of the various versions. The publisher of *An Bíobla Naofa* (*Bíobla Má Nuad*) is An Sagart, Daingean, Trá Lí, Co. Chiarraí.

The copyright of music (words and music) is held by the composers and/or publishers/agents. An annual reprint licence and once-off publication permission covering much of the music used in worship (mainly GIA, OCP, Taizé, McCrimmon, Weston Priory and many individual composers) are available from Calamus, Oak House, 70 High Street, Brandon, IP27 0AU, England (Tel. 0044 1842 819830). Another licensing agent (covering Mayhew, OUP, Stainer and Bell, Kingsway's Thankyou, etc.) is Christian Copyright Licensing International (CCLI), 26 Gildredge Road, Eastbourne, BN21 4SA (Tel. 0044 1323 417711).

LITURGICAL NOTE 23
Liturgical Websites

General Links

www.liturgy-ireland.ie
The National Centre for Liturgy has extensive Calendar information. Information on the courses offered is also given.

www.catholicbishops.ie
For information and news on the Church in Ireland, bishops and on the agencies and commissions of the Irish Bishops' Conference

www.catholicireland.net
Gives information on Mass times in parishes in Ireland. It provides news, features and liturgical material.

www.maynoothcollege.ie
This is the site of St Patrick's College, Maynooth, the home of the National Centre for Liturgy. It gives information on courses offered, including the liturgy programme of the Centre.

www.nuim.ie
Gives access to the Department of Music at NUIM where a Diploma in Arts (Church Music) is available. This part-time course is conducted in association with the National Centre for Liturgy.

www.irishchurchmusicassociation.com
The site of the Irish Church Music Association with links to other sites on liturgical music.

www.cumannnasagart.ie
The website of Cumann na Sagart provides texts for liturgy through the medium of Irish.

www.vatican.va
The website of the Holy See, including the Congregation for Divine Worship and the Discipline of the Sacraments.

Liturgy Resources

www.virc.at
Readings for Sunday Mass in several western and eastern European languages.

www.osb.org/liturgy
This is a comprehensive site for liturgical history, documentation and prayer texts.

www.nd.edu/~ndcpl
The site of the Notre Dame Centre for Pastoral Liturgy.

www.liturgyoffice.org.uk
This website gives access to the Liturgy Office of the Conference of Bishops of England and Wales.

Prayer Site

www.sacredspace.ie
This site offers Sacred Space, a daily reflection.

Irish Publishers of Books on Liturgy, etc.

Columba Press – *www.columba.ie*
Dominican Publications – *www.dominicanpublications.com*
The Furrow – *www.the furrow.ie*
Veritas Publications – *www.veritas.ie*

LITURGICAL CALENDAR FOR IRELAND
2012/2013

NOTES FOR DECEMBER 2012

THE POPE'S INTENTIONS

General – Migrants: That migrants throughout the world may be welcomed with generosity and authentic love, especially by Christian communities.

Mission – Christ, the light for all humanity: That Christ may reveal himself to all humanity with the light that shines forth from Bethlehem and is reflected in the face of his Church.

THE IRISH CALENDAR IN DECEMBER

12th: St Finnian studied in Idrone (Co. Carlow) and later, in Wales and on his return he settled in Clonard, Co. Meath, around 520, where he established a famous school. His pupils, among whom were Canice, Colum Cille, and Brendan, were the initiators of the great monastic expansion in Ireland. He died in 549 and is remembered as the tutor of the saints of Ireland.

18th: St Flannan lived in the seventh century and was the son of a king of Thomond. He entered Molua's monastery at Killaloe and became abbot there. He is remembered as a great preacher.

20th: St Fachanan. Although little is known with certainty about Fachanan, a strong tradition from early times links him with Kilfenora and records that he founded a church or monastery there in the sixth century. He is venerated as the patron of the diocese of Kilfenora, now part of Galway.

THE YEAR OF FAITH

The renewal of the Church is also achieved through the witness offered by the lives of believers: by their very existence in the world, Christians are called to radiate the word of truth that the Lord Jesus has left us. The Council itself, in the Dogmatic Constitution *Lumen Gentium*, said this: While 'Christ, 'holy, innocent and undefiled' (*Heb* 7:26) knew nothing of sin (cf. *2 Cor* 5:21), but came only to expiate the sins of the people (cf. *Heb* 2:17) ... the Church ... clasping sinners to its bosom, at once holy and always in need of purification, follows constantly the path of penance and renewal. The Church, 'like a stranger in a foreign land, presses forward amid the persecutions of the world and the consolations of God', announcing the cross and death of the Lord until he comes (cf. *1 Cor* 11:26). But by the power of the risen Lord it is given strength to overcome, in patience and in love, its sorrow and its difficulties, both those that are from within and those that are from without, so that it may reveal in the world, faithfully, although with shadows, the mystery of its Lord until, in the end, it shall be manifested in full light' (*Lumen Gentium* 8).

The Year of Faith, from this perspective, is a summons to an authentic and renewed conversion to the Lord, the one Saviour of the world. In the mystery of his death and resurrection, God has revealed in its fullness the Love that saves and calls us to conversion of life through the forgiveness of sins (cf. *Acts* 5:31). For Saint Paul, this Love ushers us into a new life: 'We were buried ... with him by baptism into death, so that as Christ was raised from the dead by the glory of the Father, we too might walk in newness of life' (*Rm* 6:4). Through faith, this new life shapes the whole of human existence according to the radical new reality of the resurrection. To the extent that he freely cooperates, man's thoughts and affections, mentality and conduct are slowly purified and transformed, on a journey that is never completely finished in this life. 'Faith working through love' (*Gal* 5:6) becomes a new criterion of understanding and action that changes the whole of man's life (cf. *Rm* 12:2; *Col* 3:9-10; *Eph* 4:20-29; *2 Cor* 5:17).

'*Caritas Christi urget nos*' (*2 Cor* 5:14): it is the love of Christ that fills our hearts and impels us to evangelise. Today as in the past, he sends us through the highways of the world to proclaim his Gospel to all the peoples of the earth (cf. *Mt* 28:19). Through his love, Jesus Christ attracts to himself the people of every generation: in every age he convokes the Church, entrusting her with the proclamation of the Gospel by a mandate that is ever new. Today too, there is a need for stronger ecclesial commitment to new evangelisation in order to rediscover the joy of believing and the enthusiasm for communicating the faith. In rediscovering his love day by day, the missionary commitment of believers attains force and vigour that can never fade away. Faith grows when it is lived as an experience of love received and when it is communicated as an experience of grace and joy. It makes us fruitful, because it expands our hearts in hope and enables us to bear life-giving witness: indeed, it opens the hearts and minds of those who listen to respond to the Lord's invitation to adhere to his word and become his disciples. Believers, so Saint Augustine tells us, 'strengthen themselves by believing' (*De Utilitate Credendi* 1:2). The saintly Bishop of Hippo had good reason to express himself in this way. As we know, his life was a continual search for the beauty of the faith until such time as his heart would find rest in God (cf. *Confessions* 1:1). His extensive writings, in which he explains the importance of believing and the truth of the faith, continue even now to form a heritage of incomparable riches, and they still help many people in search of God to find the right path towards the 'door of faith'.

Only through believing, then, does faith grow and become stronger; there is no other possibility for possessing certitude with regard to one's life apart from self-abandonment, in a continuous crescendo, into the hands of a love that seems to grow constantly because it has its origin in God.

... We want to celebrate this Year in a worthy and fruitful manner. Reflection on the faith will have to be intensified, so as to help all believers in Christ to acquire a more conscious and vigorous adherence to the Gospel, especially at a time of profound change such as humanity is currently experiencing. We will have the opportunity to profess our faith in the Risen Lord in our cathedrals and in the churches of the whole world; in our homes and among our families, so that everyone may feel a strong need to know better and to transmit to future generations the faith of all times. Religious communities as well as parish communities, and all ecclesial bodies old and new, are to find a way, during this Year, to make a public profession of the *Credo*.

We want this Year to arouse in every believer the aspiration to *profess* the faith in fullness and with renewed conviction, with confidence and hope. It will also be a good opportunity to intensify the *celebration* of the faith in the liturgy, especially in the Eucharist, which is 'the summit towards which the activity of the Church is directed ... and also the source from which all its power flows' (SC 10). At the same time, we make it our prayer that believers' witness of life may grow in credibility. To rediscover the content of the faith that is professed, celebrated, lived and prayed, and to reflect on the act of faith, is a task that every believer must make his own, especially in the course of this Year.

– Apostolic Letter, *Porta Fidei* (6–9) of Pope Benedict XVI, 11 October 2011, in which he announced the Year of Faith, beginning 11 October 2012, the 50th anniversary of the opening of the Second Vatican Council, and concluding on 24 November 2013, the solemnity of Our Lord Jesus Christ, Universal King.

DECEMBER 2012 READINGS Sunday Cycle C Psalter Week 1

2 Sunday — **FIRST SUNDAY OF ADVENT**
Violet ✠
HOURS Proper. Te Deum. Psalter Week 1
MASS Proper. No Gloria. Creed. Preface: Advent I
READINGS **Jer 33:14-16. Ps 24:4-5, 8-9, 10, 14. 1 Th 3:12-4:2. Lk 21:25-28, 34-36.** Lect I:8

The Advent spirit of waiting and longing for the Lord reminds us of the daily call to holiness. We are to be found blameless when He comes, living lives of honesty and integrity. We are to avoid the temptations to escapism from the true meaning of life. The temptations come in many guises.
No other celebrations, not even funeral Masses, are permitted today (see Lit. Note 7)
Ossory Today is the anniversary of the episcopal ordination of Most Rev. Seamus Freeman SCA, 2 December 2007.

Advent-Christmas-Epiphany Season
UNLYC, 32, 33, 39, 42
After the annual celebration of the Paschal Mystery, the Church has no more ancient custom than celebrating the memorial of the Nativity of the Lord and of his first manifestations, and this takes place in Christmas Time.
Christmas Time runs from First Vespers (Evening Prayer I) of the Nativity of the Lord up to and including the Sunday after Epiphany or after 6 January.

Advent has a twofold character, for it is a time of preparation for the Solemnities of Christmas, in which the First Coming of the Son of God to humanity is remembered, and likewise a time when, by remembrance of this, minds and hearts are led to look forward to Christ's Second Coming at the end of time. For these two reasons, Advent is a period of devout and expectant delight.
The weekdays from 17 December up to and including 24 December are ordered in a more direct way to preparing for the Nativity of the Lord.

The Mass Lectionary in Advent
Sunday Readings
Each Gospel reading has a distinctive theme: 1st Sunday – the Lord's coming at the end of time, 2nd and 3rd – John the Baptist, 4th – the events preparatory to the Lord's birth. The Old Testament readings, usually from Isaiah, are Messianic prophecies. The readings from an apostle are exhortations and proclamations in keeping with the themes of Advent.

Weekday Readings
There are two series of readings: the first continues until 16 December; the second is according to date from 17 December.
On the first days of Advent the Gospel passage is chosen in relation to the selected passage from Isaiah.
On Thursday of the second week the Gospel passages are about St John the Baptist, and the first reading is either a continuation of Isaiah or a text chosen in view of the Gospel.
From 17 December Gospel passages are chosen about the events which immediately prepared for the birth of Christ. The first readings are from different books of the Old Testament in view of the Gospel readings and include the most important Messianic prophecies. See Liturgical Note 7 in regard to commemorations of saints.

DECEMBER 2012   READINGS Sunday Cycle C   Weekday Cycle 1

Advent is a time of waiting, conversion and of hope:
- waiting-memory of the first, humble coming of the Lord in our mortal flesh; waiting-supplication for his final, glorious coming as Lord of History and universal Judge;
- conversion, to which the Liturgy at this time often refers quoting the prophets, especially John the Baptist, 'Repent for the kingdom of heaven is at hand' (*Mt* 3:2);
- joyful hope that the salvation already accomplished by Christ (cf. *Rm* 8:24-25) and the reality of grace in the world will mature and reach their fullness, thereby granting us what is promised by faith, and 'we shall become like him for we shall see him as he really is' (*Jn* 3:2).

Popular piety is particularly sensitive to Advent, especially when seen as the memory of the preparation for the coming of the Messiah. The Christian people are deeply conscious of the long period of expectation that preceded the birth of our Saviour. The faithful know that God sustained Israel's hope in the coming of the Messiah by the prophets.
Various expressions of popular piety connected with Advent have emerged throughout the centuries. These have sustained the faith of the people, and from one generation to the next, they have conserved many valuable aspects of the liturgical season of Advent.

The Advent Wreath
Placing four candles on green fronds has become a symbol of Advent in many Christian homes, especially in Germanic countries and in North America.
The Advent wreath, with the progressive lighting of its four candles, Sunday after Sunday, until the Solemnity of Christmas, is a recollection of the various stages of salvation history prior to Christ's coming and a symbol of the prophetic light gradually illuminating the long night prior to the rising of the Sun of justice (cf. *Mal* 3:20; *Lk* 1:78).

The Blessed Virgin Mary and Advent
The Liturgy frequently celebrates the Blessed Virgin Mary in an exemplary way during the season of Advent. It recalls the women of the Old Testament who prefigured and prophesied her mission; it exalts her faith and the humility with which she promptly and totally submitted to God's plan of salvation; it highlights her presence in the events of grace preceding the birth of the Saviour. Popular piety also devotes particular attention to the Blessed Virgin Mary during Advent, as is evident from the many pious exercises practised at this time, especially the novena of the Immaculate Conception and of Christmas. The novena of the Immaculate Conception, wherever it is celebrated, should highlight the prophetical texts which begin with Genesis 3:15, and end in Gabriel's salutation of the one who is 'full of grace' (*Lk* 1:31-33).

However, the significance of Advent, 'that time which is particularly apt for the cult of the Mother of God' (*Marialis cultus*, 4), is such that it cannot be represented merely as a 'Marian month'.
In the calendars of the Oriental Churches, the period of preparation for the celebration of the manifestation (Advent) of divine salvation (Theophany) in the mysteries of Christmas-Epiphany of the Only Son of God, is markedly Marian in character. Attention is concentrated on preparation for the Lord's coming in the *Deipara*. For the Orientals, all Marian mysteries are Christological mysteries since they refer to the mystery of our salvation in Christ. The Byzantine Rite prepares for Christmas with a whole series of Marian feasts and rituals.
– *Directory on Popular Piety and the Liturgy*, 96–8, 100

December 2012 Psalter Week 1

3 Monday
White

1st Week of Advent
St Francis Xavier, priest — Memorial
HOURS of the memorial. Psalter Week 1
MASS of the memorial. Preface: Advent I or of the Saint

---

4 Tuesday
Violet
White

1st Week of Advent
HOURS Psalter Week 1. MASS Proper. Preface: Advent I
Optional memorial of **St John Damascene, priest and doctor of the Church**

---

5 Wednesday
Violet

1st Week of Advent
HOURS Psalter Week 1. MASS Proper. Preface: Advent I

---

6 Thursday
Violet
White
Galway
City of Galway

1st Week of Advent
HOURS Psalter Week 1. MASS Proper. Preface: Advent I
Optional memorial of **St Nicholas, bishop**
St Nicholas, bishop — Feast
St Nicholas, bishop — Solemnity

---

7 Friday

White

1st Week of Advent
St Ambrose, bishop and doctor of the Church — Memorial
HOURS of the memorial. Psalter Week 1
MASS of the memorial. Preface: Advent I or of the Saint
FIRST EVENING PRAYER of **Immaculate Conception**

---

8 Saturday
White ✠

THE IMMACULATE CONCEPTION OF THE BLESSED VIRGIN MARY — Solemnity
HOURS Proper. Te Deum
Complementary Psalms at Day Hour
MASS Proper. Gloria. Creed. Preface: Proper
FIRST EVENING PRAYER of **Sunday**

No other celebrations, not even funeral Masses, are permitted today (see Lit. Note 7)

December 2012 READINGS Sunday Cycle C

FIRST WEEK OF ADVENT

3 Monday   Is 2:1-5. Ps 121:1-2, 4-5, 6-9. Mt 8:5-11. *Lect* I:10
On these first days of Advent the Gospel passage is chosen in consideration of the selected texts from Isaiah. For this reason the Church, especially during Advent and Lent and above all at the Easter Vigil, re-reads and re-lives the great events of salvation history in the 'today' of her liturgy.
St Francis Xavier, 1506–52, one of the first seven Jesuits, was sent to India by St Ignatius. He converted many in Goa and later in Japan. He died as he attempted to enter China. A patron of the missions.

4 Tuesday   Is 11:1-10. Ps 71:1-2, 7-8, 12-13, 17. Lk 10:21-24. *Lect* I:13
The prophet speaks of the one on whom the spirit rests. Integrity and faithfulness shall characterise him. And in those days there shall be peace. Jesus, filled with the joy of the Holy Spirit, gives thanks to the Father for revealing the fulfilment of the prophecies.
St John Damascene, 675–749, was a Syrian Christian theologian. He became a priest in the monastery of St Sabas near Jerusalem and was a leading figure in the defence of icons in the iconoclastic controversy.

5 Wednesday   Is 25:6-10. Ps 22. Mt 15:29-37. *Lect* I:15
Isaiah prophesies the banquet on the heavenly mount when all tears will be wiped away. Christ on the hillside provides bread for the people who are astonished at the Messianic signs. In the Eucharist we have a foretaste of the heavenly banquet.

6 Thursday   Is 26:1-6. Ps 117:1, 8-9, 19-21, 25-27. Mt 7:21, 24-27. *Lect* I:18
It is the upright nation, the faithful people, which will enter the kingdom. To be part of that people each one must hear the word of God and do God's will.
St Nicholas is a fourth-century bishop of Myra in modern-day Turkey of whom little is known. He is patron of Russia, of sailors, of pawnbrokers, and of children.

7 Friday   Is 29:17-24. Ps 26:1, 4, 13-14. Mt 9:27-31. *Lect* I:20
One of the signs of the Day of the Lord is that the eyes of the blind will see. Jesus cures two blind men because of their faith in him. In Christ, the true light, we can truly see, have visions, discern with wisdom.
St Ambrose, 340–97, became governor of the Roman province whose seat was in Milan. In 374, the laity insisted on his becoming bishop though he was still not baptised. He defended orthodoxy in brilliant preaching and through his writing. Patron of Milan, bee-keepers, and domestic animals.

8 Saturday   Gn 3:9-15, 20. Ps 97:1-4. Eph 1:3-6, 11-12. Lk 1:26-38. *Lect* I:1009 *or* II:1289
The Immaculate Conception of the Blessed Virgin Mary. We celebrate Mary who, from the first instant of her existence in the womb of her mother Anne, was 'by a singular grace and privilege of almighty God, and in view of the merits of Jesus Christ, Saviour of the human race, preserved free from all stain of original sin'.

Next Sunday's readings: Bar 5:1-9. Ps 125. Phil 1:3-6, 8-11. Lk 3:1-6. *Lect* I:30

December 2012 Psalter Week 2

9 Sunday **SECOND SUNDAY OF ADVENT**
Violet ✠ HOURS Proper. Te Deum. Psalter Week 2
MASS Proper. No Gloria. Creed. Preface: Advent I
No other celebrations, not even funeral Masses, are permitted today (see Lit. Note 7)
St Juan Diego Cuahtlatoatzin is not celebrated this year.

---

10 Monday **2nd Week of Advent**
Violet HOURS Psalter Week 2. MASS Proper. Preface: Advent I

---

11 Tuesday **2nd Week of Advent**
Violet HOURS Psalter Week 2. MASS Proper. Preface: Advent I
White Optional memorial of **St Damasus I, pope**

---

12 Wednesday **2nd Week of Advent**
Violet HOURS Psalter Week 2. MASS Proper. Preface: Advent I
White Optional memorial of **Our Lady of Guadalupe**
White Optional memorial of **St Finnian, bishop**
Meath **St Finnian, bishop** Feast

---

13 Thursday **2nd Week of Advent**
 St Lucy, virgin and martyr Memorial
Red HOURS of the memorial. Psalter Week 2
MASS of the memorial. Preface: Advent I or of the Saint

---

14 Friday **2nd Week of Advent**
 St John of the Cross, priest and doctor of the Church
 Memorial
White HOURS of the memorial. Psalter Week 2
MASS of the memorial. Preface: Advent I or of the Saint

---

15 Saturday **2nd Week of Advent**
Violet HOURS Psalter Week 2. MASS Proper. Preface: Advent I

Next Sunday's readings: Zeph 3:14-18. Ps Is 12:2-6. Phil 4:4-7. Lk 3:10-18. *Lect* I:51

December 2012   READINGS Sunday Cycle C

SECOND WEEK OF ADVENT

9 Sunday   Bar 5:1-9. Ps 125. Phil 1:3-6, 8-11. Lk 3:1-6. Lect I:30
God's promises to us are fulfilled in Jesus Christ. We look forward to the Kingdom when, pure and blameless, we will reach the perfect goodness which Christ produces in us.

10 Monday   Is 35:1-10. Ps 84:9-14. Lk 5:17-26. Lect I:33
The marvellous vision of God's saving love is expressed in some of the most poetic language of the prophet. This vision is realised in the life and works of Jesus Christ.

11 Tuesday   Is 40:1-11. Ps 95:1-3, 10-13. Mt 18:12-14. Lect I:35
Isaiah's words of comfort breathe the very spirit of Advent. The nation's slavery is ended and God will lead his people in a new Exodus. The road must be prepared for God to travel on.
St Damasus I, born around 304 and died on this day in 384, elected pope in 366. He insisted on the apostolic foundations of the Roman See and was active in opposing fourth century heresies. He commissioned St Jerome to prepare the Vulgate version of the Bible.

12 Wednesday Is 40:25-31. Ps 102:1-4, 8, 10. Mt 11:28-30. Lect I:38
The people are not to grow weary and tired, thinking that the Lord has deserted them. Those who hope in him will renew their strength, they will sprout wings like eagles. Jesus promises rest to the weary and overburdened.
St Finnian see *December notes*.
Our Lady of Guadalupe is patron of the Americas. This memorial recalls the apparitions in December 1531 to Juan Diego Cuahtlatoatzin on Tepeyac hill, near Mexico city.

13 Thursday   Is 41:13-20. Ps 144:1, 9-13. Mt 11:11-15. Lect I:40
From today the Gospel passages are about St John the Baptist. All the prophets before John were leading to him. His vocation is to show that Jesus is the promised one, the redeemer of humankind.
St Lucy, desiring to remain consecrated to Christ alone, was martyred in 304 in Sicily during the persecution of Diocletion.

14 Friday   Is 48:17-19. Ps 1:1-4, 6. Mt 11:16-19. Lect I:42
The people of Jesus' own time have acted in a self-willed way, never consistent nor satisfied, and have refused the offer of salvation. Neither the ascetical John, nor Jesus with his free and easy way at table with sinners, can bring them to faith.
St John of the Cross, 1542–91, a Carmelite who, despite opposition and imprisonment, worked for the reform of the Carmelites. He was a man of prayer, an outstanding poet, a spiritual writer declared doctor of the Church.

15 Saturday   Eccles (Sir) 48:1-4, 9-11. Ps 79:2-3, 15-16, 18-19. Mt 17:10-13. Lect I:44
Going before Jesus in the spirit and power of Elijah, John bears witness to Christ in his preaching, by his Baptism of conversion, and through his martyrdom.

December 2012 Psalter Week 3

16 Sunday **THIRD SUNDAY OF ADVENT** (Gaudete Sunday)
Violet or Rose ✠ HOURS Proper. Te Deum. Psalter Week 3
MASS Proper. No Gloria. Creed. Preface: Advent I
No other celebrations, not even funeral Masses, are permitted today (see Lit. Note 7)

17–24 December Preparation for Christmas

For the Liturgy of the Hours the texts are proper for each day (see Divine Office: I, pp. 117 ff.). Mass texts are proper also according to the date. Votive Masses and daily Masses for the dead are not permitted. See Liturgical Note 7 in regard to commemorations of saints.

17 Monday	**3rd Week of Advent**	
Violet	HOURS Psalter Week 3. MASS Proper. Preface: Advent II	

18 Tuesday	**3rd Week of Advent**	
Violet	HOURS Psalter Week 3. MASS Proper. Preface: Advent II	
	Memorial may be made of **St Flannan, bishop** (see Lit. Note 7)	
Killaloe	**St Flannan, bishop**	Feast

19 Wednesday	**3rd Week of Advent**	
Violet	HOURS Psalter Week 3. MASS Proper. Preface: Advent II	

20 Thursday	**3rd Week of Advent**	
Violet	HOURS Psalter Week 3. MASS Proper. Preface: Advent II	
	Memorial may be made of **St Fachanan, bishop** (see Lit. Note 7)	
Kilfenora	**St Fachanan, bishop**	Feast

21 Friday	**3rd Week of Advent**
Violet	HOURS Psalter Week 3. MASS Proper. Preface: Advent II
	Memorial may be made of **St Peter Canisius, priest and doctor of the Church** (see Lit. Note 7)

22 Saturday	**3rd Week of Advent**
Violet	HOURS Psalter Week 3. MASS Proper. Preface: Advent II

December 2012 READINGS Sunday Cycle C

THIRD WEEK OF ADVENT

16 Sunday **Zeph 3:14-18. Ps Is 12:2-6. Phil 4:4-7. Lk 3:10-18.** *Lect* I:51

John the Baptist inaugurates the Gospel, already from his mother's womb welcomes the coming of Christ and rejoices in being 'the friend of the bridegroom', whom he points out as 'the Lamb of God, who takes away the sin of the world'.

17 Monday **Gn 49:2, 8-10. Ps 71:1-4, 7-8, 17. Mt 1:17.** *Lect* I:76

'When the Church celebrates the liturgy of Advent each year, she makes present this ancient expectancy of the Messiah, for by sharing in the long preparation for the Saviour's first coming, the faithful renew their ardent desire for his second coming' (*CCC*, 524). 'Wisdom of the Most High, teach us the way of truth.'

18 Tuesday **Jer 23:5-8. Ps 71:1-2, 12-13, 18-19. Mt 1:18-24.** *Lect* I:79

In the story of Christ's birth, Matthew now stresses the divinity of Christ. St Joseph appears as a man of justice and integrity. 'Ruler of the House of Israel, who gave the law to Moses on Mount Sinai, come with outstretched arm.'

St Flannan, see *December notes.*

19 Wednesday Jg 13:2-7, 24-25. Ps 70:3-6, 16-17. Lk 1:5-25. *Lect* I:81

Samson and John are specially chosen messengers, whose births are announced by an angel. Each of us is a messenger, to tell the praise of God's glory every day. 'Root of Jesse, do not delay to come and save us.'

20 Thursday **Is 7:10-14. Ps 23:1-6. Lk 1:26-38.** *Lect* I:83

'The faithful who carry the spirit of Advent from the liturgy into their own lives perceive the inexpressible love in the Virgin Mary's welcoming of her Son. Thus the Advent liturgy leads them to keep Mary before their own eyes as a model and to prepare the way for the coming Saviour, with wonder and praise (*Marialis cultus*). 'Key of David, come to liberate those who are captive in darkness.'

St Fachanan, see *December notes.*

21 Friday **Song 2:8-14** *or* **Zeph 3:14-18. Ps 32:2-3, 11-12, 20-21. Lk 1:39-45.** *Lect* I:85

Elizabeth is honoured by a visit from the mother of her Lord, and the child leaps for joy. Our Advent joy arises from Christ's coming among us. 'Emmanuel, our king and our law-giver, come and save us, Lord our God.'

St Peter Canisius, 1521–97, was born in Holland. He intended to become a lawyer but joined the Jesuits. Through courtesy and learning he promoted the Catholic revival after the Council of Trent. His greatest work was a catechism of 211 questions and answers, published in 1555.

22 Saturday **1 Sm 1:24-28. Ps 1 Sm 2:1, 4-8. Lk 1:46-56.** *Lect* I:88

'The Almighty has done great things for me': both Hannah and Mary can sing this song to the Lord. So can all who have heard the good news of great joy. 'Root of Jesse, set up as a sign to the peoples, delay no more.'

Next Sunday's readings: Mic 5:1-4. Ps 79:2-3, 15-16, 18-19. Heb 10:5-10. Lk 1:39-44. *Lect* I:73

December 2012 READINGS Sunday Cycle C Psalter Week 4

23 Sunday **FOURTH SUNDAY OF ADVENT**
Violet ✠ HOURS Proper. Te Deum. Psalter Week 4
  MASS Proper. No Gloria. Creed. Preface: Advent II
READINGS **Mic 5:1-4. Ps 79:2-3, 15-16, 18-19. Heb 10:5-10. Lk 1:39-44.** *Lect* I:73

We prepare for Christmas with the attitudes of Elizabeth and Mary. Like Elizabeth we are open to receive the Christ with wonder and joy. Like Mary we are ready to do the will of God as it is made clear to us. That may mean standing by the cross before we come to the glory of the resurrection.

No other celebrations, not even funeral Masses, are permitted today (see Lit. Note 7)
St John of Kanty, priest is not celebrated this year.

---

24 Monday **4th Week of Advent**
Violet HOURS Psalter Week 4. MASS Proper. Preface: Advent II
READINGS **2 Sm 7:1-5, 8-12, 14, 16. Ps 88:2-5, 27, 29. Lk 1:67-79.** *Lect* I:92

Zechariah prophesies that the Rising Sun comes to give light to all in darkness and the shadow of death. The tender mercy of our God will bring the rising Sun to shine upon us, to guide our feet into the way of peace. 'Morning Star, sun of justice, come and enlighten those who live in darkness.'

THE PROCLAMATION OF CHRISTMAS

The first entry in the *Marytrologium Romanum* (Roman Martyrology) for 25 December is a proclamation of 'the Nativity of Our Lord Jesus Christ according to the flesh'. It may be used before or at the beginning of Midnight Mass. Its inclusion after Evening Prayer or at the Office of Readings is also appropriate.

The twenty-fifth day of December.
After the passage of countless centuries from the creation of the world, when in the beginning God created heaven and earth and formed man in his own image; and very many centuries from the time when after the flood the Almighty had set his bow in the clouds, a sign of the covenant and of peace;
in the twenty-first century from the migration of Abraham, our father in faith, from Ur of the Chaldees;
in the thirteenth century from the departure of the people of Israel from Egypt under the leadership of Moses;
in about the thousandth year from the anointing of David as king according to the prophecy of Daniel;
in the 194th Olympiad;
in the 752nd year from the foundation of the City of Rome;
in the forty-second year of the rule of Caesar Octavian Augustus;
while the whole world was at peace, Jesus Christ, eternal God and Son of the Eternal Father, desiring to consecrate the world by his most gracious coming, having been conceived of the Holy Spirit, and when nine months had passed after his conception, is born as man in Bethlehem of Judah from the Virgin Mary:
the Nativity of Our Lord Jesus Christ according to the flesh.

December 2012

SEASON OF CHRISTMAS
THE NATIVITY OF OUR LORD JESUS CHRIST

24 Monday   **Christmas Eve**   Solemnity with Octave
White ✠   EVENING MASS of the Vigil, Proper. Gloria. Creed. Preface: Nativity I–III. In the Roman Canon, proper form.
READINGS   **Is 62:1-5. Ps 88:4-5, 16-17, 27, 29. Acts 13:16-17, 22-25. Mt 1:1-25** (shorter form 1:18-25). Lect I:99

The Virgin will conceive and give birth to a son and they shall call him Emmanuel.
At all Masses this evening and tomorrow in the Profession of Faith all genuflect at the words: and was made man.

FIRST EVENING PRAYER of the **Nativity**

OFFICE OF READINGS should appropriately be celebrated before the Midnight Mass as a solemn Vigil.

---

25 Tuesday   **THE NATIVITY OF OUR LORD JESUS CHRIST**   Solemnity
White ✠   HOURS Proper. Te Deum
MASS, at Midnight, Dawn and Day, Proper
Gloria. Creed. Preface: Nativity I–III. In the Roman Canon, proper form
EVENING PRAYER of the **Nativity**

READINGS
Midnight Mass Is 9:1-7. Ps 95:1-3, 11-13. Ti 2:11-14. Lk 2:1-14. Lect I:104
I bring you news of great joy. This night a child is born for us, a son given to us.
Dawn Mass   **Is 62:11-12. Ps 96:1, 6, 11-12. Ti 3:4-7. Lk 2:15-20.** Lect I:107
The shepherds found Mary and Joseph and the baby: and glorified God.
Mass during the Day Is 52:7-10. Ps 97:1-6. Heb 1:1-6. Jn 1:1-18 (shorter form 1:1-5, 9-14). Lect I:109
The Word was made flesh, he lived among us, and we saw his glory.
On Christmas Day all priests may celebrate three Masses, provided that they are celebrated at the proper time. No Masses for the dead, not even funeral Masses, are permitted today (see Lit. Note 7)

December 2012

26 Wednesday ST STEPHEN, FIRST MARTYR — Feast
Red
HOURS Proper. Te Deum. Psalter Week 4 at Day Hour
MASS Proper. Gloria. Preface: Nativity I–III. In the Roman Canon, proper form
No Masses for the dead, except funeral Masses, are permitted today (see Lit. Note 7)

---

27 Thursday ST JOHN, APOSTLE AND EVANGELIST — Feast
White
HOURS Proper. Te Deum. Psalter Week 4 at Day Hour
MASS Proper. Gloria. Preface: Nativity I–III. In the Roman Canon, proper form
No Masses for the dead, except funeral Masses, are permitted today (see Lit. Note 7)

---

28 Friday THE HOLY INNOCENTS, MARTYRS — Feast
Red
HOURS Proper. Te Deum. Psalter Week 4 at Day Hour
MASS Proper. Gloria. Preface: Nativity I–III. In the Roman Canon, proper form
No Masses for the dead, except funeral Masses, are permitted today (see Lit. Note 7)

---

29 Saturday **5th Day in the Octave of Christmas**
White
HOURS Proper. Te Deum. Psalter Week 4 at Day Hour
MASS Proper. Gloria. Preface: Nativity I–III. In the Roman Canon, proper form
Memorial may be made of **St Thomas Becket, bishop and martyr** *(see Lit. Note 7)*
No Masses for the dead, except the funeral Mass and Mass on the occasion of the news of a death, final burial, or the first anniversary are permitted today (see Lit. Note 7)

ANNOUNCEMENT OF EASTER

The season of Christmas ends with the celebration of the Baptism of the Lord. As the season draws to an end, the solemnity of the Epiphany offers an opportunity to proclaim the centrality of Christ's paschal mystery: dying he destroyed our death and rising he restored our life. The Easter Triduum of the Passion, Death and Resurrection of Christ is the culmination of the entire liturgical year. The proclamation of the date of Easter may be announced on the solemnity of the Epiphany after the homily or after the Prayer after Communion. The Announcement with music is to be found in *RM* pp. 1351–2.

Know, dear brothers and sisters, that as we have rejoiced at the Nativity of our Lord Jesus Christ, so by leave of God's mercy we announce to you also the joy of his Resurrection, who is our Saviour.
On the thirteenth day of February will fall Ash Wednesday, and the beginning of the fast of the most sacred Lenten season.
On the thirty-first day of March you will celebrate with joy Easter Day, the Paschal feast of our Lord Jesus Christ.
On the twelfth day of May will be the Ascension of our Lord Jesus Christ.
On the nineteenth day of May, the feast of Pentecost.
On the second day of June, the feast of the Most Holy Body and Blood of Christ.
On the first day of December, the First Sunday of the Advent of our Lord Jesus Christ, to whom is honour and glory for ever and ever. Amen.

December 2012 READINGS Sunday Cycle C

26 Wednesday Acts 6:8-10, 7:54-59. Ps 30:3-4, 6, 8, 16-17. Mt 10:17-22. Lect I:125

St Stephen, the first Christian martyr, was one of those in charge of the poor and needy. He is outstanding for his forgiveness of his enemies. Patron of deacons, stonemasons, and bricklayers.

Since their feasts fall on the three days after Christmas, St Stephen, St John the apostle and evangelist and the Holy Innocents were given the name of *Comites Christi*, Companions of Christ, in the Middle Ages. It was also said that three forms of martyrdom are represented: voluntary and executed (Stephen), voluntary but not executed (John), and executed but not voluntary (Holy Innocents).

27 Thursday   1 Jn 1:1-4. Ps 96:1-2, 5-6, 11-12. Jn 20:2-8. Lect I:27

St John, brother of James, son of Zebedee, the disciple whom Jesus loved, is traditionally said to have died in Ephesus. He is considered to be the author of the Fourth Gospel, the Book of Revelation and three Letters. The Letters especially teach us the law of love; John is said in his old age to have preached only one message: love one another.

28 Friday   1 Jn 1:5-2:2. Ps 123:2-5, 7-8. Mt 2:13-18. Lect I:129

'The flight into Egypt and the massacre of the **Holy Innocents** make manifest the opposition of darkness to the light: "He came to his own home, and his own people received him not." Christ's whole life was lived under the sign of persecution. His own share it with him. Jesus' departure from Egypt recalls the exodus and presents him as the definitive liberator of God's people.' (CCC, 530)

29 Saturday   1 Jn 2:3-11. Ps 95:1-3, 5-6. Lk 2:22-35. Lect I:131

Christmas has its origins in a feast of light to celebrate the victory of the Sun of Justice, a light shining in the darkness.

St Thomas Becket, 1118–70, as Archbishop of Canterbury, came in conflict with King Henry II over Church rights. He was killed in his cathedral on this date.

Next Sunday's readings: Year C: 1 Sm 1:20-22, 24-28. Ps 83:2-3, 5-6, 9-10. 1 Jn 3:1-2, 21-24. Lk 2:41-52. Lect I:122 **or Eccles (Sir) 3:2-6, 12-14. Ps 127:1-5. Col 3:12-21. Mt 2:13-15, 19-23.** Lect I:114. Note: **Col 3:12-17** (first two paragraphs of Lectionary reading) is recommended as an alternative second reading. See Lit. Note 14.

NOTES FOR JANUARY 2013

THE POPE'S INTENTIONS

General – The Year of Faith: That in this Year of Faith Christians may deepen their knowledge of the mysteriy of Christ and witness joyfully to the gift of faith in him.

Mission – Christians of the Middle East: That the Christian communities of the Middle East, which frequently suffer discrimination, may receive the strength of fidelity and perseverance of the Holy Spirit.

THE IRISH CALENDAR IN JANUARY

3rd: St Munchin (Mainchin) is the patron saint of the diocese of Limerick. His traditional birthplace is Dal Cais, where a parish and old graveyard Cell Mainchin (Kilmanaheen) existed. In the seventh century he was granted Inis Sibtonn (Ibton) in the tidal waters of Limerick, in the region of which he founded a church and had a thriving religious community.

5th: (Dublin): St Charles of St Andrew. John Andrew Houben was born in Holland in 1821. He took vows as a Passionist in 1846 and came to Mount Argus in 1857. It was there he spent most of his priestly life. His ministry in the confessional was renowned and the poor of Dublin found in him a strong support. He died on 5 January 1893. St Charles was canonised on 3 June 2007.

15th: St Ita was born in Co. Waterford of noble and Christian parents. Early on she set her mind on serving Christ in religious life. She founded a monastery in Killeedy, Co. Limerick, which attracted a great variety of young people. She was given the title 'foster-mother of the saints of Ireland'. She died in 570.

16th: St Fursa was born in Ireland and became one of the great monastic missionaries abroad. He went first with his brothers Foillan and Ultan to live the monastic life in East Anglia. But as great numbers continued to visit him there he left Foillan as abbot and sought refuge in France around 644. A patron gave him a hermitage at Lagny on the Marne. He died about 650 at Mézerolles and was buried in Péronne, which became a great centre of devotion to him.

30th: St Aidan or Maedoc (Mogue) was born around 550, probably in County Cavan. Aidan studied under David in Wales, and on his return he founded a monastery at Ferns. He became bishop there and was renowned for his generosity and kindness. He died in 626 and his *Lives* testify to his popularity both in Cavan and in Ferns.

30th (Dublin, Meath): Bl. Margaret Ball was imprisoned for teaching Catholicism, harbouring priests and having Mass celebrated in her home. The harsh conditions of Dublin Castle wore down this old lady of gentle birth, and she died there in 1584. **Bl. Francis Taylor** was born in Swords, Co. Dublin and was elected Mayor of Dublin in 1595. For his Catholic faith he was put in prison for seven years and died of the hardships suffered there on 30 January 1621 at the age of seventy.

18-25 January: WEEK OF PRAYER FOR CHRISTIAN UNITY
What does God require of us? (cf. Mic 6:6-8)

To mark its centenary, the Student Christian Movement of India (SCMI) was invited to prepare the resources for the Week of Prayer for Christian Unity 2013 and they involved the All India Catholic University Federation and the National Council of Churches in India. In the preparatory process while reflecting on the significance of the Week of Prayer, it was decided that in a context of great injustice to Dalits in India and in the Church, the search for visible unity cannot be disassociated from the dismantling of casteism and the lifting up of contributions to unity by the poorest of the poor.

The Dalits in the Indian context are the communities which are considered 'outcastes'. They are the people worst affected by the caste system, which is a rigid form of social stratification based on notions of ritual purity and pollution. The Dalit communities are considered to be the most polluted and polluting and thus placed outside the caste system and were previously even called 'untouchable'. Because of casteism, the Dalits are socially marginalised, politically under-represented, economically exploited and culturally subjugated. Almost 80 per cent of Indian Christians have a Dalit background.

Casteism poses severe challenges for the unity of Christians in India and therefore, for the moral and ecclesial witness of the Church as the one body of Christ. As a church-dividing issue, casteism is consequently an acute doctrinal issue. It is in this context that this year's Week of Prayer invites us to explore the well-known biblical text of Micah 6:6-8, focusing upon the question 'what does God require of us?' as the main theme. The Dalit experience serves as the crucible from within which theological reflections on the biblical theme emerge.

Micah sets justice and peace within the history of the relationship between God and humanity but insists that this history necessitates and demands a strong ethical reference. He reminds the people that God has saved them from slavery in Egypt and called them through the covenant to live in a society built on dignity, equality and justice. Thus, true faith in God is inseparable from personal holiness and the search for social justice. More than just worship, sacrifices and burnt offerings (6:7), God's salvation from slavery and daily humiliation rather demands that we should do justice, love kindness, and walk humbly with our God (cf. 6:8).

In many ways, the situation facing the people of God in the time of Micah can be compared to the situation of the Dalit community in India. Dalits also face oppression and injustice from those who wish to deny them their rights and dignity. Micah's rejection of rituals and sacrifices which were impoverished by a lack of concern for justice, speaks of God's expectation that justice ought to be at the core of our religion and rituals. His message is prophetic in a context where discrimination against the Dalits is legitimised on the basis of religion and notions of ritual purity and pollution. Faith gains or loses its meaning in relation to justice. In the contemporary Dalit situation Micah's insistence on the moral element of our faith requires us to ask ourselves what God truly requires of us; mere sacrifices, or to walk with God in justice and peace.

Material for liturgy, which can be adapted for local use, is published jointly by the Pontifical Council for Promoting Christian Unity (www.vatican.va) and the Faith and Order Commission of the World Council of Churches (www.wcc.oikeumene.org).

December 2012 Psalter Week 1

30 Sunday — **THE HOLY FAMILY OF JESUS, MARY AND JOSEPH**
Feast
White ✠ HOURS Proper. Te Deum. Psalter Week 1 at Day Hour
MASS Proper. Gloria. Creed. Preface: Nativity I–III. In the Roman Canon, proper form

No Masses for the dead, except funeral Masses, are permitted today (see Lit. Note 7)

---

31 Monday — **7th Day in the Octave of Christmas**
White HOURS Proper. Te Deum. Psalter Week 1 at Day Hour
MASS Proper. Gloria. Preface: Nativity I–III. In the Roman Canon, proper form
Memorial may be made of **St Sylvester, pope** *(see Lit. Note 7)*
FIRST EVENING PRAYER of **Mary, Mother of God**

No Masses for the dead, except the funeral Mass and Mass on the occasion of the news of a death, final burial, or the first anniversary are permitted today (see Lit. Note 7)

JANUARY 2013

1 Tuesday — **MARY, THE HOLY MOTHER OF GOD** Solemnity
White *World Day of Peace* Octave of Christmas
HOURS Proper. Te Deum. Complementary Psalms at Day Hour
MASS Proper. Gloria. Creed. Preface of BVM I. In the Roman Canon, proper form

No Masses for the dead, not even funeral Masses, are permitted today (see Lit. note 7)

---

2 Wednesday — **Before Epiphany**
Ss Basil the Great and Gregory Nazianzen, bishops and doctors of the Church Memorial
White HOURS of the memorial. Psalter Week 1
MASS Proper. Preface: Nativity I–III or of the Saints

---

3 Thursday — **Before Epiphany**
White HOURS Psalter Week 1. MASS Proper. Preface: Nativity I–III
White Optional memorial of **The Holy Name of Jesus**
White Optional memorial of **St Munchin (Mainchin), bishop**
Limerick **St Munchin (Mainchin), bishop** Feast

---

4 Friday — **Before Epiphany**
White HOURS Psalter Week 1. MASS Proper. Preface: Nativity I–III

---

5 Saturday — **Before Epiphany**
White HOURS Psalter Week 1. MASS Proper. Preface: Nativity I–III
Dublin Optional memorial of **St Charles of St Andrew, priest**
FIRST EVENING PRAYER of the **Epiphany**
Night Prayer 1 of Sunday

Next Sunday's readings: Is 60:1-6. Ps 71:1-2, 7-8, 10-13. Eph 3:2-3, 5-6. Mt 2:1-12. *Lect* I:161

December 2012   READINGS Sunday Cycle C

30 Sunday   Year C: 1 Sm 1:20-22, 24-28. Ps 83:2-3, 5-6, 9-10. 1 Jn 3:1-2, 21-24. Lk 2:41-52. *Lect* I:122 *or* **Eccles (Sir) 3:2-6, 12-14. Ps 127:1-5. Col 3:12-21. Mt 2:13-15, 19-23.** *Lect* I:114. *Note:* **Col 3:12-17** *(first two paragraphs of Lectionary reading) is recommended as an alternative second reading. See Lit. Note 14.*

The Holy Family is seen as the model for the human family, the religious community, and the Church itself. The celebration of the Incarnation has brought us to see God's closeness. In the Holy Family we see the ordinariness of the life of Jesus, the simple acceptance by Mary and Joseph of the marvels of God. In the daily life of family and community we can touch the divine, we can come close to God. But we have to learn to live centred on God, with respect and love for each other.

31 Monday   1 Jn 2:18-21. Ps 95:1-2, 11-13. Jn 1:1-18. *Lect* I:136

'This end of the civil year affords an opportunity for the faithful to reflect on 'the mystery of time', which passes quickly and inexorably. Such should give rise to a dual feeling: of penance and sorrow for the lost occasions of grace; and of thanks to God for the graces and blessings He has given during the past year. These sentiments have given rise to two pious exercises: prolonged exposition of the Blessed Sacrament, and the singing of the Te Deum as an act of community praise and thanksgiving to God for the graces received from Him as the year draws to a close' (*Directory on Popular Piety and the Liturgy*, 126).

St Sylvester died in 335 after being Pope for twenty-one years. Being elected in the year after the Edict of Milan he was free to build many churches in Rome.

JANUARY 2013

1 Tuesday   Num 6:22-27. Ps 66:2-3, 5, 6, 8. Gal 4:4-7. Lk 2:16-21. *Lect* I:139

Mary, Mother of God. At the message of the angel, the Virgin Mary received the Word of God in her heart and in her body, and gave Life to the world. Hence she is acknowledged and honoured as being truly the Mother of God and Mother of the Redeemer (*Lumen gentium*, 52).

2 Wednesday   1 Jn 2:22-28. Ps 97:1-4. Jn 1:19-28. *Lect* I:146

'To become "children of God" we must be "born from above" or "born of God".' The mystery of Christmas is fulfilled in us when Christ is formed in us.

St Basil, 330–79, bishop of Caesarea, lived an ascetic life establishing norms for monastic life. He was a theologian of distinction. **St Gregory**, 329–89, a friend of Basil, was bishop of Sasima and later of Constantinople. He retired to live a monastic life.

3 Thursday   1 Jn 2:29-3:6. Ps 97:1, 3-6. Jn 1:29-34. *Lect* I:148

'The whole life of Jesus Christ will make manifest "how God anointed Jesus of Nazareth with the Holy Spirit and with power"' (*CCC*, 486).

The Holy Name of Jesus: Phil 2:1-11. Ps 8:4-9. Lk 2:21-24.

St Munchin (Mainchin) see *January notes*.

4 Friday   1 Jn 3:7-10. Ps 97:1, 7-9. Jn 1:35-42. *Lect* I:150

The Christmas message is that we have found the Messiah. Jesus Christ, the Incarnate Word, has appeared to undo the work of the devil.

5 Saturday   1 Jn 3:11-21. Ps 99. Jn 1:43-51. *Lect* I:152

'The Epiphany shows that "the full number of the nations" now takes its "place in the family of the patriarchs" and acquires *Israelitica dignitas* (is made "worthy of the heritage of Israel")' (*CCC*, 528).

St Charles of St Andrew see *January notes*.

Dublin Tomorrow is the anniversary of the episcopal ordination of Most Rev. Diarmuid Martin, 6 January 1999.

January 2013 Psalter Week 2

6 Sunday **THE EPIPHANY OF THE LORD** Solemnity
White ✠ HOURS Proper. Te Deum
MASS Proper. Gloria. Creed. Preface: Epiphany. In the Roman Canon, proper form
EVENING PRAYER of the Epiphany

No other celebrations, not even funeral Masses, are permitted today.
After the Gospel, the announcement of the movable feasts may be made. See Announcement of Easter, p. 34 and RM pp. 1351–2

---

7 Monday **After Epiphany**
White HOURS Psalter Week 2. MASS Proper. Preface: Epiphany or Nativity I–III
White Optional memorial of **St Raymond of Penyafort, priest**

---

8 Tuesday **After Epiphany**
White HOURS Psalter Week 2. MASS Proper. Preface: Epiphany or Nativity I–III

---

9 Wednesday **After Epiphany**
White HOURS Psalter Week 2. MASS Proper. Preface: Epiphany or Nativity I–III

---

10 Thursday **After Epiphany**
White HOURS Psalter Week 2. MASS Proper. Preface: Epiphany or Nativity I–III

---

11 Friday **After Epiphany**
White HOURS Psalter Week 2. MASS Proper. Preface: Epiphany or Nativity I–III

---

12 Saturday **After Epiphany**
White HOURS Psalter Week 2. MASS Proper. Preface: Epiphany or Nativity I–III
FIRST EVENING PRAYER of the **Baptism of the Lord**

January 2013 READINGS Sunday Cycle C

6 Sunday   Is 60:1-6. Ps 71:1-2, 7-8, 10-13. Eph 3:2-3, 5-6. Mt 2:1-12. Lect I:161

'**The Epiphany** is the manifestation of Jesus as Messiah of Israel, Son of God and Saviour of the world. The great feast of Epiphany celebrates the adoration of Jesus by the wise men (magi) from the East, together with his baptism in the Jordan and the wedding feast at Cana in Galilee. In the magi, representatives of the neighbouring pagan religions, the Gospel sees the first-fruits of the nations, who welcome the good news of salvation through the Incarnation' (CCC, 528).

7 Monday   1 Jn 3:22-4:6. Ps 2:7-8, 10-11. Mt 4:12-17, 23-25. Lect I:164

Jesus, God made man, works signs and wonders among his people. We lose the message of Christmas if we see only a baby in a crib and do not wonder at the great mystery unfolded for us.

St Raymond of Penyafort, 1175–1275, was a very brilliant lawyer when, at the age of forty-seven, he became a Dominican. Later he became Master General of the Dominicans and Archbishop of Tarragona.

8 Tuesday   1 Jn 4:7-10. Ps 71:1-4, 7-8. Mk 6:34-44. Lect I:166

The celebration of Epiphany recalls the signs given us of God's presence in our world. God's love has been revealed, and each time we celebrate the Eucharist we proclaim that manifestation, and look forward to its final revealing.

9 Wednesday   1 Jn 4:11-18. Ps 71:1-2, 10-13. Mk 6:45-52. Lect I: 168

'The signs worked by Jesus attest that the Father has sent him. They invite belief in him. To those who turn to him in faith, he grants what they ask. So miracles strengthen faith in the One who does his Father's works; they bear witness that he is the Son of God' (CCC, 548).

10 Thursday   1 Jn 4:19-5:4. Ps 71:1-2, 14-15, 17. Lk 4:14-22. Lect I: 171

The virtue of love is seen in Jesus who comes to bring freedom to captives and joy to the poor.

11 Friday   1 Jn 5:5-13. Ps 147:12-15, 19-20. Lk 5:12-16. Lect I:173

We are healed from our sinfulness through the blood of the cross and the water of baptism.

12 Saturday   1 Jn 5:14-21. Ps 149:1-6, 9. Jn 3:22-30. Lect I:175

John the Baptist rejoices to hear the bridegroom's voice. The Lord takes delight in his people and hears their prayers when they call in faith.

Next Sunday's readings: Year C: Is 40:1-5, 9-11. Ps 103:1-2, 3-4, 24-25, 27-30. Ti 2:11-14, 3:4-7. Lk 3:15-16, 21-22. Lect I:185 or 833 **or Is 42:1-4, 6-7. Ps 28:1-4, 9-10. Acts 10:34-38. Lk 3:15-16, 21-22.** Lect I:179

January 2013 Psalter Week 1

13 Sunday **THE BAPTISM OF THE LORD** Feast
White ✠ HOURS Proper. Te Deum. Psalter Week 3 at Day Hour
MASS Proper. Gloria. Creed. Preface: Proper
EVENING PRAYER of the Feast

No other celebrations, except funeral Masses, are permitted today (see Lit. Note 7)

St Hilary, bishop and doctor of the Church is not celebrated this year.

ORDINARY TIME

14 Monday **1st Week in Ordinary Time**
Green HOURS Psalter Week 1. MASS of choice

---

15 Tuesday **1st Week in Ordinary Time**
 St Ita, virgin Memorial
White HOURS of the memorial. Psalter Week 1
 MASS of the memorial. Preface: Common or of the Saint
Limerick **St Ita, virgin** Feast

---

16 Wednesday **1st Week in Ordinary Time**
Green HOURS Psalter Week 1. MASS of choice
White Optional memorial of **St Fursa, abbot and missionary**

---

17 Thursday **1st Week in Ordinary Time**
 St Anthony, abbot Memorial
White HOURS of the memorial. Psalter Week 1
 MASS of the memorial. Preface: Common or of the Saint

From 18–25 January, the Week of Prayer for Christian Unity is held. The texts for the Masses for Christian Unity are given in the Missal, pp. 1176–81. These can be used on days which allow a choice throughout the Week of Prayer. The Eucharistic Prayer for Various Needs, form I (The Church on the Path of Unity), may be used each day.

18 Friday **1st Week in Ordinary Time**
Green HOURS Psalter Week 1. MASS of choice

---

19 Saturday **1st Week in Ordinary Time**
Green HOURS Psalter Week 1. MASS of choice
White/Green Saturday Mass of the **Blessed Virgin Mary**

January 2013   READINGS Sunday Cycle C   Weekday Cycle 1

13 Sunday (Year C) Is 40:1-5, 9-11. Ps 103:1-2, 3-4, 24-25, 27-30. Ti 2:11-14, 3:4-7. Lk 3:15-16, 21-22. *Lect* I:185 *or* 833 *or* **Is 42:1-4, 6-7. Ps 28:1-4, 9-10. Acts 10:34-38. Lk 3:15-16, 21-22.** *Lect* I:179

The Baptism of the Lord. Jesus is anointed with the Spirit and his power. He is proclaimed Messiah. He now goes about doing good, working the signs that make him known as the Servant of God. He is the one who brings good news to the poor and tells of salvation. Through our baptism each one of us is ordered to the life of Christ – Priest, Prophet and King – and the Father looks on us with favour.

FIRST WEEK IN ORDINARY TIME

14 Monday   Heb 1:1-6. Ps 96:1-2, 6-7, 9. Mk 1:14-20. *Lect* II:3
The Letter to the Hebrews is to be understood as a homily, rather than a letter. Just as for the people of his time so for us today the message of forgiveness, the call to courage and to hope, the challenge to risk are relevant. For God has spoken in his Son to us today.

15 Tuesday   Heb 2:5-12. Ps 8:2, 5-9. Mk 1:21-28. *Lect* II:5
The humanity of Jesus is strongly stressed: he is immersed in our human existence. Like us he suffered and was tempted.
St Ita see *January notes.*

16 Wednesday Heb 2:14-18. Ps 104:1-4, 6-9. Mk 1:29-39. *Lect* II:7
Jesus is the pioneer of our salvation, the one who leads us forward into a new land. The new high priest, chosen from the people, has entered the presence of God, offered sacrifice for sin, and removed the burden of guilt. He continues his merciful intercession; for through his own experience he understands our temptations.
St Fursa see *January notes.*

17 Thursday   Heb 3:7-14. Ps 94:6-11. Mk 1:40-45. *Lect* II:9
Let us not be foolish and reject the word spoken to us today, and in turn lose our own entrance into God's presence, into the Promised Land.
St Anthony, died 356, 'Father of monasticism', lived a life of solitude but also attracted many others to form communities of hermits.
During the Week of Prayer for Christian Unity readings may be taken from *Lect* III:508–28.

18 Friday   Heb 4:1-5, 11. Ps 77:3-4, 6-8. Mk 2:1-12. *Lect* II:11
The temptation to give up, to disregard the word of God, to take his gifts lightly – these are dangers for Christians at all times.

19 Saturday   Heb 4:12-16. Ps 18:8-10, 15. Mk 2:13-17. *Lect* II:13
We stand before God's judgement with Jesus who feels for our weaknesses.
Ossory Tomorrow is the anniversary of the episcopal ordination of Most Rev. Laurence Forristal, 20 January 1980.
Ferns Tomorrow is the anniversary of the episcopal ordination of Most Rev. Brendan Comiskey SSCC, 20 January 1980.

Next Sunday's readings: Is 62:1-5. Ps 95:1-3, 7-10. 1 Cor 12:4-11. Jn 2:1-11. *Lect* I:838

January 2013 Psalter Week 2

20 Sunday **SECOND SUNDAY IN ORDINARY TIME**
World Day of Migrants and Refugees
Green ✠ HOURS Proper. Te Deum. Psalter Week 2
MASS Proper. Gloria. Creed. Preface: Sundays I–VIII
No Masses for the dead, except funeral Masses, are permitted today (see Lit. Note 7)
St Fabian, pope and martyr and **St Sebastian, martyr** are not celebrated this year.

---

21 Monday	**2nd Week in Ordinary Time**
	St Agnes, virgin and martyr Memorial
Red	HOURS Proper of the memorial. Psalter Week 2 at Day Hour
	MASS of the memorial. Preface: Common or of the Saint

---

22 Tuesday **2nd Week in Ordinary Time**
Green HOURS Psalter Week 2. MASS of choice
Red Optional memorial of **St Vincent, deacon and martyr**

---

23 Wednesday 2nd Week in Ordinary Time
Green HOURS Psalter Week 2. MASS of choice

---

24 Thursday **2nd Week in Ordinary Time**
St Francis de Sales, bishop and doctor of the Church
Memorial
White HOURS of the memorial. Psalter Week 2
MASS of the memorial. Preface: Common or of the Saint

---

25 Friday THE CONVERSION OF ST PAUL, APOSTLE Feast
White HOURS Proper. Te Deum. Psalter Week 2 at Day Hour
MASS Proper. Gloria. Preface: Apostles I
No Masses for the dead, except funeral Masses, are permitted today (see Lit. Note 7)

---

26 Saturday **2nd Week in Ordinary Time**
Ss Timothy and Titus, bishops Memorial
White HOURS of the memorial. Psalter Week 2
MASS of the memorial. Preface: Common or of the Saints

January 2013 READINGS Sunday Cycle C   Weekday Cycle 1

SECOND WEEK IN ORDINARY TIME

20 Sunday Is 62:1-5. Ps 95:1-3, 7-10. 1 Cor 12:4-11. Jn 2:1-11. *Lect* I:838
The fulfillment of God's promise is compared to a wedding feast. The wine that flows in plenty speaks of the joy of the kingdom.

21 Monday Heb 5:1-10. Ps 109:1-4. Mk 2:18-22. *Lect* II:15
Jesus grew in suffering and learned to obey God's will. He is the bridegroom who is always with us.
St Agnes, wealthy and beautiful, was martyred for her virginity in the last persecutions in Rome, in the early fourth century. Patron of betrothed couples, gardeners and young girls.

22 Tuesday Heb 6:10-20. Ps 100:1-2, 4-5, 9, 10. Mk 2:23-28. *Lect* II:17
'The celebration of Sunday observes the moral commandment inscribed by nature in the human heart to render to God an outward, visible, public and regular worship "as a sign of his universal beneficence to all"' (*CCC*, 2176).
St Vincent, deacon of the church of Saragossa, Spain, martyred in 304 in Valencia after prolonged torture.

23 Wednesday Heb 7:1-3, 15-17. Ps 109:1-4. Mk 3:1-6. *Lect* II:19
'Sunday worship fulfils the moral command of the Old Covenant, taking up its rhythm and spirit in the weekly celebration of the Creator and Redeemer of his people' (*CCC*, 2176).

24 Thursday Heb 7:25-8:6. Ps 39:7-10, 17. Mk 3:7-12. *Lect* II:21
'Christ always gives his Church the gift of unity, but the Church must always pray and work to maintain, reinforce, and perfect the unity that Christ wills for her' (*CCC*, 820).
St Francis de Sales, 1567–1622, bishop of Geneva, founder of the Visitation Sisters. He worked with gentleness and love to rebuild the Catholic faith after the Reformation. Patron saint of writers, editors and journalists.

25 Friday Acts 22:3-16 *or* Acts 9:1-22. Ps 116:1-2. Mk 16:15-18. *Lect* II:928
Conversion of St Paul. St Paul preached the power of God at work in the lives of each one of us. His own conversion shows that power in his own life. Out of a persecutor God made a preacher and teacher of the peoples.

26 Saturday 2 Tm 1:1-8 *or* Ti 1:1-5. Ps 95:1-3, 7-8, 10. Lk 10:1-9. *Lect* II:931
Ss Timothy and Titus were close to St Paul as followers and later in their work with him. Tradition makes Timothy the first bishop of Ephesus. And from Paul's advice to him to take some wine for his stomach's sake, he has been invoked as a patron in cases of stomach complaint. Titus was sent to organise the Church in Crete.
Achonry Tomorrow is the anniversary of the episcopal ordination of Most Rev. Brendan Kelly, 27 January 2008.

Next Sunday's readings: Neh 8:2-6, 8-10. Ps 18:8-10, 15. 1 Cor 12:12-30 (shorter form 12:12-14, 27)**. Lk 1:1-4, 4:14-21.** *Lect* I:841

NOTES FOR FEBRUARY 2013

THE POPE'S INTENTIONS

General – Migrant Families: That migrant families, in particular mothers, may be sustained and accompanied in their difficulties.

Mission – Peace: That peoples experiencing war and conflicts may lead the way in building a future of peace.

THE IRISH CALENDAR IN FEBRUARY

1st: St Brigid is renowned for her hospitality, almsgiving and care of the sick. She was born c. 454. When she was young her father wished to make a very suitable marriage for her but she insisted in consecrating her virginity to God. She received the veil and spiritual formation probably from St Mel and stayed for a period under his direction in Ardagh. Others followed her example and this led her to found a double monastery in Kildare with the assistance of Bishop Conleth. She died in 524 and her cult is widespread not only throughout Ireland but in several European lands.

7th: St Mel died in 488. He is said to have been a Briton who came to Ireland with Patrick, with whom he worked until he was ordained in Ardagh. He is one of the earliest Irish saints and gave the religious veil to Brigid.

11th: St Gobnait is one of the best loved saints in West Cork but only traditions concerning her life survive. The main part of her life was spent in Ballyvourney, Co. Cork where there has always been a deep devotion to her, and which is a place of pilgrimage on this day and on Pentecost. Her gifts of caring for and curing the sick have been a significant part of her cult through the centuries. Happily her memorial coincides with the World Day for the Sick.

17th: St Fintan was born in Leinster. He received his religious formation in Terryglass, Co. Tipperary under the abbot Colum, and was deeply influenced by his penitential practices and the severity of the Rule. Fintan made his own foundation in Clonenagh, Co. Laois. He died in 603.

3 February:
BLESSING OF THROATS ON THE MEMORIAL OF ST BLAISE

St Blaise, bishop of Sebaste in Armenia, is believed to have been martyred in the early fourth century. Very little is known about him. Tradition states that he was a physician before becoming a bishop. Since the eighth century he has been venerated as the patron of those who suffer from disease of the throat. He is said to have healed a boy who was choking. The blessing of St Blaise is a sign of our faith in God's protection and love for us and for the sick.

Using two crossed and unlighted candles, blessed on the memorial of St Blaise or on the feast of the Presentation of the Lord, the minister touches the throat of each person, saying:

Through the intercession of St Blaise, bishop and martyr, may God deliver you from all ailments of the throat and from every other evil (*or* from every disease of the throat and from every other illness): In the name of the Father, and of the Son, and of the Holy Spirit. Amen.

CATECHISM OF THE CATHOLIC CHURCH

In the Apostolic Constitution, *Fidei Depositum* on the publication of the *Catechism of the Catholic Church* (11 October 1992), Pope John Paul II said that the Catechism 'is given ... that it may be a sure and authentic reference text for teaching Catholic doctrine and particularly for preparing local catechisms. It is also offered to all the faithful who wish to deepen their knowledge of the unfathomable riches of salvation. It is meant to support ecumenical efforts that are moved by the holy desire for the unity of all Christians, showing carefully the content and wondrous harmony of the Catholic faith. The *Catechism of the Catholic Church*, lastly, is offered to every individual who asks us to give an account of the hope that is in us and who wants to know what the Catholic Church believes.'

The Apostolic Constitution outlines the content and arrangement of the Catechism: 'A catechism should faithfully and systematically present the teaching of Sacred Scripture, the living Tradition of the Church and the authentic Magisterium, as well as the spiritual heritage of the Fathers and the Church's saints, to allow for a better knowledge of the Christian mystery and for enlivening the faith of the People of God. It should take into account the doctrinal statements which down the centuries the Holy Spirit has intimated to his Church. It should also help illumine with the light of faith the new situations and problems which had not yet emerged in the past.

The catechism will thus contain the new and the old (cf. *Mt* 13:52), because the faith is always the same yet the source of ever new light.

To respond to this twofold demand, the *Catechism of the Catholic Church* on the one hand repeats the old, traditional order already followed by the Catechism of St Pius V, arranging the material in four parts: the *Creed*, the *Sacred Liturgy*, with pride of place given to the sacraments, the *Christian way of life*, explained beginning with the Ten Commandments, and finally, *Christian prayer*. At the same time, however, the contents are often expressed in a new way in order to respond to the questions of our age.

The four parts are related one to the other: the Christian mystery is the object of faith (first part); it is celebrated and communicated in liturgical actions (second part); it is present to enlighten and sustain the children of God in their actions (third part); it is the basis for our prayer, the privileged expression of which is the *Our Father*, and it represents the object of our supplication, our praise and our intercession (fourth part).

The Liturgy itself is prayer; the confession of faith finds its proper place in the celebration of worship. Grace, the fruit of the sacraments, is the irreplaceable condition for Christian living, just as participation in the Church's liturgy requires faith. If faith is not expressed in works, it is dead (cf. *Jas* 2:14-16) and cannot bear fruit unto eternal life.

In reading the *Catechism of the Catholic Church* we can perceive the wondrous unity of the mystery of God, his saving will, as well as the central place of Jesus Christ, the only-begotten Son of God, sent by the Father, made man in the womb of the Blessed Virgin Mary by the power of the Holy Spirit, to be our Saviour. Having died and risen, Christ is always present in his Church, especially in the sacraments; he is the source of our faith, the model of Christian conduct and the Teacher of our prayer.'

January 2013 Psalter Week 3

27 Sunday **THIRD SUNDAY IN ORDINARY TIME**
Green ✠ HOURS Proper. Te Deum. Psalter Week 3
MASS Proper. Gloria. Creed. Preface: Sundays I–VIII
Catholic Schools Week begins today
No Masses for the dead, except funeral Masses, are permitted today (see Lit. Note 7)
St Angela Merici, virgin is not celebrated this year

---

28 Monday	**3rd Week in Ordinary Time**
	St Thomas Aquinas, priest and doctor of the Church
	Memorial
White	HOURS of the memorial. Psalter Week 3
	MASS of the memorial. Preface: Common or of the Saint

---

29 Tuesday **3rd Week in Ordinary Time**
Green HOURS Psalter Week 3. MASS of choice

---

30 Wednesday 3rd Week in Ordinary Time
Green HOURS Psalter Week 3. MASS of choice
White Optional memorial of **St Aidan, bishop**
Ferns **St Aidan, bishop** Feast
Dublin **Bl. Margaret Ball and Francis Taylor, martyrs**
Meath **Bl. Margaret Ball and Francis Taylor, martyrs**

---

31 Thursday **3rd Week in Ordinary Time**
St John Bosco, priest Memorial
White HOURS of the memorial. Psalter Week 3
MASS of the memorial. Preface: Common or of the Saint

FEBRUARY 2013

1 Friday ST BRIGID, ABBESS, SECONDARY PATRON OF IRELAND Feast
White HOURS Proper (Divine Office, II, p. 192*)
Te Deum. Psalter Week 3 at Day Hour
MASS Proper. Gloria. Preface: Proper
EVENING PRAYER of St Brigid
No Masses for the dead, except funeral Masses, are permitted today (see Lit. Note 7)

---

2 Saturday THE PRESENTATION OF THE LORD Feast
White *World Day for Consecrated Life*
HOURS Proper. Te Deum. Psalter Week 3 at Day Hour.
MASS Proper. Gloria. Preface: Proper
BLESSING OF CANDLES AND PROCESSION. Two forms are given: a procession from a chapel or other place and a solemn entrance and gathering. Then the altar is venerated, followed by the Gloria and opening prayer of the Mass.
EVENING PRAYER of the Feast
No Masses for the dead, except funeral Masses, are permitted today (see Lit. Note 7)

January 2013 READINGS Sunday Cycle C   Weekday Cycle 1

THIRD WEEK IN ORDINARY TIME

27 Sunday   Neh 8:2-6, 8-10. Ps 18:8-10, 15. 1 Cor 12:12-30
(shorter form 12:12-14, 27)**. Lk 1:1-4, 4:14-21.** *Lect* I:841
The teaching of the Church on the Liturgy of the Word is expressed in these texts. Jesus states that the prophecy of Isaiah is fulfilled in himself: so the Scripture word is actualised for us each time it is proclaimed in church. Christ is really present in his Word. That Word challenges us to a renewal of life, as the people rediscovered their identity when Ezra read the Law to them. Those who serve as ministers of the Word will find the joy of the Lord to be their strength.

28 Monday   Heb 9:15, 24-28. Ps 97:1-6. Mk 3:22-30. *Lect* II:27
We now live in the new covenant times when Jesus has conquered sin. But we await the final consummation when he returns in glory to claim us for himself.
St Thomas Aquinas was born in Italy in 1224. He died in 1274. Thomas taught that Christian revelation and human knowledge are aspects of a single truth and cannot be in conflict with one another. One of the greatest theologians, he is patron of schools, universities, students and booksellers.
Meath Tomorrow is the anniversary of the episcopal ordination of Most Rev. Michael Smith, 29 January 1984.

29 Tuesday   Heb 10:1-10. Ps 39:2, 4, 7-8, 10, 11. Mk 3:31-35.
Lect II:29
In the story of God's relationship with his people there is an often repeated warning about sacrifices which are purely external. In Christ we have the supreme expression of conformity to God's will in a sacrificial life.

30 Wednesday Heb 10:11-18. Ps 109:1-4. Mk 4:1-20. *Lect* II: 31
The parable of sowing and harvest tells us that God's glorious kingdom is still to come. God's kingdom will surely come despite the various difficulties experienced by those who work for it. We are to prepare by an upright life.
St Aidan see *January notes*.
Bl. Margaret Ball and Francis Taylor see *January notes*.

31 Thursday   Heb 10:19-25. Ps 23:1-6. Mk 4:21-25. *Lect* II:34
We are called to an attentive hearing of God's word. So the truth will eventually be revealed. Sunday attendance at the Word and Eucharist gives life to the community – 'encourage each other to go'.
St John Bosco, 1815–88, born in Piedmont, founded the Salesians to educate boys for life. He also became involved in publishing catechetical material for youth. He is a patron saint of youth and of Catholic publishers.

FEBRUARY 2013

1 Friday   Job 31:16-20, 24-25, 31-32 *or* Eph 3:14-21. Ps 106:35-38, 41-42. Lk 6:32-38. National Proper
St Brigid see *February notes*.
Kilmore Tomorrow is the anniversary of the episcopal ordination of Most Rev. Leo O'Reilly, 2 February 1997.

2 Saturday   Mal 3:1-4 *or* Heb 2:14-18. Ps 23:7-10. Lk 2:22-40
(shorter form 2:22-32)**.** *Lect* I:967 or II:940
The Presentation of the Lord. This feast is a remembrance of the Lord and Mary, his Mother. With candles in their hands, the people go out to meet the Lord and to acclaim him with Simeon, who recognised Christ as 'a light to reveal God to the nations'.

Next Sunday's readings: Jer 1:4-5, 17-19. Ps 70:1-6, 15, 17. 1 Cor 12:31–13:13 (shorter form 13:4-13)**. Lk 4:21-30.** *Lect* I:845

February 2013 Psalter Week 4

3 Sunday **FOURTH SUNDAY IN ORDINARY TIME**
Green ✠ HOURS Proper. Te Deum. Psalter Week 4
MASS Proper. Gloria. Creed. Preface: Sundays I–VIII
No Masses for the dead, except funeral Masses, are permitted today (see Lit. Note 7)
St Blaise, bishop and martyr and **St Ansgar, bishop** are not celebrated this year.

---

4 Monday **4th Week in Ordinary Time**
Green HOURS Psalter Week 4. MASS of choice

---

5 Tuesday **4th Week in Ordinary Time**
St Agatha, virgin and martyr Memorial
Red HOURS of the memorial. Psalter Week 4
MASS of the memorial. Preface: Common or of the Saint

---

6 Wednesday **4th Week in Ordinary Time**
Ss Paul Miki and Companions, martyrs Memorial
Red HOURS of the memorial. Psalter Week 4
MASS of the memorial. Preface: Common or of the Saint

---

7 Thursday **4th Week in Ordinary Time**
Green HOURS Psalter Week 4. MASS of choice
White Optional memorial of **St Mel, bishop**
Ardagh and
Clonmacnois **St Mel, bishop** Feast

---

8 Friday **4th Week in Ordinary Time**
Green HOURS Psalter Week 4. MASS of choice
White Optional memorial of **St Jerome Emiliani**
White Optional memorial of **St Josephine Bakhita, virgin**

---

9 Saturday **4th Week in Ordinary Time**
Green HOURS Psalter Week 4. MASS of choice
White/Green Saturday Mass of the **Blessed Virgin Mary**

February 2013 READINGS Sunday Cycle C Weekday Cycle 1

FOURTH WEEK IN ORDINARY TIME

3 Sunday **Jer 1:4-5, 17-19. Ps 70:1-6, 15, 17. 1 Cor 12:31–13:13** (shorter form 13:4-13). **Lk 4:21-30.** *Lect* I:845
Jesus has come as the prophet to all nations. There is no limit to the mercy and salvation he brings, only the willingness to accept him.

4 Monday **Heb 11:32-40. Ps 30:20-24. Mk 5:1-20.** *Lect* II:40
These witnesses of faith who endured so much did not receive the promises. We are indeed blessed in that we have been chosen.

5 Tuesday **Heb 12:1-4. Ps 21:26-28, 30-32. Mk 5:21-43.** *Lect* II:42
'Jesus hears the prayer of faith, expressed in words by Jairus or in silence by the woman who touches his clothes. The urgent request of the blind men has been renewed in the traditional prayer to Jesus known as the Jesus Prayer: "Lord Jesus Christ, Son of God, have mercy on me, a sinner!"' (*CCC*, 2616).
St Agatha died a martyr for the faith at Catania in Sicily in the third Century. Patron of bell-founders.

6 Wednesday **Heb 12:4-7, 11-15. Ps 102:1-2, 13-14, 17-18. Mk 6:1-6.** *Lect* II:45
The end of Jesus' Galilean ministry sees his rejection. This foreshadows the greater rejection by Israel, and the turning to the Gentiles by the apostles.
Ss Paul Miki and Companions martyred at Nagasaki, Japan, in 1597. The six Franciscans, seventeen Franciscan Tertiaries, and three Jesuits died suspended on crosses.

7 Thursday **Heb 12:18-19, 21-24. Ps 47:2-4, 9-11. Mk 6:7-13.** *Lect* II:47
The author of Hebrews contrasts the assembly of Israel with that of the Christians. The former is of earth, while the latter is in the heavenly sanctuary, the place of the new covenant in the sacrifice of Jesus. The blood of Jesus brings forgiveness of sin and access to God.
St Mel see *February notes*.

8 Friday **Heb 13:1-8. Ps 26:1, 3, 5, 8-9. Mk 6:14-29.** *Lect* II:49
The law of love covers all situations and it remembers strangers and prisoners. The marriage state is to be honoured and authority in the Church respected.
St Jerome Emiliani, d. 1537, after a military career he founded the Clerks Regular of Somaschi for the care of orphans and the poor. Patron saint of orphans.
St Josephine Bakhita, 1868–1947, a native of Sudan, brought as a slave to Italy where she became a Christian and later entered the Institute of Canossian Daughters of Charity in Venice.

9 Saturday **Heb 13:15-17, 20-21. Ps 22. Mk 6:30-34.** *Lect* I:51
Jesus took pity on the crowd for they were like sheep without a shepherd. May the Good Shepherd make us always ready to do God's will in every kind of good action.

Next Sunday's readings: Is 6:1-8. Ps 137:1-5, 7-8. 1 Cor 15:1-11 (shorter form 15:3-8, 11). **Lk 5:1-11.** *Lect* I:849

February 2013 READINGS Sunday Cycle C Psalter Week 1

10 Sunday   **FIFTH SUNDAY IN ORDINARY TIME**
Day of Prayer for Temperance
Green ✠   HOURS Proper. Te Deum. Psalter Week 1
MASS Proper. Gloria. Creed. Preface: Sundays I–VIII
READINGS   **Is 6:1-8. Ps 137:1-5, 7-8. 1 Cor 15:1-11** (shorter form 15:3-8, 11)**. Lk 5:1-11.** *Lect* I:849

Today we look at the vocations of Isaiah and St Peter. Both are called in strange circumstances. They each recognise their unworthiness, but are reassured that God will be with them. Through our baptism we also are called to build up God's kingdom. We should fear no evil for the Lord is with us.

No Masses for the dead, except funeral Masses, are permitted today (see Lit. Note 7)
St Scholastica, virgin is not celebrated this year.

---

11 Monday   **5th Week in Ordinary Time**
World Day of the Sick
Green   HOURS Psalter Week 1. MASS of choice
White   Optional memorial of **Our Lady of Lourdes**
White   Optional memorial of **St Gobnait, virgin**
READINGS   **Gn 1:1-19. Ps 103:1-2, 5-6, 10, 12, 24, 35. Mk 6:53-56.** *Lect* II:54

The blessing of water at Baptism recalls the Spirit of God over the primitive waters from which came life. We are reborn by water and the Spirit to the new life of Christ.
Our Lady of Lourdes. On this day in 1858, Our Lady first appeared to the fourteen-year-old Bernadette Soubirous. Later Bernadette was to learn that the mysterious lady was the Blessed Virgin and to hear from her lips, 'I am the Immaculate Conception'. In 1992 Pope John Paul II instituted the World Day of the Sick to be held on the commemoration of Our Lady of Lourdes.
St Gobnait see *February notes*.

---

12 Tuesday   **5th Week in Ordinary Time**
Green   HOURS Psalter Week 1. MASS of choice
READINGS   **Gn 1:20-2:4. Ps 8:4-9. Mk 7:1-13.** *Lect* II:56

We are the crown of God's creation, yet we fail to carry out the work of conserving the earth that God gave to our stewardship. Our responsibility towards conservation of the earth's resources and beauty is a God-given trust.

SEASON OF LENT

The annual Lenten season is the fitting time to climb the holy mountain of Easter.

The Lenten season has a double character, namely to prepare both catechumens and faithful to celebrate the paschal mystery. The catechumens, both with the rite of election and scrutinies, are prepared for the celebration of the sacraments of Christian initiation; the faithful, ever more attentive to the word of God and prayer, prepare themselves by penance for the renewal of their baptismal promises.

The faithful are to be encouraged to participate in an ever more intense and faithful way in the Lenten liturgy and in penitential celebrations. They are to be clearly reminded that both according to the law and tradition they should approach the sacrament of penance during this season so that with purified heart they may participate in the paschal mysteries. (*Paschale solemnitatis*, 6, 15, *Ceremonial of Bishops*, 249, 251)

February 2013   Psalter Week 4

13 Wednesday ASH WEDNESDAY Day of Fast and Abstinence
Violet   HOURS Psalter Week 4
                   Psalms of Friday Week 3 may be used at Morning Prayer
                   MASS Proper. Preface: Lent III or IV.
READINGS   **Jl 2:12-18. Ps 50:3-6, 12-14, 17. 2 Cor 5:20-6:2. Mt 6:1-6, 16-18.** *Lect* I:191

In the readings today there is a great consciousness of our sinfulness as we pray, 'Have mercy on us, O Lord, for we have sinned.' There is also a sense that the time to repent and turn back is now. The Gospel tells us how to approach that renewal of our lives. It puts before us the remedy in prayer, fasting and almsgiving. These three strands of Lenten observance are as ancient as Christianity itself. There is no substitute for them. 'Fasting is the soul of prayer, mercy is the lifeblood of fasting. If we have not all three together, we have nothing,' says St Peter Chrysologus.
No Masses for the dead, except funeral Masses, are permitted today (see Lit. Note 7)

---

14 Thursday   SS CYRIL, MONK, AND METHODIUS, BISHOP,
                    PATRONS OF EUROPE   Feast
White   HOURS Proper. Te Deum. Psalter Week 4 at Day Hour
                   MASS Proper. Gloria. Preface: Saints
READINGS   **Acts 13:46-49. Ps 116. Lk 10:1-9.** *Lect* II:957

St Cyril, 826–69, and **St Methodius**, 815–85, were brothers from Thessalonica in Greece. They preached the gospel in Moravia using their own translation of the Scriptures and the liturgy in the local language. These translations into Slavonic were in an alphabet, now called Cyrillic, which they devised. They are honoured as apostles of the Slavic peoples and in 1980 Pope John Paul II declared them Patrons of Europe.
No Masses for the dead, except funeral Masses, are permitted today (see Lit. Note 7)

---

15 Friday   **After Ash Wednesday**
Violet   HOURS Psalter Week 4
                   MASS Proper. Preface: Lent I–IV
READINGS   **Is 58:1-9. Ps 50:3-6, 18-19. Mt 9:14-15.** *Lect* I:196

Christian fasting began as a voluntary practice, as a support to prayer, as penance for sin, as a way to save something for the poor, and as a way to prepare for a feast. It was a suitable practice to prepare for the celebration of Easter. The need for fasting is still there.

---

16 Saturday   **After Ash Wednesday**
Violet   HOURS Psalter Week 4.
                   MASS Proper. Preface: Lent I–IV
READINGS   **Is 58:9-14. Ps 85:1-6. Lk 5:27-32.** *Lect* I:198

Isaiah calls out for greater service of God and fellow human beings. Lent gives us the opportunity to jettison much that is unnecessary and unhelpful in our way of life. The following of Christ implies a leaving behind of much that causes unhappiness in our own lives and in the lives of others.

Next Sunday's readings: Deut 26:4-10. Ps 90:1-2, 10-15. Rm 10:8-13. Lk 4:1-13. *Lect* I:207

February 2013 Psalter Week 1

17 Sunday **FIRST SUNDAY OF LENT**
Violet ✠ HOURS Psalter Week 1
MASS Proper. No Gloria. Creed. Preface: Proper
The Rite of Election of Catechumens is celebrated today

No other celebrations, not even funeral Masses, are permitted today (see Lit. Note 7)
St Fintan, abbot and **Seven Holy Founders of the Servite Order** are not celebrated this year.

---

18 Monday **1st Week of Lent**
Violet HOURS Psalter Week 1. MASS Proper. Preface: Lent I–IV

---

19 Tuesday **1st Week of Lent**
Violet HOURS Psalter Week 1. MASS Proper. Preface: Lent I–IV

---

20 Wednesday 1st Week of Lent
Violet HOURS Psalter Week 1. MASS Proper. Preface: Lent I–IV

---

21 Thursday **1st Week of Lent**
Violet HOURS Psalter Week 1. MASS Proper. Preface: Lent I–IV
Memorial may be made of **St Peter Damian, bishop and doctor of the Church** (see *Lit. Note 7*)

---

22 Friday THE CHAIR OF ST PETER, APOSTLE Feast
White HOURS Proper. Psalter Week 1 at Day Hour
MASS Proper. Gloria. Preface: Apostles I

No Masses for the dead, except funeral Masses, are permitted today (see Lit. Note 7)

---

23 Saturday **1st Week of Lent**
Violet HOURS Psalter Week 1. MASS Proper. Preface: Lent I–IV
Memorial may be made of **St Polycarp, bishop and martyr** (see *Lit. Note 7*)

February 2013 READINGS Sunday Cycle C

FIRST WEEK OF LENT

17 Sunday   Deut 26:4-10. Ps 90:1-2, 10-15. Rm 10:8-13. Lk 4:1-13. *Lect* I:207

'Jesus' temptation reveals the way in which the Son of God is Messiah, contrary to the way Satan proposes to him and the way men wish to attribute to him. This is why Christ vanquished the Tempter for us' (*CCC* 540).

18 Monday   Lev 19:1-2, 11-18. Ps 18:8-10, 15. Mt 25:31-46. *Lect* I:210

The Gospel reminds us that Jesus came to preach good news to the poor. At the beginning of Lent we again get a reminder that good works are essential to our proper observance of the season, along with prayer and fasting.

Armagh Tomorrow is the anniversary of the episcopal ordination of His Eminence Cardinal Seán Brady, 19 February 1995.

19 Tuesday   Is 55:10-11. Ps 33:4-7, 16-19. Mt 6:7-15. *Lect* I:212

The model for our prayer is the Lord's Prayer. It is a summary of the whole Gospel, the most perfect of all prayers. Being taught and given to us by our Lord it is indeed the Word of God that goes out and succeeds in what it was sent to do. It is the foundation of the daily prayer of all Christians.

Achonry Tomorrow is the anniversary of the episcopal ordination of Most Rev. Thomas Flynn, 20 February 1977.

20 Wednesday Jon 3:1-10. Ps 50:3-4, 12-13, 18-19. Lk 11:29-32. *Lect* I:214

In Lent our eyes are fixed on the Cross of Christ from which comes our salvation, and the grace to accept it.

21 Thursday   Est 4:17. Ps 137:1-3, 7-8. Mt 7:7-12. *Lect* I:216

Queen Esther knew the practical things to be done and did them, but she did not rely on them. Her prayer shows that her confidence was in God: 'I have no one but you, Lord.' We can show a practical lack of faith. Sometimes we are hesitant to ask in prayer, maybe because it is only our last resort.

St Peter Damian, 1007–72, gave up teaching to become a hermit. Later he was Cardinal-bishop of Ostia. He was an outstanding reformer of Church life and discipline.

22 Friday   1 Pt 5:1-4. Ps 22. Mt 16:13-19. *Lect* II:962

The Chair of St Peter. This ancient feast relates to early Roman custom at this time of year of remembering the ancestors of the family, those who presided over the family fortunes. The texts today celebrate Peter as Bishop of Rome. We recall Christ's choice of Peter for service to the whole Church.

23 Saturday   Deut 26:16-19. Ps 118:1-2, 4-5, 7-8. Mt 5:43-48. *Lect* I:221

The Lord Jesus, the divine Teacher and Model of all perfection, preached holiness of life to each and every one of his disciples of every condition. He himself stands as the author and consummator of this holiness of life (*Lumen gentium*, 40).

St Polycarp was bishop of Smyrna or Izmir in modern Turkey. Born around the year 69, he was a disciple of St John the Apostle. He was martyred in 155.

Next Sunday's readings: Gn 15:5-12, 17-18. Ps 26:1, 7-9, 13-14. Phil 3:17-4:1 (shorter form 3:20-4:1). **Lk 9:28-36.** *Lect* I:228

NOTES FOR MARCH 2013

THE POPE'S INTENTIONS

General – Respect for Nature: That respect for nature will grow with the awareness that all creation is the work of God entrusted to human responsibility.
Mission – Bishops, Priests and Deacons: That bishops, priests and deacons may be tireless proclaimers of the Gospel to the ends of the earth.

THE IRISH CALENDAR IN MARCH

1st: St David is the patron saint of Wales, where he was an abbot and bishop in the sixth century. Several Irish saints were his pupils and he influenced monastic development in Ireland. He died around 601.

5th: St Kieran. Kieran of Saigir was born in Cape Clear, Co. Cork. He is numbered among the pre-Patrician saints of Ireland. He went to the Continent, where he was baptised and later ordained priest and bishop. He returned to his father's territory, Ossory, where he lived as a hermit. Disciples soon joined him and Saigir became a well-known monastery.

8th: St Senan was born near Kilrush, Co. Clare. His family were prosperous farmers. His vocation seems to have resulted from an experience of danger from the sea. His early studies were mainly made at the monastery of Kilnamanagh. His principal monastic foundation was on Scattery Island, near Kilrush, in the Shannon Estuary. He was anamchara to Ciaran of Clonmacnois and Brendan, and died in 544.

11th: St Aengus (Oengus) was a monk in Clonenagh, Co. Laois, who came to the monastery at Tallaght at the end of the eighth century during the abbacy of Maelruain to spend a period under his direction. He was renowned for his devotion to both foreign and native saints and composed two martyrologies. He returned to Clonenagh, where he became abbot and bishop. He died around 830.

17th: St Patrick was born very probably in the early years of the fifth century in Britain. He was taken captive at the age of sixteen and brought to Ireland where he worked as a slave. His captivity had a very positive effect on his spiritual life. He escaped back home at the age of twenty-two. It was obvious to him that God was calling him to return to convert the Irish. He studied probably in France, returned to Ireland c. 457–61 and made a tremendous number of converts. He died in 491.

21st: St Enda is considered to be one of the three great late vocations (athlaech) of Ireland. His sister, Faenche, a nun, set his thoughts on a religious vocation. He made a small foundation in Cell Aine, Co. Louth and, after studies in Scotland under Ninian, made several foundations in the Boyne valley. On Faenche's urging he went to Aran. He died probably in 520 and is considered as one of the early models of ascetic monasticism in Ireland.

24th: St Macartan belongs to a very early generation of saints in Ireland and is recognised as the first Bishop of Clogher. He is known as Patrick's 'Strong Man' for his dedication and faithfulness.

DATES OF PASSOVER AND EASTER

At the Council of Nicea in 325, the date for Easter was fixed as the Sunday after the full moon following the spring equinox. Sunday, 31 March 2013 is the feast of Easter. Eastern Christians calculate the date of Easter according to the Julian Calendar, the calendar in general use before the Gregorian reform of 1582. One of the reforms was the removal of ten days from the calendar and this discrepancy between the Julian and Gregorian Calendar results often in a difference in the date for Easter in East and West as they follow the two Calendars. Sunday, 5 May 2013 is the feast of Easter for Eastern Christians.

The feast of Passover is celebrated on 26 March (15 Nisan 5773), beginning at sundown on the previous evening and continuing for seven days.

50th ANNIVERSARY OF OPENING OF SECOND VATICAN COUNCIL

The Council, according to Pope John XXIII, wanted 'to transmit doctrine, pure and whole, without attenuations or misrepresentations', in such a way that 'this sure and immutable teaching, which must be respected faithfully, is elaborated and presented in a way which corresponds to the needs of our time'. In this regard, the opening words of the Dogmatic Constitution *Lumen gentium* remain of primary importance: 'Christ is the Light of nations. Because this is so, this Sacred Synod gathered together in the Holy Spirit eagerly desires, by proclaiming the Gospel to every creature, (cf. Mk 16:15) to bring the light of Christ to all men, a light brightly visible on the countenance of the Church' (*LG* 1). Beginning with the light of Christ, which purifies, illuminates and sanctifies in the celebration of the sacred liturgy (cfr. Constitution, *Sacrosanctum Concilium*) and with His divine word (cf. Dogmatic Constitution, *Dei Verbum*), the Council wanted to elaborate on the intimate nature of the Church (cf. Dogmatic Constitution, *Lumen gentium*) and its relationship with the contemporary world (cf. Pastoral Constitution, *Gaudium et spes*). Around these four Constitutions, the true pillars of the Council, are arranged the Declarations and Decrees which address some of the major challenges of the day.

– Congregation for the Doctrine of the Faith,
Note on Pastoral Recommendations for the Year of Faith, 6 January 2012

DOCUMENTS OF SECOND VATICAN COUNCIL

The Constitution on the Sacred Liturgy, *Sacrosanctum concilium*, 4 December 1963
Decree on the Means of Social Communication, *Inter mirifica*, 4 December 1963
Dogmatic Constitution on the Church, *Lumen Gentium*, 21 November 1964
Decree on the Catholic Eastern Churches, *Orientalium Ecclesiarum*, 21 November 1964
Decree on Ecumenism, *Unitatis redintegratio*, 21 November 1964
Decree on the Pastoral Office of Bishops in the Church, *Christus Dominus*, 28 October 1965
Decree on the Renewal of Religious Life, *Perfectae caritatis*, 28 October 1965
Decree on the Training of Priests, *Optatam totius*, 28 October 1965
Decree on Christian Education, *Gravissimum educationis*, 28 October 1965
Decree on the Relation of the Church to Non-Christian Religions, *Nostra aetate*, 28 October 1965
Dogmatic Constitution on Divine Revelation, *Dei verbum*, 18 November 1965
Decree on the Apostolate of Lay People, *Apostolicam actuositatem*, 18 November 1965
Declaration on Religious Freedom, *Dignitatis humanae*, 7 December 1965
Decree on the Church's Missionary Activity, *Ad gentes divinitus*, 7 December 1965
Decree on the Ministry and Life of Priests, *Presbyterorum ordinis*, 7 December 1965
Pastoral Constitution on the Church in the Modern World, *Gaudium et spes*, 7 December 1965

February 2013 Psalter Week 2

24 Sunday **SECOND SUNDAY OF LENT**
Violet ✠ HOURS Psalter Week 2
MASS Proper. No Gloria. Creed. Preface: Proper
No other celebrations, not even funeral Masses, are permitted today (see Lit. Note 7)

---

25 Monday **2nd Week of Lent**
Violet HOURS Psalter Week 2. MASS Proper. Preface: Lent I–IV

---

26 Tuesday **2nd Week of Lent**
Violet HOURS Psalter Week 2. MASS Proper. Preface: Lent I–IV

---

27 Wednesday 2nd Week of Lent
Violet HOURS Psalter Week 2. MASS Proper. Preface: Lent I–IV

---

28 Thursday **2nd Week of Lent**
Violet HOURS Psalter Week 2. MASS Proper. Preface: Lent I–IV

MARCH 2013

1 Friday **2nd Week of Lent**
Violet HOURS Psalter Week 2. MASS Proper. Preface: Lent I–IV
Memorial may be made of **St David, bishop** (see *Lit. Note 7*)

---

2 Saturday **2nd Week of Lent**
Violet HOURS Psalter Week 2. MASS Proper. Preface: Lent I–IV

February 2013 READINGS Sunday Cycle C

SECOND WEEK OF LENT

24 Sunday   Gn 15:5-12, 17-18. Ps 26:1, 7-9, 13-14. Phil 3:17-4:1 (shorter form 3:20-4:1)**. Lk 9:28-36.** *Lect* I:228

The vision of Christ transfigured in glory is given to the three apostles, who will see him suffering in the Garden. This vision is also for our encouragement at the beginning of Lent. Through suffering and the cross we come to the crown of glory in heaven. A Lent well spent will bring us to a joyful celebration of Easter.

25 Monday   Dn 9:4-10. Ps 78:8-9, 11, 13. Lk 6:36-38. *Lect* I:231

Daniel sees the goodness and generous love of God and contrasts the wickedness and betrayal of the people. He recognises the community aspect of that sin that has brought punishment on all the people high and low. And only God can heal them for to him alone mercy and pardon belong.

26 Tuesday   Is 1:10, 16-20. Ps 49:8-9, 16-17, 21, 23. Mt 23:1-12. *Lect* I:232

Lent meaning 'springtime' calls to mind new beginnings. Spring-cleaning destroys the dirt and grime of dark winter. The harrowing by penance and prayer prepares the Christian for the implanting of the seed that will bring an abundant harvest.

27 Wednesday Jer 18:18-20. Ps 30:5-6, 14-16. Mt 20:17-28. *Lect* I:234

'Save me in your love, O Lord.' This prayer to be saved reminds us that salvation comes from God alone. The mother of the two apostles was looking for security for her sons. Jesus had to tell her that her understanding of such safety was wrong. He required abandonment to God's will as the best security.

28 Thursday   Jer 17:5-10. Ps 1:1-4, 6. Lk 16:19-31. *Lect* I:236

The Gospel story of the poor man Lazarus is about the choice that each one has to make of life or death. It is a responsible choice because we have Moses and the prophets, and Jesus himself, to show us the alternatives.

MARCH 2013

1 Friday   Gn 37:3-4, 12-13, 17-28. Ps 104:16-21. Mt 21:33-43, 45-46. *Lect* I:239

Joseph is sold into slavery for twenty pieces of silver. The servants in the vineyard kill the heir. Jesus, the Son of God, is also sold and sent to death. But the stone rejected becomes the cornerstone.
St David see *March notes*.

2 Saturday   Mic 7:14-15, 18-20. Ps 102:1-4, 9-12. Lk 15:1-3, 11-32. *Lect* I:241

In the story of the father welcoming back his son, Jesus shows us in a very human way that we can be like that.

Next Sunday's readings: Ex 3:1-8, 13-15. Ps 102:1-4, 6-8, 11. 1 Cor 10:1-6, 10-12. Lk 13:1-9. *Lect* I:255

March 2013 Psalter Week 3

3 Sunday **THIRD SUNDAY OF LENT**
Violet ✠ HOURS Psalter Week 3
 MASS Proper. No Gloria. Creed. Preface: Lent I–II
 The First Scrutiny is celebrated today
No other celebrations, not even funeral Masses, are permitted today (see Lit. Note 7)

---

4 Monday **3rd Week of Lent**
Violet HOURS Psalter Week 3. MASS Proper. Preface: Lent I–IV
 Memorial may be made of **St Casimir** (see *Lit. Note 7*)

---

5 Tuesday **3rd Week of Lent**
Violet HOURS Psalter Week 3. MASS Proper. Preface: Lent I–IV
 Memorial may be made of **St Kieran, bishop** (see *Lit. Note 7*)
Ossory **St Kieran, bishop** Feast

---

6 Wednesday **3rd Week of Lent**
Violet HOURS Psalter Week 3. MASS Proper. Preface: Lent I–IV

---

7 Thursday **3rd Week of Lent**
Violet HOURS Psalter Week 3. MASS Proper. Preface: Lent I–IV
 Memorial may be made of **Ss Perpetua and Felicity, martyrs** (see *Lit. Note 7*)

---

8 Friday **3rd Week of Lent**
Violet HOURS Psalter Week 3. MASS Proper. Preface: Lent I–IV
 Memorial may be made of **St John of God, religious** (see *Lit. Note 7*)
 Memorial may be made of **St Senan, bishop** (see *Lit. Note 7*)

---

9 Saturday **3rd Week of Lent**
Violet HOURS Psalter Week 3. MASS Proper. Preface: Lent I–IV
 Memorial may be made of **St Frances of Rome, religious** (see *Lit. Note 7*)

Next Sunday's readings: Jos 5:9-12. Ps 33:2-7. 2 Cor 5:17-21. Lk 15:1-3, 11-32. *Lect* I:284

March 2013 READINGS Sunday Cycle C
THIRD WEEK OF LENT
3 Sunday **Ex 3:1-8, 13-15. Ps 102:1-4, 6-8, 11. 1 Cor 10:1-6, 10-12. Lk 13:1-9.** Lect I:255

Jesus illustrates from the recent local news how uncertain life can be; accidents and disasters continually remind us of that. We have indeed learnt that there is no such thing as an unsinkable ship, and so we are warned to work at our salvation. The image of the fruitless fig tree is used by Jesus to call us to repentance.
The readings in Year A may be used today as alternative readings: **Ex 17:3-7. Ps 94:1-2, 6-9. Rm 5:1-2, 5-8. Jn 4:5-42** (shorter form 4:5-15, 19-26, 39-42)**.** Lect I:245
The readings **Ex 17:1-7. Ps 94:1-2, 6-9. Jn 4:5-42.** Lect I:258 may be used instead of the Lenten readings any day this week.

4 Monday **2 Kg 5:1-15. Pss 41:2-3; 42:3-4. Lk 4:24-30.** Lect I:262
Naaman, the Syrian, learned to obey God's will, and went and washed in the Jordan. He was cleansed. Jesus reminds us that salvation is a gift of God. These are reminders to us the baptised and to those preparing for baptism.
St Casimir, 1458–84, strove to promote peace and the unity of Western Europe. Though a young prince, he chose a life of prayer and penance. Patron saint of Poland.

5 Tuesday **Dn 3:25, 34-43. Ps 24:4-9. Mt 18:21-35.** Lect I:264
It is in the memory of past favours that Azariah has the confidence to pray to God. His prayer is suitable for all times. God is faithful to his covenant, and Jesus Christ intercedes for us always.
St Kieran see *March notes*.
Dublin Tomorrow is the anniversary of the episcopal ordination of His Eminence Cardinal Desmond Connell, 6 March 1988.

6 Wednesday **Deut 4:1, 5-9. Ps 147:12-13, 15-16, 19-20. Mt 5:17-19.** Lect I:267
The Law is a great treasure to be safely guarded and to be handed on as a sacred trust. In the new Jerusalem, the Church, the laws of Christ are not to be seen as burdens or out of date. They are the evidence of the love of Christ for us.

7 Thursday **Jer 7:23-28. Ps 94:1-2, 6-9. Lk 11:14-23.** Lect I:268
Hardness of heart is the characteristic of those who have refused to listen to God. Listening to the lies of Satan led human beings to disobey God in the beginning. Satan still acts in our world out of hatred of God and his kingdom in Jesus Christ.
St Perpetua, a young upper-class married woman and **St Felicity,** a slave girl were martyred in Carthage, 203.

8 Friday **Hos 14:2-10. Ps 80:6, 8-11, 14, 17. Mk 12:28-34.** Lect I:271
We are called to return in faithfulness to God who made us. We are reminded not to have other gods before him. 'We will say no more, "Our God", to the work of our hands.'
St John of God, 1495–1550, devoted his life to the care of the poor and the sick. He is patron saint of nurses, the sick, heart patients, printers, and booksellers.
St Senan see *March notes*.
Cashel and Emly Tomorrow is the anniversary of the episcopal ordination of Most Rev. Dermot Clifford, 9 March 1986.

9 Saturday **Hos 5:15-6:6. Ps 50:3-4, 18-21. Lk 18:9-14.** Lect I:273
'Only when we humbly acknowledge that "we do not know how to pray as we ought"' are we ready to receive freely the gift of prayer. "Man is a beggar before God"' (CCC 2559).
St Frances of Rome, d. 1440, lived a happily married life in Rome where she was especially concerned for the poor.

March 2013 Psalter Week 4

10 Sunday **FOURTH SUNDAY OF LENT** (Laetare Sunday)
Violet or Rose ✠ HOURS Psalter Week 4
MASS Proper. No Gloria. Creed. Preface: Lent I–II
The Second Scrutiny is celebrated today
No other celebrations, not even funeral Masses, are permitted today (see Lit. Note 7)

---

11 Monday **4th Week of Lent**
Violet HOURS Psalter Week 4. MASS Proper. Preface: Lent I–IV
Memorial may be made of **St Aengus, bishop and abbot** (see *Lit. Note 7*)

---

12 Tuesday **4th Week of Lent**
Violet HOURS Psalter Week 4. MASS Proper. Preface: Lent I–IV

---

13 Wednesday **4th Week of Lent**
Violet HOURS Psalter Week 4. MASS Proper. Preface: Lent I–IV

---

14 Thursday **4th Week of Lent**
Violet HOURS Psalter Week 4. MASS Proper. Preface: Lent I–IV

---

15 Friday **4th Week of Lent**
Violet HOURS Psalter Week 4. MASS Proper. Preface: Lent I–IV

---

16 Saturday **4th Week of Lent**
Violet HOURS Psalter Week 4. MASS Proper. Preface: Lent I–IV
FIRST EVENING PRAYER of **St Patrick, bishop**

Next Sunday's readings: Is 43:16-21. Ps 125. Phil 3:8-14. Jn 8:1-11. *Lect* I:313

March 2013 READINGS Sunday Cycle C

FOURTH WEEK OF LENT

10 Sunday **Jos 5:9-12. Ps 33:2-7. 2 Cor 5:17-21. Lk 15:1-3, 11-32.** Lect I:284

Sinners and outcasts are at ease with Jesus, and his story of the prodigal son tells why. Today's readings are a source of hope and consolation for all who have sinned in any way. Our Lord's eating with sinners is a sign of God breaking through his own laws in order to save those who are in danger of being lost.

The readings in Year A may be used today as alternative readings: **1 Sm 16:1, 6-7, 10-13. Ps 22. Eph 5:8-14. Jn 9:1-41** (shorter form 9:1, 6-9, 13-17, 34-38)**.** Lect I:276

The readings **Mic 7:7-9. Ps 26:1, 7-9, 13-14. Jn 9:1-41.** Lect I:287 may be used instead of the Lenten readings any day this week.

11 Monday **Is 65:17-21. Ps 29:2, 4-6, 11-13. Jn 4:43-54.** Lect I:290

The echoes of an ancient, shorter Lent are still found in the semi-continuous reading of St John's Gospel beginning today. The hope expressed in Jesus' words, 'Your son will live' is the desire of all who are coming from sin to forgiveness, from death to new life, in Baptism and Reconciliation.

St Aengus see *March notes*.

12 Tuesday **Ez 47:1-9, 12. Ps 45:2-3, 5-6, 8-9. Jn 5:1-3, 5-16.** Lect I:292

The water of Baptism gives great joy to the Church. By this water we are healed and saved. By Baptism all sins are forgiven, original sin and all personal sins, as well as punishments for sin. Nothing remains that would impede the baptised from entry into the Kingdom of God.

13 Wednesday Is 49:8-15. Ps 144:8-9, 13-14, 17-18. Jn 5:17-30. Lect I:294

Pride and joy in belonging to the Church should be part of our inheritance. Today the readings in so many metaphors express the fullness of life in the Church, of the life of God's chosen people. 'Baptism is the sacrament by which its recipients are incorporated into the Church and are built up together in the Spirit into a house where God lives, into a holy nation and a royal priesthood' (*Rite of Baptism*).

14 Thursday **Ex 32:7-14. Ps 105:19-23. Jn 5:31-47.** Lect I:297

Jesus puts before his listeners the remembrance of Moses pleading for his people. The repeated failure of God's people to live up to the covenant serves as a warning for all generations. We also must call on God to give us the grace to turn back again.

15 Friday **Wis 2:1, 12-22. Ps 33:16, 18, 19-21, 23. Jn 7:1-2, 10, 25-30.** Lect I:300

A word of warning today. To take on the Christian way of life is to risk enmity and death. The opposition to Christianity has been violent and bloodstained in many periods of history. Today, the opposition may be by other means – slander and ribaldry, ridicule and negative publicity.

16 Saturday **Jer 11:18-20. Ps 7:2-3, 9-12. Jn 7:40-52.** Lect I:303

Jesus is the Paschal Lamb. He bears the sins of the multitude as he allows himself to be silently led to the Cross. The whole life of Jesus is thus characterised as one in which his mission is 'to serve, and to give his life as a ransom for many'.

Cloyne Tomorrow is the anniversary of the episcopal ordination of Most Rev. John Magee, 17 March 1987.

March 2013   Psalter Week 1

17 Sunday   **FIFTH SUNDAY OF LENT**
                     ST PATRICK, bishop, Principal Patron of Ireland
                     Solemnity

White ✠   HOURS Proper (Divine Office, II, p.209*)
                     Te Deum. Psalter Week 1 at Day Hour
                     MASS Proper. Gloria, Creed. Preface: Proper
                     The Third Scrutiny is celebrated today
                     EVENING PRAYER of **St Patrick**

Emigrants are remembered in a special way today
No other celebrations, not even funeral Masses, are permitted today (see Lit. Note 7)

---

18 Monday   **5th Week of Lent**
Violet   HOURS Psalter Week 1. Hymns may be of Passiontide
                     MASS Proper. Preface: Passion I
                     Memorial may be made of **St Cyril of Jerusalem, bishop and doctor of the Church** (see *Lit. Note 7*)
                     FIRST EVENING PRAYER of **St Joseph**

---

19 Tuesday   **ST JOSEPH, HUSBAND OF THE BLESSED VIRGIN MARY**
                     Solemnity

White   HOURS Proper. Te Deum. Complementary Psalms at Day Hour
                     MASS Proper. Gloria. Creed. Preface: Proper
                     EVENING PRAYER of **St Joseph**

No Masses for the dead, except funeral Masses, are permitted today (see Lit. Note 7)

---

20 Wednesday **5th Week of Lent**
Violet   HOURS Psalter Week 1. Hymns may be of Passiontide
                     MASS Proper. Preface: Passion I

---

21 Thursday   **5th Week of Lent**
Violet   HOURS Psalter Week 1. Hymns may be of Passiontide
                     MASS Proper. Preface: Passion I
                     Memorial may be made of **St Enda, abbot** (see *Lit. Note 7*)

---

22 Friday   **5th Week of Lent**
Violet   HOURS Psalter Week 1. Hymns may be of Passiontide
                     MASS Proper. Preface: Passion I

---

23 Saturday   **5th Week of Lent**
Violet   HOURS Psalter Week 1. Hymns may be of Passiontide
                     MASS Proper. Preface: Passion I
                     Memorial may be made of **St Turibius of Mongrovejo, bishop** (see *Lit. Note 7*)

March 2013 READINGS Sunday Cycle C
FIFTH WEEK OF LENT
17 Sunday Is 43:16-21. Ps 125. Phil 3:8-14. Jn 8:1-11. Lect I:313
'What marvels the Lord worked for us.' We all need forgiveness. As we approach Easter we see more clearly what Jesus Christ has done for us in his death and rising. He has brought the sum of God's forgiving mercy and love into our lives. Like water into a dry and parched land his mercy flows in abundance.
The readings in Year A may be used today as alternative readings: **Ez 37:12-14. Ps 129. Rm 8:8-11. Jn 11:1-45** (shorter form 11:3-7, 17, 20-27, 33-45). Lect I:305
The readings **2 Kg 4:18-21, 32-37. Ps 16:1, 6-8, 15. Jn 11:1-45.** Lect I:316 may be used instead of the Lenten readings any day this week.
St Patrick see *March notes.*

18 Monday Dn 13:1-9, 15-17, 19-30, 33-62 (shorter form 13:41-62)**. Ps 22. Jn 8:12-20.** Lect I:319
Both women in today's readings suffered in their experience of condemnation, whether guilty or innocent. They were led to the tribunals of judgement and felt defenceless. Their liberation is an act of God's mercy and provision of help.
St Cyril of Jerusalem, 315–86, bishop of Jerusalem. He excelled as a catechist and administrator, and suffered exile in his fight against Arianism.

19 Tuesday 2 Sm 7:4-5, 12-14, 16. Ps 88:2-5, 27, 29. Rm 4:13, 16-18, 22. Mt 1:16, 18-21, 24 *or* **Lk 2:41-51.** Lect I:970 *or* II:980
'The virtues of **St Joseph** have been the object of ecclesial reflection down through the centuries, especially the more recent centuries. Among those virtues the following stand out: faith, with which he fully accepted God's salvific plan; prompt and silent obedience to the will of God; love for and fulfilment of the law, true piety, fortitude in time of trial; chaste love for the Blessed Virgin Mary, a dutiful exercise of his paternal authority, and fruitful reticence' (*Directory on Popular Piety and the Liturgy*, 219).
Derry Tomorrow is the anniversary of the episcopal ordination of Most Rev. Francis Lagan, 20 March 1988.

20 Wednesday Dn 3:14-20, 24-25, 28. Ps Dn 3:52-56. Jn 8:31-42.
Lect I:328
The three young men refused to obey an unjust law – a higher moral law was at stake. God rewarded their faithfulness to the truth and their courage in making a stand for conscience's sake.

21 Thursday Gn 17:3-9. Ps 104:4-9. Jn 8:51-59. Lect I:331
Jesus declares that before Abraham, with whom God made a covenant, 'I am'.
St Enda see *March notes.*

22 Friday Jer 20:10-13. Ps 17:2-7. Jn 10:31-42. Lect I:333
To God we must turn in time of trial. It is God who will be the final judge of the rightness of the cause. Both Jesus and Jeremiah faced a lack of belief but were supported by the knowledge that the Lord was on their side

23 Saturday Ez 37:21-28. Ps Jer 31:10-13. Jn 11:45-56. Lect I:336
In order to gather together scattered humanity, God called Abraham, a wandering Aramean shepherd, to be the father of a multitude of nations. To the people descended from him would be entrusted the promise that one day God would gather all his children into the unity of the Church.
St Turibius, 1538–1606, was a layman when he was appointed archbishop of Lima, Peru by King Philip II. He combated all the abuses of the conquerors in Peru and built up the Church there.

March 2013　　　READINGS Sunday Cycle C　　　Psalter Week 2

24 Sunday　　**PALM SUNDAY OF THE LORD'S PASSION**
Red ✠　　　　HOURS Psalter Week 2
　　　　　　MASS Proper. No Gloria. Creed. Preface: Proper
No other celebrations, not even funeral Masses, are permitted today (see Lit. Note 7)
READINGS　　Procession **Lk 19:28-40**. *Lect* I:345
　　　　　　Mass **Is 50:4-7. Ps 21: 8-9, 17-20, 23-24. Phil 2:6-11. Lk 22:14-23:56** (shorter form 23:1-49). *Lect* I:346
St Macartan, bishop is not celebrated this year.

Palm Sunday of the Lord's Passion

Holy Week begins on this Sunday, which joins the foretelling of Christ's regal triumph and the proclamation of the Passion. The connection between both aspects of the paschal mystery should be shown and explained in the celebration and catechesis of this day. The commemoration of the entrance of the Lord into Jerusalem is celebrated with a solemn procession which may take place only once, before the Mass which has the largest attendance, even if this should be the evening of Saturday or Sunday. In this procession the faithful carry palm or other branches. The priest and the ministers, also carrying branches, precede the people. The palms or branches are blessed so that they can be carried in the procession. The palms should be taken home, where they will serve as a reminder of the victory of Christ which they celebrated in the procession. Pastors should make every effort to ensure that this procession in honour of Christ the King be so prepared and celebrated that it is of great spiritual significance in the life of the faithful.

The Proclamation of the Passion

The Passion narrative occupies a special place. It should be sung or read in the traditional way, that is, by three persons who take the part of Christ, the narrator, and the people. The Passion is proclaimed by deacons or priests, or by lay readers; in the latter case the part of Christ should be reserved to the priest. The proclamation of the Passion should be without candles and incense, the greeting and the sign of the cross on the book are omitted. For the spiritual good of the faithful the Passion should be proclaimed in its entirety, and the readings which precede it should not be omitted. After the Passion has been proclaimed, a homily is to be given.

Holy Week

During Holy Week the Church celebrates the mysteries of salvation accomplished by Christ in the last days of his life on earth, beginning with his messianic entrance into Jerusalem. The Lenten season lasts until the Thursday of this week. The Easter Triduum begins with the evening Mass of the Lord's Supper. The days of Holy Week, from Monday to Thursday inclusive, have precedence over all other celebrations. It is not fitting that Baptism and Confirmation be celebrated on these days.

End of Lent

It is fitting that the Lenten season should be concluded, both for the individual Christian as well as for the whole Christian community, with a penitential celebration, so that they may be helped to prepare to celebrate more fully the paschal mystery. These celebrations, however, should take place before the Easter Triduum, and should not immediately precede the evening Mass of the Lord's Supper.

March 2013 **HOLY WEEK**

25 **MONDAY IN HOLY WEEK**
Violet HOURS Psalter Week 2
MASS Proper. Preface: Passion II
No other celebrations, except funeral Masses, are permitted today (see Lit. Note 7)
READINGS **Is 42:1-7. Ps 26:1-3, 13-14. Jn 12:1-11.** *Lect* I:374
Our attention is now focused on the great mystery of Christ, dying and rising. The sense of impending doom hovers over the actions of Jesus. Like a lamb led to the slaughter, Christ does not cry out or shout aloud. Mary's anointing becomes one of preparation of the body for burial after death. All things are being readied for the final hour. The chrism is prepared for blessing by the bishop this week: it will be used to sign new Christians with the cross, to seal them for Christ. This sweet-smelling oil will remind them that they are, as St Paul says, to be the 'aroma of Christ' spreading a fragrance wherever they go (*2 Cor* 2:14-15).

---

26 **TUESDAY IN HOLY WEEK**
Violet HOURS Psalter Week 2
MASS Proper. Preface: Passion II
No other celebrations, except funeral Masses, are permitted today (see Lit. Note 7)
READINGS **Is 49:1-6. Ps 70:1-6, 15, 17. Jn 13:21-33, 36-38.** *Lect* I:376
The words of Isaiah speak beautifully of our vocation in Christ. Chosen before birth, given great gifts of body and mind, called to be servant of the Most High, and destined to be a light of the nations so that Christ's salvation may be brought to the ends of the earth. Such is our destiny. And yet, we can fail. We can reject this calling, give way to weakness. Both Judas and Peter in their weakness are put before us today, one to betray, the other to deny. So close to Jesus and yet capable of losing him.

---

27 **WEDNESDAY IN HOLY WEEK**
Violet HOURS Psalter Week 2
MASS Proper. Preface: Passion II
No other celebrations, except funeral Masses, are permitted today (see Lit. Note 7)
READINGS **Is 50:4-9. Ps 68:8-10, 21-22, 31, 33-34. Mt 26:14-25.** *Lect* I:379
Spy Wednesday we call it – for Judas has left his mark on our calendars. The pain of his betrayal is to be felt in the account of St Matthew's Gospel. And thirty pieces of silver goes into language currency ever since. At the end of this Lent which has seen us trying to purify ourselves of all that is not Christian, these thirty pieces of silver come before us as a warning.
Derry Tomorrow is the anniversary of the episcopal ordination of Most Rev. Seamus Hegarty, 28 March 1982.

March 2013

28   HOLY THURSDAY
Morning

Violet   HOURS Readings: Ants and Pss may be taken from Friday Week 3

Morning Prayer and Day Hour: Psalter Week 2

White   The CHRISM MASS is the only one that takes place in the morning

Gloria. No Creed. Preface: Priesthood

The following READINGS (*Lect* I:382) are proper:

Is 61:1-3, 6a, 8b-9. This passage is seen as Jesus' own description of his mission. It serves to highlight the vocation of those who follow him in priestly ministry. The priests of the Lord are to bring comfort, healing, and joy.

Ps 88:21-22, 25, 27. The priest's vocation is given by God in love. That love supports him always.

Apoc 1:5-8. Christ loved us and gave his life for us. Through that redeeming act we have become a community that shares his kingly and priestly identity.

Lk 4:16-21. Christ uses the text of Isaiah to tell his hearers that the words are now an actual event before them. The priest shares in Christ's ministry, has received the same spirit, is anointed for service.

'This Mass, which the bishop concelebrates with his college of presbyters and at which he consecrates the holy chrism and blesses the other oils, manifests the communion of the presbyters with their bishop.

The holy chrism consecrated by the bishop is used to anoint the newly baptised, to seal the candidates for confirmation, and to anoint the hands of presbyters and the heads of bishops at their ordination, as well as in rites of anointing pertaining to the dedication of churches and altars. The oil of catechumens is used in the preparation of the catechumens for their baptism. The oil of the sick is used to bring comfort and support to the sick in their infirmity.

Presbyters are brought together and concelebrate this Mass as witness and co-operators with their bishop in the consecration of the chrism because they share in the sacred office of the bishop in building up, sanctifying and ruling the people of God. This Mass is therefore a clear expression of the unity of the priesthood and sacrifice of Christ, which continue to be present in the Church.

To show the unity of the college of presbyters, the presbyters who concelebrate with the bishop should come from different parts of the diocese.

Presbyters who take part, but for some reason do not concelebrate, may receive communion under both kinds.

If it is difficult for the clergy and the people to assemble with the bishop on Holy Thursday morning, the blessing of oils may be held on an earlier day, near Easter, with the celebration of the proper Chrism Mass.

Because of its meaning and pastoral importance in the life of the diocese, the Chrism Mass should be celebrated as a stational Mass in the cathedral church, or, for pastoral reasons, in another church.' (*Ceremonial of Bishops*)

During today and the Sacred Triduum all other celebrations, even funeral Masses, are prohibited. For the Liturgy of the Dead, see Liturgical Note 9.

THE EASTER TRIDUUM

The Fathers of the Church saw this celebration as a unitive commemoration: St Augustine spoke of 'the most holy triduum of the crucified, buried and risen Lord'. Over Friday, Saturday, and Sunday we celebrate a single, indivisible mystery. The Easter Triduum begins with the evening Mass of the Lord's Supper, reaches its high point in the Easter Vigil, and closes with evening prayer on Easter Sunday (*GNLY*, 18–19).

> Christ redeemed us all and gave perfect glory to God principally through his paschal mystery: dying he destroyed our death and rising he restored our life. Therefore the Easter Triduum of the passion and resurrection of Christ is the culmination of the entire liturgical year. Thus the solemnity of Easter has the same kind of pre-eminence in the liturgical year that Sunday has in the week.
>
> The celebration of the paschal mystery is not simply a recalling of past events in history. It is a sacramental celebration that renders present and actualises the saving power of Christ's death and resurrection to the Church.

Active participation
For the celebration of the Easter Triduum, a sufficient number of ministers and assistants should be prepared for their role. The faithful should be instructed on the meaning of each part of the celebration so that they can take part more fully and fruitfully. The chants for the people are of special importance for their participation and should not be lightly omitted.

Where the number of participants and ministers is so small that the celebrations of the Easter Triduum cannot be carried out with the requisite solemnity, such groups of the faithful should assemble in a larger church. It is fitting that small religious communities should participate in neighbouring principal churches.

The Paschal Fast
The Easter Fast is sacred on the first two days of the Triduum, in which, according to ancient tradition, the Church fasts 'because the Spouse has been taken away' (Mk 2:19-20).

Good Friday is a day of fasting and abstinence; it is also recommended that Holy Saturday be so observed, 'so that the Church, with uplifted and welcoming heart, be ready to celebrate the joys of the Sunday of the Resurrection' (*Sacrosanctum concilium*, 110).

The Liturgy of the Hours during the Easter Triduum
The Office is proper for each day.

On Good Friday and Holy Saturday the Office of Readings should be celebrated publicly with the people before Morning Prayer, as far as this is possible.

Evening Prayer is not said by those who attend the Evening Mass on Holy Thursday or the Commemoration of the Passion on Good Friday.

The Easter Vigil takes the place of the Office of Readings. Morning Prayer for Easter Sunday is said by all.

It is fitting that Evening Prayer of Easter Sunday be celebrated in a more solemn way to mark the ending of the Triduum and to commemorate the occasions when the Lord showed himself to his disciples.

March 2013 **EASTER TRIDUUM**

28 **HOLY THURSDAY**
Evening Mass of the Lord's Supper

White MASS Proper. Gloria. No Creed. Preface: Eucharist I
In the Roman Canon proper forms

READINGS **Ex 12:1-8, 11-14. Ps 115:12-13, 15-18. 1 Cor 11:23-26. Jn 13:1-15.** *Lect* I:387

The scripture readings this evening direct our minds at the opening of the great Paschal celebration to the meaning of what we celebrate. We are entering into this mystery in such a way that when we break bread and share the cup this evening we once more proclaim the death of the Lord.

The Evening Mass of the Lord's Supper should be celebrated with the full participation of the whole community, with all the priests concelebrating. The pastoral reasons that permit another Mass should be seriously considered before breaking the unity of the celebration.

The hearing of Confessions should not take place during Mass; the faithful should be encouraged to approach the Sacrament earlier in Lent.

At the Evening Mass, the tabernacle should be entirely empty; a sufficient amount of bread should be consecrated at this Mass for the communion of all on this day and tomorrow.

Bells may be rung during the Gloria and are not rung again until the Paschal Vigil.

'With this Mass, celebrated in the evening of the Thursday in Holy Week, the Church begins the sacred Easter Triduum and devotes itself to the remembrance of the Last Supper. At this supper on the night he was betrayed, the Lord Jesus, loving those who were his own in the world even to the end, offered his body and blood to the Father under the appearances of bread and wine, gave them to the apostles to eat and drink, then enjoined the apostles and their successors in the priesthood to offer them in turn.

This Mass is, first of all, the memorial of the institution of the eucharist, that is, of the memorial of the Lord's Passover, by which under sacramental signs he perpetuated among us the sacrifice of the New Law. The Mass of the Lord's Supper is also the memorial of the institution of the priesthood, by which Christ's mission and sacrifice are perpetuated in the world. In addition, this Mass is the memorial of that love by which the Lord loved us even to death. The bishop should see to it that all these considerations are suitably presented to the faithful through the ministry of the word so that by their devotion they may be able to deepen their grasp of such great mysteries and reflect them more faithfully in the conduct of their lives.' (*Ceremonial of Bishops*, 298)

EVENING PRAYER is omitted by those who attend the Evening Mass.
Solemn adoration of the Blessed Sacrament should end at midnight.
After the Evening Mass the altar is stripped privately, and crucifixes, if not removed from the church, are veiled.
Night Prayer 2 of Sunday.

THE EASTER TRIDUUM

Celebrating the Evening Mass of the Lord's Supper

Unity of the Celebration
The Mass of the Lord's Supper is celebrated in the evening, at a time more convenient for the full participation of the whole local community. All priests may concelebrate, even if they have already celebrated. Where pastoral considerations require it, the local ordinary may permit another Mass to be celebrated, but not for the benefit of private persons or small groups or to the detriment of the main Mass. All Masses without the participation of the people are forbidden on this day.

The Mandatum
The gospel account of the Mandatum is actualised when the ceremony is carried out. The tradition of the washing of the feet should be maintained, and its proper significance explained. Gifts for the poor, especially those collected during Lent as the fruit of penance, may be presented in the procession of gifts.

The Sick and Infirm
It is appropriate that the Eucharist be borne directly from the altar by the deacons or acolytes or extraordinary ministers at the moment of Communion, for the sick and infirm who must communicate at home, so that in this way they may be more closely united to the celebrating church.

Place of Repose
For the reservation of the Blessed Sacrament that will be distributed in Communion on Good Friday, a place should be prepared and adorned in such a way as to be conducive to prayer and meditation. The Blessed Sacrament should be reserved in a closed tabernacle or pyx. When the tabernacle is located in a chapel separated from the central part of the church, it is appropriate to prepare there the place of repose or adoration. The faithful should be encouraged to spend some period of the time there during the night before the Blessed Sacrament. This adoration may be accompanied by the reading of some part of the Gospel of St John, chapters 13-17. From midnight onwards the adoration should be made without solemnity, for the day of the Lord's Passion has begun. After Mass the altar should be stripped. It is fitting that any crosses in the church be covered with a red or purple veil. Lamps should not be lit before the images of saints.

The Lectionary for the Easter Triduum
On Holy Thursday at the evening Mass the readings direct attention to the supper preceding Christ's departure. On Good Friday the liturgical service has as its centre John's narrative of the passion of him who was portrayed in Isaiah as the Servant of God and who became the one High Priest by offering himself to the Father. On the holy night of the Easter Vigil there are seven Old Testament readings recalling the wonderful works of God in the history of salvation. The New Testament readings announce the resurrection and speak of baptism as the sacrament of Christ's resurrection. On Easter Day, the Gospel reading is from John on the finding of the empty tomb, or the Easter Vigil Gospel may be used. In the evening Luke's story of the disciples on the road to Emmaus may be used.

March 2013   **EASTER TRIDUUM**

29   **GOOD FRIDAY**
Red   **Celebration of the Lord's Passion**
Day of Fast and Abstinence
LITURGY OF THE HOURS. Proper Offices

The Office of Readings and Morning Prayer should, if possible, be celebrated publicly and with the participation of the people.

CELEBRATION OF THE LORD'S PASSION. Proper

This celebration takes place in the afternoon, about three o'clock, unless pastoral reasons suggest a later hour. The celebration consists of three parts: liturgy of the word, veneration of the cross, and holy communion (Ceremonial of Bishops, 313).

READINGS *Lect* I:390

Is 52:13-53:12. This servant song, applied to Christ, gives a horrifying account of his sufferings, and the cause of them – our sins.

Ps 30: 2, 6, 12-13, 15-17, 25. A lament for the sufferings of the just one, and an expression of trust in God who is faithful.

Heb 4:14-16, 5:7-9. Christ embraced our human state and lived through our hardships. Because he was a man without sin God heard him, and all the human race as well on his behalf.

Jn 18:1-19:42. St John's account of the Passion is more reflective and theological. He emphasises Jesus' obedience to the Father's will. The kingship of Jesus is asserted: the crucifixion is a victory, the hour of death is also the hour of triumph. 'Christ gives his life, he is "lifted up" on the cross, but willingly, and only in order to enter into his glory, a glory that is made visible even in this world to the confusion of unbelievers and ending in the defeat of Satan once and for all.' (*New Jerusalem Bible*)

After the proclamation of the Passion, a homily should be given, at the end of which the faithful may be invited to spend a short time in meditation.

'On this day, when "Christ our paschal lamb was sacrificed" what had long been promised in signs and figures was at last revealed and brought to fulfilment. The true lamb replaced the symbolic lamb, and the many offerings of the past gave way to the single sacrifice of Christ.

The wonderful works of God among the people of the Old Testament were a prelude to the work of Christ the Lord. He achieved his task of redeeming humanity and giving perfect glory to God, principally by the paschal mystery of his blessed passion, resurrection from the dead, and glorious ascension, whereby dying he destroyed our death and rising he restored our life (Preface of Easter). For it was from the side of Christ as he slept the sleep of death upon the cross that there came forth the sublime sacrament of the whole Church.

In contemplating the cross of its Lord and Bridegroom, the Church commemorates its own origin and its mission to extend to all peoples the blessed effects of Christ's passion that it celebrates on this day in a spirit of thanksgiving for his marvellous gift.' (*Ceremonial of Bishops*, 312)

EVENING PRAYER is omitted by those who attend the Celebration of the Lord's Passion.
Night Prayer 2 of Sunday.

THE EASTER TRIDUUM

The Celebration of Good Friday
On this day when 'Christ our passover was sacrificed' (*1 Cor* 5:7), the Church meditates on the Passion of her Lord and Spouse, venerates the Cross, commemorates her origin from the side of Christ on the Cross, and intercedes for the salvation of the whole world. On this day, in accordance with ancient tradition, the Church does not celebrate Eucharist; Holy Communion is distributed to the faithful during the celebration of the Lord's Passion alone, though it may be brought at any time of the day to the sick who cannot take part in the celebration.

Day of Penance
Good Friday is a day of penance to be observed as of obligation in the whole Church, and indeed through abstinence and fasting. All celebration of the sacraments on this day is strictly prohibited, except for the Sacraments of Penance and Anointing of the Sick. Funerals are to be celebrated without singing, music, or tolling of bells.

Times of Celebrations
The Office of Readings and Morning Prayer should take place in the morning. The Celebration of the Lord's Passion is to take place in the afternoon, around three o'clock. For pastoral reasons, in order to allow the faithful to assemble more easily, another time may be chosen, such as shortly after midday, or in the late evening, but not later than nine o'clock.

Celebration of the Lord's Passion
The order for the celebration of the Lord's Passion, which stems from an ancient tradition of the Church, should be observed faithfully and religiously. The priest and ministers proceed to the altar in silence and without any singing. If any words of introduction are to be said, they should be pronounced before the ministers enter. The rite of prostration should be strictly observed as it signifies human abasement, and the grief of the Church. The general intercessions are to follow the wording and form handed down by ancient tradition, maintaining the full range of intentions.

Veneration of the Cross
For the veneration of the Cross, let a cross be used that is of appropriate size and beauty. The rite should be carried out with the splendour worthy of the mystery of our salvation. After each sung invitation and response, the celebrant holds the raised Cross for a period of respectful silence. The Cross is to be presented to each of the faithful individually for their veneration, since the personal veneration of the Cross is a most important feature in this celebration, and only when necessitated by the large numbers of faithful present should the rite of veneration be made simultaneously by all present. Only one Cross should be used for the veneration, as this contributes to the full symbolism of the rite. After the celebration, an appropriate place (for example, the chapel of repose used for reservation of the Eucharist on Holy Thursday) can be prepared, and there the Lord's Cross is placed with four candles, so that the faithful may venerate and kiss it, and spend some time in meditation.

Popular Devotions
Devotions, such as the Way of the Cross and Prayer around the Cross, are not to be neglected. The texts and songs should be appropriate to the spirit of this day. Such devotions should be assigned to a time of the day that makes it quite clear that the liturgical celebration by its very nature far surpasses them in importance (*Sacrosanctum concilium*, 13).

March 2013   **EASTER TRIDUUM**

30   **HOLY SATURDAY**
Violet   LITURGY OF THE HOURS Proper

It is highly recommended that on this day the OFFICE OF READINGS and MORNING PRAYER be celebrated with the participation of the people. Where this cannot be done, there should be some celebration of the Word of God, or some act of devotion suited to the mystery celebrated on this day.

NIGHT PRAYER 2 of Sunday is said only by those who do not attend the Paschal Vigil.

'Let the PASCHAL FAST be kept sacred. Let it be observed everywhere on Good Friday and, where possible, prolonged throughout Holy Saturday, as a way of coming to the joys of the Sunday of the resurrection with uplifted and welcoming heart' (*Sacrosanctum concilium*, 110).

On **Holy Saturday** the Church is as it were at the Lord's tomb, meditating on his passion and death, and on his descent into hell, and awaiting his resurrection with prayer and fasting. The image of Christ crucified or lying in the tomb, or the descent into hell, which mystery Holy Saturday recalls, as also an image of the Sorrowful Virgin Mary can be placed in the church for the veneration of the faithful.

On this day the Church abstains strictly from the celebration of the Sacrifice of the Mass. Holy Communion may be given only in the form of Viaticum. The celebration of marriages is forbidden, as also the celebration of other sacraments, except Penance and Anointing of the Sick.

The faithful are to be instructed on the special character of Holy Saturday. Festive customs and traditions associated with this day on account of the former practice of anticipating the celebration of Easter on Holy Saturday should be reserved for Easter night and the day that follows.

By means of a more intensive pastoral care and a deeper spiritual effort, all who celebrate the Easter feasts will by the Lord's grace experience their effect in their daily lives.

Announcing the Easter Vigil

In announcements concerning the Easter Vigil the participation of the faithful should be promoted; care should be taken to present it not as the concluding period of Holy Saturday, but rather it should be stressed that the Easter Vigil is celebrated 'during Easter night and that it is one single act of worship. The faithful who are absent from their parish on vacation should be urged to participate in the liturgy of the place where they happen to be'.

Time of celebration
'The entire celebration of the Easter Vigil takes place at night. It should not begin before nightfall; it should end before daybreak on Sunday' (*Ceremonial of Bishops*, 333). This rule is to be taken according to its strictest sense. Reprehensible are those abuses and practices which have crept in in many places whereby the Easter Vigil is celebrated at the time of day that it is customary to celebrate anticipated Sunday Masses' (*Paschale solemnitatis*, 78).

Sunset on Saturday, 30 March 2013 is calculated as 6.55 p.m. for Belfast, 6.57 p.m. Dublin, 7.04 p.m. Galway and 7.05 p.m. Cork. Darkness can be calculated as about forty-five minutes to an hour after sunset.

Derry Tomorrow is the anniversary of the episcopal ordination of Most Rev. Edward Daly, 31 March 1974.

THE EASTER TRIDUUM

THE EASTER VIGIL

This is the night when the Church keeps vigil, waiting for the resurrection of the Lord, and celebrates the sacraments of Christian Initiation.

The Passover Vigil, in which the Hebrews kept watch for the Lord's passover which was to free them from slavery to Pharaoh, prefigured the true Pasch of Christ that was to come. For the resurrection of Christ, in which he 'broke the chains of death and rose triumphant from the grave', is the foundation of our faith and hope, and through Baptism and Confirmation we are inserted into the paschal mystery of Christ, dying, buried, and raised with him, and with him we shall also reign.

The full meaning of this Vigil is a waiting for the coming of the Lord.

The Paschal Candle, for effective symbolism must be made of wax, never be artificial, be renewed each year, be only one in number, and be of sufficiently large size so that it may evoke the truth that Christ is the Light of the World. The Paschal Candle has its proper place either by the ambo or by the altar and should be lit at least in all the more solemn liturgical celebrations until Pentecost Sunday, whether at Mass or at Morning and Evening Prayer.

After the Easter season, the Candle should be kept with honour in the baptistery and it should not otherwise be lit or placed in the sanctuary outside the Easter season.

Baptismal Promises

The Sunday assembly commits us to an inner renewal of our baptismal promises, which are in a sense implicit in the recitation of the Creed and are an explicit part of the liturgy of the Easter Vigil and whenever baptism is celebrated during Mass. In this context, the proclamation of the Word in the Sunday Eucharist celebration takes on the solemn tone found in the Old Testament at moments when the covenant was renewed, when the law was proclaimed and the community of Israel was called – like the people in the desert at the foot of Sinai (see *Ex* 19:7-8, 24:3-7) – to repeat its 'yes', renewing its decision to be faithful to God and to obey his commandments. In speaking his word, God awaits our response: a response which Christ has already made for us with his 'Amen' and which echoes in us through the Holy Spirit so that what we hear may involve us at the deepest level (*Dies Domini*, 41).

A Fifty-Day Celebration

The celebration of Easter is prolonged throughout the Easter season. The fifty days from Easter Sunday to Pentecost Sunday are celebrated as one feast day, the 'Great Sunday'.

The Sundays of Easter have precedence over all feasts of the Lord and over all solemnities.

During Easter time, pastors should instruct the faithful on the meaning of the Church's precept concerning the reception of Holy Communion during this period (*CIC* can. 920). It is highly recommended that Communion be brought frequently to the sick also, especially during the Easter octave.

The custom of blessing houses at Easter gives an opportunity for exercising a pastoral ministry. The pastor should go to each house for the purpose of undertaking a pastoral visitation. He will speak with each family and pray with them using texts from the Book of Blessings. In larger cities consideration should be given to the gathering of several families for a common celebration of the blessing for all.

EASTER SUNDAY
THE RESURRECTION OF THE LORD

White **THE EASTER VIGIL**

In accord with ancient tradition, this night is one of vigil for the Lord.
St Augustine called it the 'mother of all vigils'. The Gospel of St Luke (12:35 ff.) reminds the faithful to have their lamps burning ready, awaiting their master's return, so that when he arrives he will find them wide awake and will seat them at his table.

There are **four parts to the Rite**:

SERVICE OF LIGHT

The **new fire** should be blessed outside the church, and its flames should be such that they genuinely dispel the darkness and light up the night. During the procession into the church, there is no reason why to each response 'Thanks be to God' there should not be added some acclamation in honour of Christ. All present should hold candles to which the light of the **Paschal Candle** is gradually passed. A cantor may sing the Exsultet, or **Easter Proclamation**, if no deacon or the celebrant can do so. The Proclamation may be adapted by inserting acclamations from the people.

LITURGY OF THE WORD

In the **Readings** from Sacred Scripture, the Church 'beginning with Moses and all the Prophets' explains Christ's paschal mystery. This is 'the fundamental element of the Easter Vigil'. Consequently wherever this is possible all the readings should be read, in order that the character of the Easter Vigil, which demands the time necessary, be respected at all costs. The reading from Exodus ch. 14 with its canticle must never be omitted. It will be helpful to introduce the people to the meaning of each reading by means of a brief introduction, given by the priest himself or by a deacon. Each reading is followed by **the singing of a psalm**, for which melodies should be provided that foster the people's participation and devotion. Great care must be taken that trivial songs do not take the place of the psalms. The Resurrection of the Lord is proclaimed from the **Gospel** as the high point of the whole Liturgy of the Word. After the Gospel, a **homily** is to be given, no matter how brief.

LITURGY OF BAPTISM

In the Baptismal liturgy, Christ's resurrection and ours is celebrated. This is given full expression when the **Christian initiation** of adults is held or at least the Baptism of infants. Through the sprinkling with blessed water and the **renewal of baptismal vows**, the faithful recall the Baptism they have received.

LITURGY OF THE EUCHARIST

MASS Proper. Gloria. No Creed. Preface: Easter I. Proper forms in Roman Canon. This most solemn and joyful celebration fulfils the Sunday obligation. Priests who celebrate or concelebrate the Mass at night may celebrate or concelebrate the second Mass of Easter Sunday.

The celebration of the **Eucharist** is in the fullest sense the Easter Sacrament, that is to say, the commemoration of the sacrifice of the Cross and the presence of the Risen Christ, the completion of Christian initiation, and the foretaste of the eternal pasch. Great care must be taken that it is not celebrated in haste; all the rites and words must be given their full force. It is fitting that in the Communion of the Easter Vigil full expression be given to the symbolism of the Eucharist, namely, by consuming the Eucharist under the species of both bread and wine.

EASTER SUNDAY: THE RESURRECTION OF THE LORD
THE EASTER VIGIL READINGS

I Genesis 1:1-2:2 (shorter form 1:1, 26-31). *About creation. Lect* I:399
Psalm 103 or **32**

God saw all that he had made, and indeed it was very good.
The understanding of Baptism as our new creation in the image of God makes this first reading appropriate on this night. This is a proclamation to the catechumens and the already baptised of God's creative work at all times.

II Genesis 22:1-18 (shorter form 1-2, 9-13, 15-18). *About Abraham's sacrifice. Lect* I:403
Psalm 15

The sacrifice of Abraham, our father in faith.
The Isaac story has been seen by Christians from the beginning as a type of Christ's sacrifice. The carrying of the wood represents the cross, and his reprieve from death is seen as a kind of resurrection.

III Exodus 14:15-15:1. *About the passage through the Sea. Lect* I:405
Psalm from **Exodus 15**

The Israelites went on dry ground right through the sea.
This is the most important reading of the night. The crossing of the sea is the type of Christ's death and resurrection, and of the Christian's journey in baptism through dying and rising with Christ.

IV Isaiah 54:5-14. *About the new Jerusalem. Lect* I:407
Psalm 29

With everlasting love I will have compassion on you, says the Lord, your Redeemer.
This passage in which Deutero-Isaiah speaks of the return from exile, has several pictures. In the exodus God had taken Israel as a bride; in the exile he had rejected her, but only for a moment; in his compassion he brings her back. Christ's compassion for his Church is seen in his death and resurrection. The new kingdom is rebuilt with precious stones, the Church shines forth in splendour.

V Isaiah 55:1-11. *About salvation freely offered to all. Lect* I:408
Psalm from **Isaiah 12**

Incline your ear, and come to me; listen, so that you may live. I will make with you an everlasting covenant.
The Easter Eucharist this night is a foretaste of the eschatological banquet to which all are invited, and to which all Lenten preparation has been directed. This is why God's word has gone out and has not returned empty.

VI Baruch 3:9-15, 32-4:4. *About the fountain of wisdom. Lect* I:410
Psalm 18

Walk towards the shining of her light.
The images of Egyptian captivity and Babylonian exile are used tonight to speak to us of alienation from God. We are called to return to him from the land of our enemies, to enter into the full life of the Church.

VII Ezekiel 36:16-28. *About a new heart and a new spirit. Lect* I:412
Psalm 41 or **50**

I shall pour clean water over you and you will be cleansed; I shall give you a new heart, and put a new spirit in you.
Exile was a punishment for Israel's sin; return demands purification, new heart, new spirit. This is achieved for the Christian through Baptism, in which new birth and a new spirit is achieved through Christ's death and resurrection.

VIII Romans 6:3-11. *About the new life through Baptism. Lect* I:414
Psalm 117

This reading prepares us for the celebration and renewal of baptismal vows. In union with Christ we imitate his death and rising. We go from death to life, from darkness to light, from captivity to freedom, from the old way of life to the new.

IX Luke 24:1-12. *Why look among the dead for someonewho is alive? Lect* I:416

(Taken from *In the Light of Christ: The Old Testament Readings for the Easter Vigil.* Commentaries by Brian Magee CM, Anne F. Kelly, Andrew McGrady, Anne Looney & Donal Neary SJ, Veritas, 1994).

March 2013 READINGS Sunday Cycle C Psalter Proper
THE EASTER SEASON
31 Sunday **EASTER DAY OF THE LORD'S RESURRECTION**
Solemnity with Octave
White ✠ HOURS Proper. The Office of Readings is omitted by those who have attended the Easter Vigil. If celebrated – Te Deum
MASS in the Day. Proper. Gloria. Sequence. Creed
Preface of Easter I. In the Roman Canon, proper forms

The penitential act may be replaced by the form of sprinkling with water blessed at the Vigil.

The Rite of Renewal of Baptismal Promises is desirable after the homily.

It is fitting that EVENING PRAYER should be celebrated in a more solemn manner to mark the close of the Easter Triduum and to commemorate the apparitions in which our Lord showed himself to his disciples. (GILH 213)

READINGS **Acts 10:34, 37-43. Ps 117:1-2, 16-17, 22-23. Col 3:1-4 or 1 Cor 5:6-8. Jn 20:1-9.** Lect I:417

The Gospel from the Easter Vigil, **Lk 24:1-12***, Lect I:416, may be used at the Day Mass as an alternative.*

'Christ is risen, alleluia!' This is the ancient Christian greeting on this day of great joy and happiness for all. 'Easter is not simply one feast among others, but the "Feast of feasts". The mystery of the Resurrection, in which Christ crushed death, permeates with its powerful energy our old time, until all is subjected to him' (CCC, 1169).

Evening Mass: Gospel: **Lk 24:13-35.** *Lect I:428 may be used as an alternative.*

Night Prayer 1 or 2 of Sunday is used at choice throughout the Octave.

No other celebrations, not even funeral Masses, are permitted today (see Lit. Note 7)

APRIL 2013

1 Monday **EASTER MONDAY**
White HOURS Proper. Te Deum
MASS Proper. Gloria. Preface: Easter 1. Sequence optional. In the Roman Canon, proper forms
READINGS **Acts 2:14, 22-33. Ps 15:1-2, 5, 7-11. Mt 28:8-15.** Lect I:423

The women clasp the feet of the real body of the risen Lord who is thus identified with the earthly Jesus. But they are not to cling on in signs of love. His appearances are for the purpose of sending them on mission, to tell others.

No other celebrations, except funeral Masses, are permitted today (see Lit. Note 7)

St Ceallach (Celsus) is not celebrated this year.

---

2 Tuesday **EASTER TUESDAY**
White HOURS Proper. Te Deum
MASS Proper. Gloria. Preface: Easter 1. Sequence optional. In the Roman Canon, proper forms
READINGS **Acts 2:36-41. Ps 32:4-5, 18-20, 22. Jn 20:11-18.** Lect I:425

Mary Magdalen is told that the old relationship is now changed, she is not to cling on, for Jesus has to return to the Father, to fulfil what he had been sent to do.

No other celebrations, except funeral Masses, are permitted today (see Lit. Note 7)

St Francis of Paola, hermit is not celebrated this year.

April 2013 READINGS Sunday Cycle C Psalter Proper

3 Wednesday EASTER WEDNESDAY
White HOURS Proper. Te Deum
MASS Proper. Gloria. Preface: Easter 1. Sequence optional. In the Roman Canon, proper forms
READINGS **Acts 3:1-10. Ps 104:1-4, 6-9. Lk 24:13-35.** Lect I:427
Two disillusioned followers who cannot understand are met by someone who opens their minds and hearts by showing how God's word can give meaning to their lives. Invited to share their table, he takes bread, blesses it, breaks it, and gives it to them, and they know the Lord Jesus in that fourfold action. With joy they go back to tell the good news.
No other celebrations, except funeral Masses, are permitted today (see Lit. Note 7)

---

4 Thursday EASTER THURSDAY
White HOURS Proper. Te Deum
MASS Proper. Gloria. Preface: Easter I. Sequence optional. In the Roman Canon, proper forms
READINGS **Acts 3:11-26. Ps 8:2, 5-9. Lk 24:35-48.** Lect I:430
'Immediately they touched him, and through this contact with his flesh and spirit, they believed' (Ignatius of Antioch). And Jesus, though in his risen body he did not need food, shows them the courtesy of sharing their food.
No other celebrations, except funeral Masses, are permitted today (see Lit. Note 7)
St Isidore, bishop and doctor of the Church is not celebrated this year.

---

5 Friday EASTER FRIDAY
White HOURS Proper. Te Deum
MASS Proper. Gloria. Preface: Easter 1. Sequence optional. In the Roman Canon, proper forms
READINGS **Acts 4:1-12. Ps 117:1-2, 4, 22-27. Jn 21:1-14.** Lect I:432
The appearance at the lakeside – perhaps on a Sunday morning after a Sabbath rest from work – has echoes of the meals that Jesus shared during his earthly life. It recalls the sign of the Eucharist in the multiplication of the loaves and fishes.
No other celebrations, except funeral Masses, are permitted today (see Lit. Note 7)
St Vincent Ferrer, priest is not celebrated this year.

---

6 Saturday EASTER SATURDAY
White HOURS Proper. Te Deum
MASS Proper. Gloria. Preface: Easter 1. Sequence optional. In the Roman Canon, proper forms
READINGS **Acts 4:13-21. Ps 117:1, 14-21. Mk 16:9-15.** Lect I:435
The news of the resurrection brings belief or incredulity. Jesus has to reproach his disciples for being so slow to believe. They are to go out with the Good News, and the response to their preaching will be again belief or unbelief. Only those who believe will be saved.
No other celebrations, except funeral Masses, are permitted today (see Lit. Note 7)
Killala Tomorrow is the anniversary of the episcopal ordination of Most Rev. John Fleming, 7 April 2002.

Next Sunday's readings: Acts 5:12-16. Ps 117:2-4, 22-27. Apoc 1:9-13, 17-19. Jn 20:19-31. Lect I:444

NOTES FOR APRIL 2013

THE POPE'S INTENTIONS

General – Life-giving Worship: That the prayerful and public celebration of the faith may be a source of life for the faithful.

Mission – Churches in Mission Territories: That the Churches in mission territories may be a sign and instrument of hope and resurrection.

THE IRISH CALENDAR IN APRIL

1st: St Ceallach (Celsus) was born in 1080. He became abbot of Armagh in 1105 and was ordained priest. He was influenced by the reform then in progress in Munster. He presided at the synod of Rathbreasail in 1111. In 1129 on a visitation of Munster he died and is buried in Lismore in accordance with his own request.

18th: St Laserian (Molaise) worked in both Ireland and Scotland in the seventh century and later entered the monastery at Leighlin, where he became abbot. His monastery thrived and gave its name to the diocese established in 1110. He adapted church discipline in accordance with the practices of Rome and introduced the Roman method of dating the celebration of Easter. Laserian died in 639.

27th: St Asicus was St Patrick's expert craftsman in metal work and accompanied him on his journeys. He was left in charge of the church in Elphin which Patrick is said to have founded.

RITE OF BLESSING AND SPRINKLING OF WATER

The Rite of Blessing and Sprinkling of Water, is given in an appendix of the *Missal, RM* pp. 1353–6, the rubric on p. 379 notes that it may take place 'from time to time on Sundays, especially in Easter Time, instead of the customary Penitential Act ... as a reminder of Baptism'.

The Book of Blessings says, 'Holy Water reminds the faithful of Christ, who is given to us as the supreme divine blessing, who called himself the living water, and who in water established baptism for our sake as the sacramental sign of the blessing that brings salvation' (1388).

This Rite may also be an option in ritual Masses such as Ordinations and Religious Professions.

EASTER TIME

The celebration of Easter is prolonged throughout the Easter season. The fifty days from Easter Sunday to Pentecost Sunday are celebrated as one feast day, the 'great Sunday'.

The Sundays of this season are regarded as Sundays of Easter and are so termed; they have precedence over all feasts of the Lord and over all solemnities. Solemnities that fall on one of these Sundays are anticipated on the Saturday. Celebrations in honour of the Blessed Virgin Mary or the saints that fall during the week may not be transferred to one of these Sundays.

For adults who have received Christian initiation during the Easter Vigil, the whole of this period is given over to mystagogical catechesis. Therefore, wherever there are neophytes, the prescriptions of the *Rite of Christian Initiation of Adults* should be observed. Intercession should be made in the Eucharistic Prayer for the newly baptised through the Easter octave in all places.

Throughout the Easter season, the neophytes should be assigned their own special place among the faithful. All neophytes should endeavour to participate at Mass along with their godparents. In the homily and, according to local circumstances, in the General Intercessions, mention should be made of them. Some celebration should be held to conclude the period of mystagogical catechesis on or about Pentecost Sunday, depending upon local custom. It is also appropriate that children receive their first communion on one or other of the Sundays of Easter.

During Easter time, pastors should instruct the faithful who have been already initiated into the Eucharist on the meaning of the Church's precept concerning the reception of Holy Communion during this period. It is highly recommended that communion also be brought to the sick, especially during the Easter octave.

Where there is the custom of blessing houses in celebration of the resurrection, this blessing is to be imparted after the Solemnity of Easter and not before, by the parish priest or other priest or deacon delegated by him. This is an opportunity for exercising a pastoral ministry. The parish priest should go to each house for the purpose of undertaking a pastoral visitation of each family. There, he will speak with the residents and spend a few moments with them in prayer, using texts to be found in the *Book of Blessings*. In larger cities, consideration should be given to the gathering of several families for a common celebration of the blessing for all.

According to the differing circumstances of places and peoples, there are found a number of popular practices linked to celebrations of the Easter season, which in some instances attract greater numbers of the people than the sacred liturgy itself. These practices are not in any way to be undervalued, for they are often well adapted to the religious mentality of the faithful. Let episcopal conferences and local ordinaries, therefore, see to it that practices of this kind, which seem to nourish popular piety, be harmonised in the best way possible with the sacred liturgy, be imbued more distinctly with the spirit of the liturgy, be in some way derived from it, and lead the people to it.

This sacred period of fifty days concludes with Pentecost Sunday, when the gift of the Holy Spirit to the apostles, the beginnings of the Church, and the start of its mission to all tongues and peoples and nations are commemorated.

Encouragement should be given to the prolonged celebration of Mass in the form of a Vigil, whose character is not baptismal as in the Easter Vigil, but is one of urgent prayer, after the example of the apostles and disciples, who persevered together in prayer with Mary, the Mother of Jesus, as they awaited the Holy Spirit.

'It is proper to the paschal festivity that the whole Church rejoices at the forgiveness of sins, which is not only for those who are reborn in Holy Baptism, but also for those who have long been numbered among the adopted children' (St Leo the Great). By means of a more intensive pastoral care and a deeper spiritual effort, all who celebrate the Easter feasts will, by the Lord's grace, experience their effect in their daily lives.

– Congregation for Divine Worship, *Paschale solemnitatis*, letter on the preparation and celebration of the Easter feasts, 100–8.

April 2013 Psalter Week 2

7 Sunday **SECOND SUNDAY OF EASTER**
Divine Mercy Sunday
White ✠ HOURS Proper. Te Deum
MASS Proper. Gloria. Sequence optional. Creed. Preface: Easter I. In the Roman Canon, proper forms
No other celebrations, not even funeral Masses, are permitted today (see Lit. Note 7)
St John Baptist de la Salle, priest is not celebrated this year.

---

8 Monday **THE ANNUNCIATION OF THE LORD** Solemnity
White HOURS Proper. Te Deum. Complementary Psalms at Day Hour
MASS Proper. Gloria. Creed. Preface: Proper
In the Profession of Faith, all genuflect at the words: and was made man.
No Masses for the Dead, except funeral Masses, are permitted today (see Lit. Note 7)

---

9 Tuesday **2nd Week of Easter**
White HOURS Psalter Week 2
MASS Proper. Preface: Easter I–V

---

10 Wednesday 2nd Week of Easter
White HOURS Psalter Week 2
MASS Proper. Preface: Easter I–V

---

11 Thursday **2nd Week of Easter**
St Stanislaus, bishop and martyr Memorial
Red HOURS of the memorial. Psalter Week 2
MASS Proper. Preface: Easter I–V or of the Saint

---

12 Friday **2nd Week of Easter**
White HOURS Psalter Week 2
MASS Proper. Preface: Easter I–V

---

13 Saturday **2nd Week of Easter**
White HOURS Psalter Week 2
MASS Proper. Preface: Easter I–V
Red Optional memorial of **St Martin I, pope and martyr**

April 2013 READINGS Sunday Cycle C

SECOND WEEK OF EASTER

7 Sunday Acts 5:12-16. Ps 117:2-4, 22-27. Apoc 1:9-13, 17-19. Jn 20:19-31. *Lect* I:444

The account of the doubts of the apostle Thomas sets out to answer the question of how we can believe as firmly as those first disciples who had seen the Lord. And we are shown first that those first disciples did not come easily to faith. Because their faith was tested and tried we can have confidence in their testimony.

8 Monday Is 7:10-14, 8:10. Ps 39:7-11 Heb 10:4-10. Lk 1:26-38. *Lect* II:985

The Annunciation of the Lord. 'Giving her consent to God's word, Mary becomes the mother of Jesus. Espousing the divine will for salvation wholeheartedly, without a single sin to restrain her, she gave herself entirely to the person and to the work of her Son; she did so in order to serve the mystery of redemption with him and dependant on him, by God's grace' (CCC, 494).

Clonfert Tomorrow is the anniversary of the episcopal ordination of Most Rev. John Kirby, 9 April 1988.

9 Tuesday Acts 4:32-37. Ps 91:1-2, 5. Jn 3:7-15. *Lect* I:449

Jesus is the perfect revealer of God whose revelation reaches its climax in his exaltation on the cross. Faith is an active response to Jesus.

Ardagh and Clonmacnois. Tomorrow is the anniversary of the episcopal ordination of Most Rev. Colm O'Reilly, 10 April 1983.

10 Wednesday Acts 5:17-26. Ps 33:2-9. Jn 3:16-21. *Lect* I:452

God's love calls for a response of faith in Jesus. This faith results in making the truth part of one's living. To refuse faith is to be self-condemned.

11 Thursday Acts 5:27-33. Ps 33:2, 9, 17-20. Jn 3:31-36. *Lect* I:454

St Peter speaking before the officials says clearly that the apostles are the authentic witnesses to the events which are God's Spirit at work.

St Stanislaus became bishop of Krakow, Poland in 1072. His outspoken condemnation of corruption resulted in his murder in 1097.

12 Friday Acts 5:34-42. Ps 26:1, 4, 13-14. Jn 6:1-15. *Lect* I:456

Jesus communicates his life-giving power through his living word and the gift of his own life in the eucharistic bread.

Dublin Tomorrow is the anniversary of the episcopal ordination of Most Rev. Dermot O'Mahony, 13 April 1975.

13 Saturday Acts 6:1-7. Ps 32:1-2, 4-5, 18-19. Jn 6:16-21. *Lect* I:459

The Church continues to grow and the apostles re-order the ministries to cope with different needs. The Spirit works in the Church, and brings peace.

St Martin I died in 655 from harsh treatment in exile and prison.

Next Sunday's readings: Acts 5:27-32, 40-41. Ps 29:2, 4-6, 11-13. Apoc 5:11-14. Jn 21:1-19 (shorter form 21:1-14). *Lect* I:468

April 2013 Psalter Week 3

14 Sunday White ✠	**THIRD SUNDAY OF EASTER** HOURS Proper. Te Deum. Psalter Week 3 MASS Proper Gloria. Creed. Preface: Easter I–V

No other celebrations, not even funeral Masses, are permitted today (see Lit. Note 7)

15 Monday White	**3rd Week of Easter** HOURS Psalter Week 3 MASS Proper. Preface: Easter I–V

16 Tuesday White	**3rd Week of Easter** HOURS Psalter Week 3 MASS Proper. Preface: Easter I–V

17 Wednesday White	**3rd Week of Easter** HOURS Psalter Week 3 MASS Proper. Preface: Easter I–V

18 Thursday White	**3rd Week of Easter** HOURS Psalter Week 3 MASS Proper. Preface: Easter I–V	
White	Optional memorial of **St Laserian, bishop**	
Leighlin	**St Laserian, bishop**	Feast

19 Friday White	**3rd Week of Easter** HOURS Psalter Week 3 MASS Proper. Preface: Easter I–V

Today is the anniversary of the election in 2005 of **Pope Benedict XVI** as Supreme Pastor of the Church. An intention for the Holy Father should be included in the Prayer of the Faithful at all Masses.

20 Saturday White	**3rd Week of Easter** HOURS Psalter Week 3 MASS Proper. Preface: Easter I–V

April 2013 READINGS Sunday Cycle C

THIRD WEEK OF EASTER

14 Sunday **Acts 5:27-32, 40-41. Ps 29:2, 4-6, 11-13. Apoc 5:11-14. Jn 21:1-19** (shorter form 21:1-14). *Lect* I:468

In the gospels the disciples never catch fish without the help of Jesus. So when they are told to go out and preach, to make disciples, and to feed the flock, they know that they will do so with his help. For now he is with us always.

15 Monday **Acts 6:8-15. Ps 118:23-24, 26-27, 29-30. Jn 6:22-29.** *Lect* I:472

Stephen, filled with grace and power, witnesses to Christ, becomes a threat to the synagogue, and is arrested. Jesus tells the people to look beyond the bread they eat to the mystery, and to seek him in faith.

16 Tuesday **Acts 7:51-8:1. Ps 30:3-4, 6-8, 17, 21. Jn 6:30-35.** *Lect* I:474

Stephen becomes the first to die for Christ, echoing his Master's words of forgiveness for his executioners. Jesus is the Father's gift, sent to us on a life-giving mission.

17 Wednesday Acts 8:1-8. Ps 65, 1-7. Jn 6:35-40. *Lect* I:476

The persecution of the Church in Jerusalem under Saul sends the Christians to preach the Good News elsewhere.
Limerick Tomorrow is the anniversary of the episcopal ordination of Most Rev. Donal Murray, 18 April 1982.

18 Thursday **Acts 8:26-40. Ps 65:8-9, 16-17, 20. Jn 6:44-51.** *Lect* I:479

The Ethiopian official was humble enough to ask to have the scriptures explained to him. Philip's opening up of the word of God brought the man to faith and baptism. We also ought to search the scriptures daily.
St Laserian see *April notes*.

19 Friday **Acts 9:1-20. Ps 116. Jn 6:52-59.** *Lect* I:481

The conversion of St Paul comes through his meeting with the risen Lord on the Road to Damascus. It is the same risen Lord who gives himself to believers in the Eucharist in a personal communion. That communion is a pledge of an eternal communion with Jesus and the Father.

20 Saturday **Acts 9:31-42. Ps 115:12-17. Jn 6:60-69.** *Lect* I:484

The churches built themselves up and were filled with the consolation of the Holy Spirit. Peter raises Dorcas to life on his apostolic journey. The words of Jesus lead to life, and give life if accepted in faith.
Armagh Tomorrow is the anniversary of the episcopal ordination of Most Rev. Gerard Clifford, 21 April 1991.

Next Sunday's readings: Acts 13:14, 43-52. Ps 99:1-3, 5. Apoc 7:9, 14-17. Jn 10:27-30. *Lect* I:493

April 2013 Psalter Week 4

21 Sunday **FOURTH SUNDAY OF EASTER**
Day of Prayer for Vocations
White ✠ HOURS Proper. Te Deum. Psalter Week 4
MASS Proper. Gloria. Creed. Preface: Easter I–V
No other celebrations, not even funeral Masses, are permitted today (see Lit. Note 7)
St Anselm, bishop and doctor of the Church is not celebrated this year.
Derry **Dedication of the Cathedral** (see *Lit. Note 11*)

---

22 Monday **4th Week of Easter**
White HOURS Psalter Week 4
MASS Proper. Preface: Easter I–V

---

23 Tuesday **4th Week of Easter**
White HOURS Psalter Week 4
MASS Proper. Preface: Easter I–V
Red Optional memorial of **St George, martyr**
Red Optional memorial of **St Adalbert of Prague, bishop and martyr**

---

24 Wednesday 4th Week of Easter
White HOURS Psalter Week 4
MASS Proper. Preface: Easter I–V
Red Optional memorial of **St Fidelis of Sigmaringen, priest and martyr**
Today is the anniversary of the solemn inauguration in 2005 of **Pope Benedict XVI** as Supreme Pastor of the Church. His election took place on 19 April 2005. An intention for the Holy Father should be included in the Prayer of the Faithful at all Masses.

---

25 Thursday ST MARK, EVANGELIST Feast
Red HOURS Proper. Te Deum. Psalter Week 4 at Day Hour
MASS Proper. Gloria. Preface: Apostles II.
No Masses for the dead, except funeral Masses, are permitted today (see Lit. Note 7)

---

26 Friday **4th Week of Easter**
White HOURS Psalter Week 4
MASS Proper. Preface: Easter I–V

---

27 Saturday **4th Week of Easter**
White HOURS Psalter Week 4
MASS Proper. Preface: Easter I–V
White Optional memorial of **St Asicus, bishop**
Elphin **St Asicus, bishop** Feast

April 2013 READINGS Sunday Cycle C
FOURTH WEEK OF EASTER

21 Sunday **Acts 13:14, 43-52. Ps 99:1-3, 5. Apoc 7:9, 14-17. Jn 10:27-30.** Lect I:493

This is Good Shepherd Sunday, a day of special prayer for vocations to the work of service in the Church. There is the enduring command of Christ to his Church to go out and preach to all people. There is need for people of faith to respond to that command, people who are prepared to dedicate their lives to this work for the sake of the gospel.

Dublin Tomorrow is the anniversary of the episcopal ordination of Most Rev. Eamonn Walsh, 22 April 1990.

22 Monday **Acts 11:1-18. Pss 41:2-3, 42:3-4. Jn 10:1-10.** Lect I:496

'The Church is, accordingly, a sheepfold, the sole and necessary gateway to which is Christ. It is also the flock, of which God himself foretold that he would be the shepherd, and whose sheep, even though governed by human shepherds, are unfailingly nourished and led by Christ himself, the Good Shepherd, Prince of Shepherds, who gave his life for his sheep' (*Lumen gentium*, 6).

Ferns Tomorrow is the anniversary of the episcopal ordination of Most Rev. Denis Brennan, 23 April 2006

23 Tuesday **Acts 11:19-26. Ps 86:1-7. Jn 10:22-30.** Lect I:499

At Antioch the Good News is first preached to the pagans and the disciples are first called 'Christians'. Those who receive Jesus as their shepherd receive his protection and the gift of eternal life.

St George was venerated as a soldier saint at Lydda in the Holy Land where he was probably martyred around the year 300. His cult may have been popularised in England and Ireland by returning crusaders. He is patron saint of England, Portugal, of soldiers, and of the Scout Movement.

St Adalbert, born 956, after being bishop of Prague, went as a missionary among the Prussians on the Polish coast where he was martyred in 997.

24 Wednesday Acts 12:24-13:5. Ps 66:2-3, 5-6, 8. Jn 12:44-50. Lect I:501

Barnabas and Saul start their work together as they travel to Cyprus. Jesus in his last public message teaches that those who believe in him will be freed from darkness and liberated from sin, unbelief and separation from God.

St Fidelis of Sigmaringen, 1578–1622, a Capuchin who preached to the Calvinists in Switzerland, where he was killed by a group of extremists.

25 Thursday **1 Pt 5:5-14. Ps 88:2-3, 6-7, 16-17. Mk 16:15-20.** Lect II:1005

St Mark was closely connected with the preaching of Ss Peter, Paul, and Barnabas. His Gospel was probably written at Rome when he was with Paul, and is traditionally viewed as representing St Peter's approach to the preaching of the good news. Later tradition has him as an interpreter for St Peter. His symbol is a winged lion.

26 Friday **Acts 13:26-33. Ps 2:6-11. Jn 14:1-6.** Lect I:505

'I am the Way, the Truth and the Life.' Jesus encourages peace in our hearts in times of trouble. There remains for us a place of rest in his Father's house. Following him who is the Way, we come to the Father.

27 Saturday **Acts 13:44-52. Ps 97:1-4. Jn 14:7-14.** Lect I:508

Prayer in the name of Jesus, animated by the Spirit, will lead us to think and desire as he does.

St Asicus see *April notes*.

Next Sunday's readings: Acts 14:21-27. Ps 144:8-13. Apoc 21:1-5. Jn 13:31-35. Lect I:517

NOTES FOR MAY 2013

THE POPE'S INTENTIONS

General – The Administrators of Justice: That those who administer justice will always act with integrity and upright conscience.

Mission – Seminarians: That seminarians, especially from mission Churches, may always be pastors according to the heart of Christ, fully devoted to the proclamation of the Gospel.

THE IRISH CALENDAR IN MAY

4th: St Conleth is believed to have come from the Wicklow area. While living as a hermit he was persuaded by Brigid to act as priest for her community in Kildare. He was venerated as a great saint and Cogitosus in his *Life of Brigid* calls him bishop and abbot of the monks of Kildare. He was buried beside Brigid in the great church there.

5th: Bl. Edmund Ignatius Rice (1762–1844) came from Callan, Co. Kilkenny. After his young wife's early death, he sold his possessions and dedicated his life to the education of the poor. To advance the work, he gathered other like-minded men who took religious vows together to work for the Catholic education of boys. He is a model of patient and cheerful acceptance of the sufferings God sends, a true lay apostle and a deeply committed religious.

10th: St Comgall was born around 516 in Co. Antrim. His father was a soldier and wished his son to follow in his steps but Comgall wished to become a soldier of Christ. He studied under Finnian of Moville and deepened his life of prayer to counteract his temptations to boredom and homesickness. He was persuaded to become a priest and then established a monastery at Bangor around 555-8, which attracted people like Columbanus. He also founded a monastery at Tiree in Scotland. He died after a long illness at Pentecost 602 or 605.

15th: St Carthage (or Mochuta) hailed from a rich family in Kerry. As he loved the chanting of the psalms the local king arranged for him to become a priest. Having spent a year possibly at Bangor he founded his own monastery at Rahan in 595. It grew rapidly. But opposition made him move southwards around 637. He, with hundreds of monks and their patients from the leper colony, finally arrived at Lismore, where he made a foundation. He died in 638.

16th: St Brendan was a Kerryman who was born in 486. He studied at Clonard under Finnian. His name is connected with many places in Kerry such as Ardfert and Mount Brandon. He visited Scotland and reached the Hebrides and possibly areas beyond. He founded a monastery in Clonfert in 568 and died there in 578.

24 May:
DAY OF PRAYER FOR THE CHURCH IN CHINA – OUR LADY OF SHESHAN

In a Letter written to the faithful of the Catholic Church in China in May 2007, Pope Benedict XVI expressed the hope that 24 May, liturgical memorial of Our Lady Help of Christians who is venerated with such devotion at the Marian shrine of Sheshan in Shanghai, would become a day of prayer for the Church in China.

SOLEMN OPENING OF SECOND VATICAN COUNCIL

Today is a day of joy for Mother Church: through God's most kindly providence the longed-for day has dawned for the solemn opening of the Second Vatican Ecumenical Council, here at Saint Peter's shrine. And Mary, God's Virgin Mother, on this feast day of her noble motherhood, gives it her gracious protection.

Certain it is that the critical issues, the thorny problems that wait upon human solution, have remained the same for almost twenty centuries. And why? Because the whole of history and of life hinges on the person of Jesus Christ. Either people anchor themselves on Him and His Church, and thus enjoy the blessings of light and joy, right order and peace; or they live their lives apart from Him; many positively oppose Him, and deliberately exclude themselves from the Church. The result can only be confusion in their lives, bitterness in their relations with one another, and the savage threat of war.

But the function of every ecumenical council has always been to make a solemn proclamation of the union that exists between Christ and His Church; to diffuse the light of truth; to give right guidance to men both as individuals and as members of a family and a society; to evoke and strengthen their spiritual resources; and to set their minds continually on those higher values which are genuine and unfailing.

No study of human history during these twenty centuries of Christendom can fail to take note of the evidence of this extraordinary teaching authority of the Church as voiced in her general councils. The documents are there, whole volumes of them; a sacred heritage housed in the Roman archives and in the most famous libraries of the world.

As regards the immediate cause for this great event, which gathers you here together at our bidding, it is sufficient for us to put on record once more something which, though trifling in itself, made a deep impression on us personally. The decision to hold an ecumenical council came to us in the first instance in a sudden flash of inspiration. We communicated this decision, without elaboration, to the Sacred College of Cardinals on that memorable 25 January 1959, the feast of Saint Paul's Conversion, in his patriarchal basilica in the Ostien Way. The response was immediate. It was as though some ray of supernatural light had entered the minds of all present: it was reflected in their faces; it shone from their eyes. At once the world was swept by a wave of enthusiasm, and people everywhere began to wait eagerly for the celebration of this Council.

For three years the arduous work of preparation continued. It consisted in making a detailed and accurate analysis of the prevailing condition of the faith, the religious practice, and the vitality of the Christian, and particularly the Catholic, body.

We are convinced that the time spent in preparing for this Ecumenical Council was in itself an initial token of grace, a gift from heaven.

For we have every confidence that the Church, in the light of this Council, will gain in spiritual riches. New sources of energy will be opened to her, enabling her to face the future without fear. By introducing timely changes and a prudent system of mutual cooperation, we intend that the Church shall really succeed in bringing men and women, families and nations to the appreciation of supernatural values.

Thus the celebration of this Council becomes a compelling motive for wholehearted thanksgiving to God, the giver of every good gift, and for exultantly proclaiming the glory of Christ the Lord, the triumphant and immortal King of ages and peoples.

– From the address of Pope John XXIII at the opening of the Second Vatican Council on 11 October 1962

April 2013 Psalter Week 1

28 Sunday **FIFTH SUNDAY OF EASTER**
White ✠ HOURS Proper. Te Deum. Psalter Week 1
MASS Proper Gloria. Creed. Preface: Easter I–V
No other celebrations, not even funeral Masses, are permitted today (see Lit. Note 7)
St Peter Chanel, priest and martyr and **St Louis Marie Grignion de Montfort, priest** are not celebrated this year.

---

29 Monday ST CATHERINE OF SIENA, VIRGIN AND DOCTOR OF THE CHURCH, PATRON OF EUROPE Feast
White HOURS Proper. Psalter Week 1 at Day Hour
MASS Proper. Gloria. Preface: Saint
No Masses for the dead, except funeral Masses, are permitted today (see Lit. Note 7)

---

30 Tuesday **5th Week of Easter**
White HOURS Psalter Week 1
MASS Proper. Preface: Easter I–V
White Optional memorial of **St Pius V, pope**

MAY 2013

1 Wednesday **5th Week of Easter**
White HOURS Psalter Week 1
MASS Proper. Preface: Easter I–V
White Optional memorial of **St Joseph the Worker**

---

2 Thursday **5th Week of Easter**
St Athanasius, bishop and doctor of the Church
Memorial
White HOURS of the memorial. Psalter Week 1
MASS Proper. Preface: Easter I–V or of the Saint

---

3 Friday SS PHILIP AND JAMES, APOSTLES Feast
Red HOURS Proper. Psalter Week 1 at Day Hour
MASS Proper. Gloria. Preface: Apostles I–II
No Masses for the dead, except funeral Masses, are permitted today (see Lit. Note 7)

---

4 Saturday **5th Week of Easter**
White HOURS Psalter Week 1
MASS Proper. Preface: Easter I–V
White Optional memorial of **St Conleth, bishop**
Kildare **St Conleth, bishop** Feast

April 2013 READINGS Sunday Cycle C
FIFTH WEEK OF EASTER
28 Sunday **Acts 14:21-27. Ps 144:8-13. Apoc 21:1-5. Jn 13:31-35.** *Lect* I:517

Love shown in the members of the Church enables the community to be seen as disciples of Christ. Mutual love within the community overflows to the whole world. Christian charity helps to ease the burden of suffering and eliminate many of its causes.
Cork and Ross Tomorrow is the anniversary of the episcopal ordination of Most Rev. John Buckley, 29 April 1984.
Down and Connor Tomorrow is the anniversary of the episcopal ordination of Most Rev. Donal McKeown, 29 April 2001.

29 Monday **1 Jn 1:5-2:2. Ps 102:1-4, 8-9, 13-14, 17-18. Mt 11:25-30.** *Lect* II:1009

St Catherine of Siena, 1347–80, humble and dauntless Dominican tertiary who brought peace to her native Siena, to Italy, and to fourteenth-century Europe, spent all her energies for the Church, being able to achieve the Pope's return from Avignon to Rome. She is remembered also as a mystic and reformer of religious life. Proclaimed Doctor of the Church in 1970 and Patron of Europe in 2000.

30 Tuesday **Acts 14:19-28. Ps 144:10-13, 21. Jn 14:27-31.** *Lect* I:522

'As witnesses of the Risen One, the apostles – and Peter in particular – remain the foundation stones of his Church' (*CCC*, 642).
St Pius V, 1504–72. Dominican, elected pope in 1565, he implemented the reforms of the Council of Trent, including the Breviary, Missal and Catechism. He is noted for his defence of Christendom against the Ottoman empire.

MAY 2013

1 Wednesday **Acts 15:1-6. Ps 121:1-5. Jn 15:1-8.** *Lect* I:524

The apostles and teachers come together in search of unity of faith. The branches must remain part of the vine so that life will flow to them and they will bear fruit.
St Joseph the Worker: Gn 1:26-2:3 *or* **Col 3:14-15, 17, 23-24. Ps 89:2-4, 12-14, 16. Mt 13:54-58.** *Lect* II:1013

2 Thursday **Acts 15:7-21. Ps 95:1-3, 10. Jn 15:9-11.** *Lect* I:526

Jesus loves his disciples with that same gift of love with which the Father loves him. Genuine love means attending to the needs and weaknesses of others.
St Athanasius. Born at Alexandria in 295, he fought ceaselessly against the Arian heresy, defending the true and equal divinity of Christ. As a result he had to endure much tribulation and he was several times sent into exile.

3 Friday **1 Cor 15:1-8. Ps 18:2-5. Jn 14:6-14.** *Lect* II:1017

St Philip asks to see and, having seen, he tells the Good News to others. He was born at Bethsaida. Formerly a disciple of John the Baptist, he became a follower of Christ. **St James**, the son of Alphaeus and a cousin of the Lord, ruled the Church at Jerusalem, wrote an Epistle, and led a life of penance. He converted many of the people of Jerusalem to the faith and was martyred in the year 62.

4 Saturday **Acts 16:1-10. Ps 99:1-3, 5. Jn 15:18-21.** *Lect* I:531

The conflict between the believer and the world is part of the Christian's inheritance. The disciple cannot expect other than what his Master also received. It is better to be persecuted for doing right than simply to conform to the ways of the world.
St Conleth see *May notes*.

Next Sunday's readings: Acts 15:1-2, 22-29. Ps 66:2-3, 5-6, 8. Apoc 21:10-14, 22-23. Jn 14:23-29. *Lect* I:539

The second reading and Gospel of the Seventh Sunday of Easter may be used with the first reading and psalm of the Sixth Sunday: **Acts 15:1-2, 22-29. Ps 66:2-3, 5-6, 8.** *Lect* I:539 **Apoc 22:12-14, 16-17, 20. Jn 17:20-26.** *Lect* I:574

May 2013 Psalter Week 2

5 Sunday **SIXTH SUNDAY OF EASTER**
White ✠ HOURS Proper. Te Deum. Psalter Week 2
MASS Proper Gloria. Creed. Preface: Easter I–V
No other celebrations, not even funeral Masses, are permitted today (see Lit. Note 7)
Bl. Edmund Rice, religious is not celebrated this year.

---

6 Monday **6th Week of Easter**
White HOURS Psalter Week 2
MASS Proper. Preface: Easter I–V

---

7 Tuesday **6th Week of Easter**
White HOURS Psalter Week 2
MASS Proper. Preface: Easter I–V

---

8 Wednesday **6th Week of Easter**
White HOURS Psalter Week 2
MASS Proper. Preface: Easter I–V

---

9 Thursday **6th Week of Easter**
White HOURS Psalter Week 2
MASS Proper. Preface: Easter I–V

---

10 Friday **6th Week of Easter**
White HOURS Psalter Week 2
MASS Proper. Preface: Easter I–V
White Optional memorial of **St Comgall, abbot**

---

11 Saturday **6th Week of Easter**
White HOURS Psalter Week 2
MASS Proper. Preface: Easter I–V
FIRST EVENING PRAYER of the **Ascension**

May 2013 READINGS Sunday Cycle C

SIXTH WEEK OF EASTER

5 Sunday **Acts 15:1-2, 22-29. Ps 66:2-3, 5-6, 8. Apoc 21:10-14, 22-23. Jn 14:23-29.** Lect I:539

The Holy Spirit guides the Church from its beginnings. The promise of the gift of the Spirit is a comfort to the disciples as the Lord leaves them.

The second reading and Gospel of the Seventh Sunday of Easter may be used with the first reading and psalm of the Sixth Sunday: **Acts 15:1-2, 22-29. Ps 66:2-3, 5-6, 8.** Lect I:539 **Apoc 22:12-14, 16-17, 20. Jn 17:20-26.** Lect I:574

6 Monday **Acts 16:11-15. Ps 149:1-6, 9. Jn 15:26-16:4.** Lect I:542

Jesus understands the fear of his disciples as they face the world. The Spirit of truth is with us to help us to speak up for our faith in the face of opposition, ridicule or indifference.

7 Tuesday **Acts 16:22-34. Ps 137:1-3, 7-8. Jn 16:5-11.** Lect I:544

'God is Love' and love is his first gift, containing all others. Because we are dead or at least wounded by sin, the first effect of the gift of love is the forgiveness of our sins. The communion of the Holy Spirit in the Church restores to the baptised the divine likeness lost through sin (CCC, 733–4).

8 Wednesday **Acts 17:15, 22-18:1. Ps 148:1-2, 11-14. Jn 16:12-15.** Lect I:546

St Paul preached to the citizens of Athens about their unknown God, but they preferred to think about it all at a later time. The Spirit continues with the Church, helping us to interpret the signs of the times. We must be always ready to listen.

9 Thursday **Acts 18:1-8. Ps 97:1-4. Jn. 16:16-20.** Lect I:560

St Paul gives the example of missionary work, devoting all his time to preaching. As a result a great many Corinthians embrace the faith. 'Faith comes from hearing.'

10 Friday **Acts 18:9-18. Ps 46:2-7. Jn 16:20-23.** Lect I:562

'On the day of Pentecost when the seven weeks of Easter had come to an end, Christ's Passover is fulfilled in the outpouring of the Holy Spirit, manifested, given and communicated as a divine person: of his fullness, Christ, the Lord, pours out the Spirit in abundance' (CCC, 731)

St Comgall, abbot see *May notes.*

11 Saturday **Acts 18:23-28. Ps 46:2-3, 8-10. Jn 16:23-28.** Lect I:564

The conflict between the believer and the world is part of the Christian's inheritance. The disciple can not expect other than what his Master also received. It is better to be persecuted for doing right than simply to conform to the ways of the world.

Next Sunday's readings: Acts 1:1-11. Ps 46:2-3, 6-7, 8-9. Eph 1:17-23 *or* Heb 9:24-28, 10:19-23. Lk 24:46-53. Lect I:556

May 2013 Weekdays Cycle C Psalter Week 3

12 Sunday **THE ASCENSION OF THE LORD** Solemnity
World Communications Day
White ✠ HOURS Proper. Te Deum.
MASS Proper. Gloria. Creed. Preface: Ascension I–II. In the Roman Canon, proper form
READINGS **Acts 1:1-11. Ps 46:2-3, 6-7, 8-9. Eph 1:17-23 *or* Heb 9:24-28, 10:19-23. Lk 24:46-53.** *Lect* I:556

'**The Ascension** of Christ means our own salvation as well; where the glorious Head has gone before, the body is called to follow in hope. Let us therefore exult, beloved, as is fitting, and let us rejoice in devout thanksgiving. For on this day not only have we been confirmed in our possession of paradise, but we have even entered heaven in the person of Christ; through his grace we have regained far more than we had lost through the devil's hatred' (St Leo the Great, *Sermon* 73:4).
No other celebrations, not even funeral Masses, are permitted today (see Lit. Note 7)
The week of prayer for the coming of the Holy Spirit recalls the waiting in prayer of the disciples with Mary.
Ss Nereus and Achilleus, martyrs and **St Pancras, martyr** are not celebrated this year.

---

13 Monday **7th Week of Easter**
White HOURS Psalter Week 3
MASS Proper. Preface: Easter I–V/Ascension I–II
White Optional memorial of **Our Lady of Fatima**
READINGS **Acts 19:1-8. Ps 67:2-7. Jn 16:29-33.** Lect I:576
Jesus understands the fear of his disciples as they face the world. The Spirit of truth is with us to help speak up for our faith in the face of opposition, ridicule, or indifference.
Our Lady of Fatima: Is 61:9-11. Ps 44. Lk 11:27-28.

---

14 Tuesday ST MATTHIAS, APOSTLE Feast
Red HOURS Proper. Psalter Week 3 at Day Hour
MASS Proper. Gloria. Preface: Apostles I–II
READINGS **Acts 1:15-17, 20-26. Ps 112:1-8. Jn 15:9-17.** *Lect* II:1023
St Matthias, like all the apostles, was chosen to become 'a witness with us of Christ's resurrection'. The story of his election as one of the apostles is given in the first reading. He seems to have spent a great deal of time working in Judea; then he travelled east to Cappadocia (now Turkey), where it is said that he was the vital instrument in bringing many pagans to the faith. He is said to have been martyred at Colchis on the Black Sea and his relics brought to Rome by St Helena.
No Masses for the dead, except funeral Masses, are permitted today (see Lit. Note 7)
Down and Connor Tomorrow is the anniversary of the episcopal ordination of Most Rev. Patrick Walsh and Most Rev. Anthony Farquhar, 15 May 1983.

---

15 Wednesday 7th Week of Easter
White HOURS Psalter Week 3
MASS Proper. Preface: Easter I–V/Ascension I–II
White Optional memorial of **St Carthage, bishop**
Waterford and Lismore **St Carthage, bishop** Feast
READINGS **Acts 20:28-38. Ps 67:29-30, 33-36. Jn 17:11-19.** *Lect* I:580
St Paul warns the Ephesians of the false teachers that will come, and calls them to be on their guard.
St Carthage see *May notes*.

May 2013 Weekdays Cycle C Psalter Week 3

16 Thursday	**7th Week of Easter**	
White	HOURS Psalter Week 3	
	MASS Proper. Preface: Easter I–V/Ascension I–II	
White	Optional memorial of **St Brendan, abbot**	
Clonfert	**St Brendan, abbot**	Feast
Kerry	**St Brendan, abbot**	Feast
READINGS	**Acts 22:30, 23:6-11. Ps 15:1-2, 5, 7-11. Jn 17:20-26.** Lect I:583	

Jesus prays for the gift of unity among his followers – a unity that will mirror the unity of the Trinity.
St Brendan see May notes.

---

17 Friday	**7th Week of Easter**
White	HOURS Psalter Week 3
	MASS Proper. Preface: Easter I–V/Ascension I–II
READINGS	**Acts 25:13-21. Ps 102:1-2, 11-12, 19-20. Jn. 21:15-19.** Lect I:585

Paul is now on his way to Rome to meet his death there. Jesus foretells Peter's last days which will also be in Rome.

---

18 Saturday	**7th Week of Easter**
White	HOURS Psalter Week 3
	MASS Proper. Preface: Easter I–V/Ascension I–II
Red	Optional memorial of **St John I, pope and martyr**
READINGS	**Acts 28:16-20, 30-31. Ps 10:4-5, 7. Jn 21:20-25.** Lect I:588

St Paul teaches the truth about Jesus until the end. St John's Gospel reminds us at the end that much more happened and was said than is written in the books.
St John I was the first bishop of Rome to visit Constantinople. He was involved in Arian controversies and imprisoned at Ravenna, where he died in 526.

FEAST OF PENTECOST

The Fifty Days of Easter conclude with the celebration of Pentecost Sunday. It is appropriate to celebrate the Vigil with an extended Liturgy of the Word at the Evening Mass. See May Notes.

Red ✠	EVENING MASS of the Vigil. Proper. Gloria. Creed
	Preface: Pentecost. In the Roman Canon, proper form
	FIRST EVENING PRAYER: Proper
	Night Prayer 1 of Sunday
READINGS	**Saturday Evening: Vigil of Pentecost**

Vigil Mass as in Missal and Lectionary (Lect I:596)
(extended form RM p. 315; simple form RM p. 319)

Next Sunday's readings: Year C: Acts 2:1-11. Ps 103:1, 24, 29-31, 34. Rm 8:8-17. Jn 14:15-16, 23-26. Lect I :601 & 606 **or Acts 2:1-11. Ps 103:1, 24, 29-31, 34. 1 Cor 12:3-7, 12-13. Jn 20:19-23.** Lect I:601

May 2013 Psalter Week 3

19 Sunday Red ✠	**PENTECOST SUNDAY** HOURS Proper. Te Deum MASS Proper Gloria. Sequence. Creed. Preface: Pentecost. In the Roman Canon, proper forms EVENING PRAYER of Pentecost

No other celebrations, not even funeral Masses, are permitted today (see Lit. Note 7)
At the end of the Easter season, the Paschal Candle should be kept in the baptistery. It is lit during Baptisms and from it the candles of the newly baptised are lighted. At funerals the Easter candle should be placed near the coffin, to signify that Christian death is a true Passover.

Ardagh and Clonmacnois   **Dedication of the Cathedral** (see Lit. Note 11)

ORDINARY TIME
Ordinary Time resumes this year with Week 7.
Volume III of the Divine Office is used from today.

20 Monday
Green — **7th Week in Ordinary Time**
HOURS Psalter Week 3. MASS of choice
White — Optional memorial of **St Bernadine of Siena, priest**

21 Tuesday
Green — **7th Week in Ordinary Time**
HOURS Psalter Week 3. MASS of choice
Red — Optional memorial of **Ss Christopher Megallánes, priest and Companions, martyrs**

22 Wednesday **7th Week in Ordinary Time**
Green — HOURS Psalter Week 3. MASS of choice
White — Optional memorial of **St Rita of Cascia, religious**

23 Thursday **7th Week in Ordinary Time**
Green — HOURS Psalter Week 3. MASS of choice

24 Friday **7th Week in Ordinary Time**
Green — HOURS Psalter Week 3. MASS of choice

25 Saturday **7th Week in Ordinary Time**
Green — HOURS Psalter Week 3. MASS of choice
White — Optional memorial of **St Bede the Venerable, priest and doctor of the Church**
White — Optional memorial of **St Gregory VII, pope**
White — Optional memorial of **St Mary Magdalene de' Pazzi, virgin**
White/Green — Saturday Mass of the **Blessed Virgin Mary**
FIRST EVENING PRAYER of **Trinity Sunday**

Next Sunday's readings: Prov 8:22-31. Ps 8:4-9. Rm 5:1-5. Jn 16:12-15. *Lect* I:615

May 2013 Weekdays Cycle 1
FEAST OF PENTECOST
19 Sunday **Year C: Acts 2:1-11. Ps 103:1, 24, 29-31, 34. Rm 8:8-17. Jn 14:15-16, 23-26.** Lect I:601 & 606 or **Acts 2:1-11. Ps 103:1, 24, 29-31, 34. 1 Cor 12:3-7, 12-13. Jn 20:19-23.** Lect I:601

The day of **Pentecost** brings the Paschal Mystery to completion and the Church is made manifest to the world.

SEVENTH WEEK IN ORDINARY TIME
20 Monday **Eccles (Sir) 1:1-10. Ps 92:1-2, 5. Mk 9:14-29.** Lect II:81

The wisdom which Ben Sira commends comes from God. It is the source of happiness, and the young should form their character from it. This Wisdom is closely associated with the Law of Moses, especially in carrying out religious duties, notably the liturgy.

St Bernadine was born in Siena in 1380. He became a Franciscan, travelled through Italy, preaching with great success. He promoted devotion to the Holy Name and to St Joseph. He died in 1444.

21 Tuesday **Eccles (Sir) 2:1-11. Ps 36:3-4, 18-19, 27-28, 39-40. Mk 9:30-37.** Lect II:83

Fear of the Lord is the key to endurance. In time of trial we must stand firm, there must be no giving way to apostasy. Jesus himself is our example, being delivered into the hands of men who put him to death.

Ss Christopher Magallánes and Companions. These twenty-five priests and laymen were executed in 1927 in Mexico.

22 Wednesday Eccles (Sir) 4:11-19. Ps 118:165, 168, 171-172, 174-175. Mk 9:38-40. Lect II:85

Wisdom is personified, and her children are those who seek out wisdom and live it out in their daily lives. From true wisdom comes happiness and joy in living, even though that means going through trials. True wisdom is being for God, not against.

St Rita of Cascia, 1381–1457, was married for eighteen years. Her husband, an ill-tempered and abusive man, was murdered. Later Rita entered the Augustinian convent in Cascia and spent forty years in prayer and charity and working for peace in the region.

23 Thursday **Eccles (Sir) 5:1-8. Ps 1:1-4, 6. Mk 9:41-50.** Lect II:87

Jesus reproaches the Scribes and Pharisees because of the scandal given by those who by their position are obliged to teach and educate others. Elsewhere he likens them to wolves in sheep's clothing.

24 Friday **Eccles (Sir) 6:5-17. Ps 118:12, 16, 18, 27, 34-35. Mk 10:1-12.** Lect II:89

Good human relationships result from making sound judgements and in persevering effort. To find a loyal friend is to find a treasure. And to be united in marriage is to become one body.

25 Saturday **Eccles (Sir) 17:1-15. Ps 102:13-18. Mk 10:13-16.** Lect II:91

God the creator made human beings responsible for their actions. Following Genesis 1, Ben Sira describes the creation of stars, plants and animals and, finally, human beings whose ways are always under his eyes. Their destiny is to belong to the kingdom of God.

St Bede, 673–735, monk of Jarrow, historian and biblical commentator. Patron of scholars.

St Gregory VII, 1028–85, Hildebrand of Tuscany, was a Cluniac monk in Rome who, on becoming Pope, worked for reform, and died in exile at Salerno.

St Mary Magdalene de' Pazzi, 1566–1607, a Carmelite in Florence, offered her life for the spiritual renewal of the Church.

NOTES FOR JUNE 2013

THE POPE'S INTENTIONS

General – A Culture of Mutual Respect: That a culture of dialogue, listening and mutual respect may prevail among the nations.

Mission – New Evangelisation: That where secularisation is strongest, Christian communities may learn to effectively promote a new evangelisation.

THE IRISH CALENDAR IN JUNE

3rd: St Kevin was a native of Leinster and grew up in Kilnamanagh, where he received his early religious formation. Wishing to be a hermit, he crossed the mountains to Glendalough and settled in Disert Caoimhghin at the foot of the upper lake. But disciples began to gather round him. Gradually the great monastic settlement grew, and spread through the glen after his death in 618.

6th: St Jarlath is said to have been a disciple of St Enda, and was taught also by St Benignus. He became abbot-bishop of the monastery he founded at Tuam in the sixth century.

7th: St Colman (Mocholmoc) of Dromore, Co. Down spent most of his life in that area. Possibly he studied under Caetan of Nendrom, Co. Down and was persuaded by St Mac Nissi to settle at Dromore c. 514.

9th: St Columba, also known as Colum Cille, was born in Gartan, Co. Donegal in 521 and was of royal lineage. He studied under St Finnian of Moville and St Finnian of Clonard. He founded monasteries in Derry, Durrow, Iona and possibly Kells. He left Ireland, either for penance or to be a pilgrim for Christ, but Iona became his principal foundation. From it missionaries undertook the conversion of Northumbria. Columba is noted for his great love for people and for all living creatures. He died 9 June 597.

14th: St Davnet lived and died at Tydavnet at Sliabh Beagh, Co. Monaghan. Tradition speaks of St Davnet as a virgin and founder of a church or monastery. A bachall (staff) said to have been hers has been preserved and in the past it was used as a test of truth.

20th: Bl. Irish Martyrs. Seventeen Irish martyrs, men and women, cleric and lay, put to death for the Catholic faith between 1579 and 1654 were beatified by Pope John Paul II in 1992: Dermot Hurley, Archbishop of Cashel, hanged 20 June 1584 at Hoggen Green. Conor O'Devany, Bishop of Down and Connor, hanged, drawn and quartered. Patrick O'Loughran, chaplain to the O'Neill family and Maurice McKenraghty, chaplain to the earl of Desmond, both hanged. Also hanged were Dominicans Terence O'Brien and Peter Higgins, Franciscans John Kearney, Patrick O'Healy and Conrad O'Rourke, Augustinian William Tirry, and a Jesuit lay brother, Dominic Collins. Lay people Francis Taylor, mayor of Dublin, and Margaret Bermingham died of ill treatment: a baker, Matthew Lambert, and a group of sailors, Robert Meyler, Edward Cheevers and Patrick Cavanagh were hanged, drawn and quartered on 5 July 1581. Six Catholics of Irish birth or connection executed for the faith in England had already been beatified in 1929 and 1987: John Roche (alias Neale), John (Terence) Carey, Patrick Salmon, John Cornelius (alias John Conor O'Mahoney), Charles Meehan, Ralph Corby (Corbington).

EUCHARISTIC ADORATION

Adoration of the Blessed Sacrament is a form of Eucharistic cult which is particularly widespread in the Church and earnestly recommended to her Pastors and faithful. Its initial form derives from Holy Thursday and the altar of repose, following the celebration of the *Coena Domini* Mass. This adoration is a most apt way of expressing the connection between the celebration of the memorial of the Lord's Sacrifice and his continued presence in the Sacrament of the Altar. The reservation of the Sacred Species, so as to be able to administer Viaticum to the sick at any time, encouraged the practice among the faithful of recollection before the tabernacle and to worship Christ present in the Sacrament.

Indeed, this worship of adoration has a sound and firm foundation, especially since faith in the Lord's real presence has as its natural consequence the outward and public manifestation of that belief. Therefore, the devotion prompting the faithful to visit the blessed sacrament draws them into an ever deeper share in the paschal mystery and leads them to respond gratefully to the gift of him who through his humanity constantly pours divine life into the members of his Body. Abiding with Christ the Lord, they enjoy his intimate friendship and pour out their hearts before him for themselves and for those dear to them and they pray for the peace and salvation of the world. Offering their entire lives with Christ to the Father in the Holy Spirit, they derive from this sublime colloquy an increase of faith, hope and charity. Thus they foster those right dispositions that enable them with due devotion to celebrate the memorial of the Lord and receive frequently the bread given us by the Father.

In adoration of the Blessed Sacrament, which can take different forms, several elements deriving from the Liturgy and from popular piety come together and it is not always easy to determine their limits:

- a simple visit to the Blessed Sacrament: a brief encounter with Christ inspired by faith in the real presence and characterised by silent prayer;

- adoration of the Blessed Sacrament exposed for a period of time in a monstrance or pyx in accordance with liturgical norm (178);

- perpetual adoration or the *Quarantore*, involving an entire religious community, or Eucharistic association, or parish, which is usually an occasion for various expressions of Eucharistic piety.

The faithful should be encouraged to read the Scriptures during these periods of adoration, since they afford an unrivalled source of prayer. Suitable hymns and canticles based on those of the Liturgy of the Hours and the liturgical seasons could also be encouraged, as well as periods of silent prayer and reflection. Gradually, the faithful should be encouraged not to do other devotional exercises during exposition of the Blessed Sacrament. Given the close relationship between Christ and Our Lady, the rosary can always be of assistance in giving prayer a Christological orientation, since it contains meditation of the Incarnation and the Redemption.

– Congregation for Divine Worship and the Discipline of the Sacraments, *Directory on Popular Piety and the Liturgy, principles and guidelines,* 164–5.

May 2013 Psalter Week 4

26 Sunday   **THE MOST HOLY TRINITY**   Solemnity
White ✠   HOURS Proper (Vol III p.7). Te Deum
Psalter Week 1 at Day Hour
MASS Proper (*RM* p. 361). Gloria. Creed. Preface: Trinity
No other celebrations, not even funeral Masses, are permitted today (see Lit. Note 7)
St Philip Neri is not celebrated this year.

---

27 Monday	**8th Week in Ordinary Time**
Green	HOURS Psalter Week 4. MASS of choice
White	Optional memorial of **St Augustine of Canterbury, bishop**

---

28 Tuesday	**8th Week in Ordinary Time**
Green	HOURS Psalter Week 4. MASS of choice

---

29 Wednesday 8th Week in Ordinary Time
Green   HOURS Psalter Week 4. MASS of choice

---

30 Thursday	**8th Week in Ordinary Time**
Green	HOURS Psalter Week 4. MASS of choice

---

31 Friday   THE VISITATION OF THE BLESSED VIRGIN MARY   Feast
White   HOURS Proper. Te Deum. Psalter Week 4 at Day Hour
MASS Proper. Gloria. Preface: BVM II
No Masses for the dead, except funeral Masses, are permitted today (see Lit. Note 7)

JUNE 2013

1 Saturday	**8th Week in Ordinary Time**
	St Justin, martyr Memorial
Red	HOURS of the memorial. Psalter Week 4
	MASS of the memorial. Preface: Common or of the Saint
	FIRST EVENING PRAYER of the **Body and Blood of Christ**

May 2013 READINGS Sunday Cycle C Weekday Cycle 1

EIGHTH WEEK IN ORDINARY TIME

26 Sunday   Prov 8:22-31. Ps 8:4-9. Rm 5:1-5. Jn 16:12-15. *Lect* I:615

The Holy Trinity. At the Last Supper Christ explained to the Apostles that he could not teach them everything because they were not, during his lifetime, sufficiently receptive. The Holy Spirit will be charged with continuing Christ's work for all the days of the future Church. It is the love of the Father that gives us his Son, while the Holy Spirit is ever leading us to know more of the truth.

27 Monday   Eccles (Sir) 17:24-29. Ps 31:1-2, 5-7. Mk 10:17-27. *Lect* II:94

The demands of the kingdom begin with the need to turn away from sin and back to the ever-merciful God, then to leave all behind and follow Christ, with a detachment of the heart from the attractions of the world.

St Augustine of Canterbury was a monk in Rome when sent by Pope Gregory the Great to preach to the English. He set up his see at Canterbury and had much success in converting the south of England.

28 Tuesday   Eccles (Sir) 35:1-12. Ps 49:5-8, 14, 23. Mk 10:28-31. *Lect* II:96

Generosity in the service of the Lord is rewarded. Token sacrifices are not enough, there has to be a complete giving, with cheerful heart. Leaving everything to follow Christ brings its own reward.

29 Wednesday Eccles (Sir) 36:1, 4-5, 10-17. Ps 78:8-9, 11, 13. Mk 10:32-45. *Lect* II:98

James and John have to learn the lesson of dedicated service. Their desire to reign with Christ in glory gives him the opportunity to speak about service and the cross.

30 Thursday   Eccles (Sir) 42:15-25. Ps 32:2-9 Mk 10:46-52. *Lect* II:100

The words spoken in the account of the cure of the blind man, Bartimaeus, are prayers and reflections for our own needs and expressions of faith.

31 Friday   Zeph 3:14-18 *or* Rm 12:9-16. Ps Is 12:2-6. Lk 1:39-56. *Lect* II:1040

The Visitation of the Blessed Virgin Mary. Today's liturgy recalls the 'Blessed Virgin Mary carrying her Son within her' and visiting Elizabeth to offer charitable assistance and to proclaim the mercy of God the Saviour (*Marialis Cultus*).

JUNE 2013

1 Saturday   Eccles (Sir) 51:12-20. Ps 18:8-11. Mk 11:27-33. *Lect* II:105

True wisdom is to be found in keeping the law of God. Searching for the will of God is an occupation for a lifetime.

St Justin was born in the Holy Land and settled in Rome. He became a Christian and is remembered for his defence of Christian belief and practice. He was martyred c. 165.

Next Sunday's readings: Gn 14:18-20. Ps 109:1-4. 1 Cor 11:23-26. Lk 9:11-17. *Lect* I:625

June 2013   Psalter Week 1

2 Sunday   **THE MOST HOLY BODY AND BLOOD OF CHRIST**
(Corpus Christi)   Solemnity
White ✠   HOURS Proper. Te Deum. Psalter Week 1 at Day Hour
MASS Proper (*RM* p. 365). Gloria. Sequence optional. Creed
Preface: Eucharist I–II

No other celebrations, not even funeral Masses, are permitted today (see Lit. Note 7)
Ss Marcellinus and Peter, martyrs are not celebrated this year.

---

3 Monday   **9th Week in Ordinary Time**
St Kevin, abbot   Memorial
White   HOURS of the memorial. Psalter Week 1
MASS of the memorial. Preface: Common or of the Saint
Dublin   **St Kevin, abbot**   Feast

---

4 Tuesday   **9th Week in Ordinary Time**
Ss Charles Lwanga and Companions, martyrs
Red   HOURS of the memorial. Psalter Week 1
MASS of the memorial. Preface: Common or of the Saint

---

5 Wednesday   **9th Week in Ordinary Time**
St Boniface, bishop and martyr   Memorial
Red   HOURS of the memorial. Psalter Week 1
MASS of the memorial. Preface: Common or of the Saint

---

6 Thursday   **9th Week in Ordinary Time**
Green   HOURS Psalter Week 1. MASS of choice
White   Optional memorial of **St Norbert, bishop**
White   Optional memorial of **St Jarlath, bishop**
Tuam   **St Jarlath, bishop**   Feast
FIRST EVENING PRAYER of **The Sacred Heart**

---

7 Friday   **THE MOST SACRED HEART OF JESUS**   Solemnity
White   HOURS Proper. Te Deum. Complementary Psalms at Day Hour
MASS Proper (*RM* p. 368). Gloria. Creed. Preface: Proper

No Masses for the dead, except funeral Masses, are permitted today (see Lit. Note 7)
St Colman, bishop is not celebrated this year.

---

8 Saturday   **9th Week in Ordinary Time**
The Immaculate Heart of the Blessed Virgin Mary
   Memorial
White   HOURS of the memorial. Psalter Week 1
MASS of the memorial (*RM* p. 767). Preface: Blessed Virgin Mary
Dromore   **St Colman, bishop**   Feast

June 2013 READINGS Sunday Cycle C Weekday Cycle 1

2 Sunday   Gn 14:18-20. Ps 109:1-4. 1 Cor 11:23-26. Lk 9:11-17. *Lect* I:625
'From this feast of **Corpus Christi** have originated many practices of eucharistic devotion that, under the inspiration of divine grace, have increased from day to day and that the Catholic Church uses eagerly to show ever greater homage to Christ, to thank him for so great a gift and to implore his mercy' (Pope Paul VI).

3 Monday   Tob 1:3, 2:1-8. Ps 111:1-6. Mk 12:1-12. *Lect* II:107
Tobit is exiled at Nineveh with his tribe of Naphthali after the fall of Israel. The Book of Tobit calls for a renewal of faith at a difficult time for the people who fear that God has abandoned them. It stresses community and family solidarity in times of trouble, the maintenance of the purity of religious belief in the midst of pagan ways of life, the mediation of God through angels, and the importance of Israel for the salvation of other nations.
St Kevin see *June notes.*

4 Tuesday   Tob 2:9-14. Ps 111:1-2, 7-9. Mk 12:13-17. *Lect* II:110
Tobit is blinded but does not blame God. He seeks always to be just and honest.
Ss Charles Lwanga and Companions, twenty-two Ugandan youths martyred 1886.

5 Wednesday   Tob 3:1-11, 16-17. Ps 24:2-9. Mk 12:18-27. *Lect* II:112
Tobit gives an example of prayer in the home, and Sarah has recourse also to the Lord. Their prayer finds favour before the Lord.
St Boniface, 673–754, was born at Crediton in Devonshire and educated in monastery schools in England. He went as a missionary to Germany. He founded monasteries in Bavaria, including Fulda in 735.

6 Thursday   Tob 6:10-11, 7:1, 9-14, 8:4-9. Ps 127:1-5. Mk 12:28-34. *Lect* II:115
Tobias, Tobit's son, goes off to find a bride, guided by the angel Raphael. In Raguel's home he accepts Sarah as his bride. She had had seven husbands one after another killed by the demon, Asmadeus. They pray with the best of intentions for God's protection.
St Norbert, 1080–1134, archbishop of Magdeburg, founder of the Norbertine canons.
St Jarlath see *June notes.*

7 Friday   Ez 34:11-16. Ps 22. Rm 5:5-11. Lk 15:3-7. *Lect* I:634
The Sacred Heart of Jesus. 'Understood in the light of the Scriptures, the term "Sacred Heart of Jesus" denotes the entire mystery of Christ: Son of God, uncreated wisdom; infinite charity, principle of the salvation and sanctification of mankind' (*Directory on Popular Piety and the Liturgy*, 166).

8 Saturday   Is 61:9-11. Ps 1 Sm 2:1, 4-8. Lk 2:41-51. *Lect* II:1043
'The Church celebrates the liturgical memorial of the **Immaculate Heart of Mary** the day after the Solemnity of the Sacred Heart of Jesus. The contiguity of both celebrations is in itself a liturgical sign of their close connection: the *mysterium* of the Heart of Jesus is projected onto and reverberates in the Heart of his Mother, who is also one of his followers and a disciple. (*Directory on Popular Piety and Liturgy*, 174)

Next Sunday's readings: 1 Kg 17:17-24. Ps 29:2, 4-6, 11-13. Gal 1:11-19. Lk 7:11-17. *Lect* I:863

June 2013   Psalter Week 2

9 Sunday   **TENTH SUNDAY IN ORDINARY TIME**
Green ✠   HOURS Proper. Te Deum. Psalter Week 2
                 MASS Proper. Gloria. Creed. Preface: Sundays I–VIII
No Masses for the dead, except funeral Masses, are permitted today (see Lit. Note 7)
St Columba (Colum Cille), abbot and missionary is not celebrated this year.
Derry   **St Columba (Colum Cille), abbot and missionary**
                                                       This year as Solemnity

---

10 Monday   **10th Week in Ordinary Time**
Green   HOURS Psalter Week 2. MASS of choice

---

11 Tuesday   **10th Week in Ordinary Time**
                  St Barnabas, apostle   Memorial
Red   HOURS of the memorial. Psalter Week 2
                  MASS of the memorial. Preface: Apostles I–II

---

12 Wednesday 10th Week in Ordinary Time
Green   HOURS Psalter Week 2. MASS of choice

---

13 Thursday   **10th Week in Ordinary Time**
                  St Anthony of Padua, priest and doctor of the Church
                                                                  Memorial
White   HOURS of the memorial. Psalter Week 2
                  MASS of the memorial. Preface: Common or of the Saint

---

14 Friday   **10th Week in Ordinary Time**
Green   HOURS Psalter Week 2. MASS of choice
White   Optional memorial of **St Davnet, virgin**

---

15 Saturday   **10th Week in Ordinary Time**
Green   HOURS Psalter Week 2. MASS of choice
White/Green   Saturday Mass of the **Blessed Virgin Mary**

June 2013   READINGS Sunday Cycle C   Weekday Cycle 1

TENTH WEEK IN ORDINARY TIME

9 Sunday   1 Kg 17:17-24. Ps 29:2, 4-6, 11-13. Gal 1:11-19. Lk 7:11-17. Lect I:863

God has visited his people. Christ has come to conquer death and give life. We must have a profound respect for life. We also believe in a deeper life of the spirit, constantly being raised to new life through the sacraments. Each Christian is a witness to life poured out through Christ's resurrection.

St Columba (Colum Cille) see June notes.

10 Monday   2 Cor 1:1-7. Ps 33:2-9. Mt 5:1-12. Lect II:124

This letter of Paul provides an inspiring example of a person committed to and concerned for his community. Paul draws on his understanding of Christ and its implications for his life and, therefore, also for his readers.

11 Tuesday   Acts 11:21-26, 13:1-3. Ps 97:1-6. Mt 10:7-13. Lect II:1058

St Barnabas was born on the island of Cyprus. He was one of the first converts in Jerusalem and preached at Antioch. He became a companion of St Paul and went with him on his first missionary journey, and he took part in the Council of Jerusalem. He returned to his native land to preach the gospel and there he died.

12 Wednesday 2 Cor 3:4-11. Ps 98:5-9. Mt 5:17-19. Lect II:128

The life of a Christian is marked by faith and service.

13 Thursday   2 Cor 3:15-4:1, 3-6. Ps 84:9-14. Mt 5:20-26. Lect II:130

The Old Law brought death, the New Covenant brings freedom from death. As Christians we see here by faith, advancing in perfection until we see Christ as he is.

St Anthony died in Padua in 1231 at the age of thirty-six. Born in Portugal he had joined the Franciscans and preached against heresy throughout France and Italy.

14 Friday   2 Cor 4:7-15. Ps 115:10-11, 15-18. Mt 5:27-32. Lect II:132

We hold a treasure in earthen vessels. Since we are so fragile it shows the power of God working in us. In our bodies we carry the death of Jesus in order that his life may be in all. We die to sin that we may live to God.

St Davnet see June notes.

15 Saturday   2 Cor 5:14-21. Ps 102:1-4, 8-9, 11-12. Mt 5:33-37. Lect II;134

There is now a change in the relationship of humanity to God. It is the end of a relationship of enmity, replaced now with one of peace and goodwill. Reconciliation has come about through the mediatorship of Christ.

Next Sunday's readings: 2 Sm 12:7-10, 13. Ps 31:1-2, 5, 7, 11. Gal 2:16, 19-21. Lk 7:36-8:3 (shorter form 7:36-50)**.** Lect I:866

June 2013 Psalter Week 3

16 Sunday **ELEVENTH SUNDAY IN ORDINARY TIME**
Green ✠ HOURS Proper. Te Deum. Psalter Week 3
  MASS Proper. Gloria. Creed. Preface: Sundays I–VIII
No Masses for the dead, except funeral Masses, are permitted today (see Lit. Note 7)
Raphoe **Dedication of the Cathedral** (see *Lit. Note 11*)

---

17 Monday **11th Week in Ordinary Time**
Green HOURS Psalter Week 3. MASS of choice

---

18 Tuesday **11th Week in Ordinary Time**
Green HOURS Psalter Week 3. MASS of choice

---

19 Wednesday **11th Week in Ordinary Time**
Green HOURS Psalter Week 3. MASS of choice
White Optional memorial of **St Romuald, abbot**
Limerick **Dedication of the Cathedral** (see *Lit. Note 11*)

---

20 Thursday **11th Week in Ordinary Time**
  The Irish Martyrs Memorial
Red HOURS of the memorial. Psalter Week 3
  MASS of the memorial. Preface: Common or Martyrs

---

21 Friday **11th Week in Ordinary Time**
  St Aloysius Gonzaga, religious Memorial
White HOURS of the memorial. Psalter Week 3
  MASS of the memorial. Preface: Common or of the Saint

---

22 Saturday **11th Week in Ordinary Time**
Green HOURS Psalter Week 3. MASS of choice
White Optional memorial of **St Paulinus of Nola, bishop**
Red Optional memorial of **Ss John Fisher, bishop and Thomas More, martyrs**
White/Green Saturday Mass of the **Blessed Virgin Mary**
Cashel and
Emly **Dedication of the Cathedral** (see *Lit. Note 11*)

June 2013 READINGS Sunday Cycle C Weekday Cycle 1

ELEVENTH WEEK IN ORDINARY TIME

16 Sunday   2 Sm 12:7-10, 13. Ps 31:1-2, 5, 7, 11. Gal 2:16, 19-21. Lk 7:36-8:3 (shorter form 7:36-50). *Lect* I:866
When David admitted his sin and showed sorrow God forgave him fully. The woman who showed Jesus her sorrow by tears and anointing was forgiven much for her great love.

17 Monday   2 Cor 6:1-10. Ps 97:1-4. Mt 5:38-42. *Lect* II:136
Let us prove ourselves to be servants of God by living in the way that Christ has taught. Paul himself shows by his way of life that he is a servant following Christ who came only to serve.

18 Tuesday   2 Cor 8:1-9. Ps 145:2, 5-9. Mt 5:43-48. *Lect* II:138
Christ became poor for our sakes that we might become rich. The more we grow in love so much the more we become perfect as God is perfect.

19 Wednesday 2 Cor 9:6-11. Ps 111:1-4, 9. Mt 6:1-6, 16-18. *Lect* II:140
God who provides seed for the sower and bread for food gives ungrudgingly. God loves a cheerful giver. He sees all that is done in secret and will bestow his reward.
St Romuald was a monk who lived a life of strict penance and solitude. He established many monasteries, most notably at Camaldoli in Tuscany. He died in 1027.

20 Thursday   2 Cor 11:1-11. Ps 110:1-4, 7-8. Mt 6:7-15. *Lect* II:142
The Lord's Prayer shows us that many words are not necessary. In it we praise God's glory, and ask for our human needs: 'provision, pardon and protection.'
The Irish Martyrs see *June notes*.

21 Friday   2 Cor 11:18, 21-30. Ps 33:2-7. Mt 6:19-23. *Lect* I:144
Paul gave example in his own life by unselfishly serving his disciples. He has suffered much for them and his concern for them is his daily burden. They are his treasure, close to his heart.
St Aloysius Gonzaga joined the Jesuits. As a model novice he worked in the plague hospital and caught the fever, dying in 1691 at the age of twenty-three. Patron of youth.

22 Saturday   2 Cor 12:1-10. Ps 33:8-13. Mt 6:24-34. *Lect* II:146
Set your hearts on God's kingdom! Fears about our weaknesses or our daily needs will distract us unduly. By depending on God we become strong.
St Paulinus, 355–431, bishop of Nola in the Campania.
St John Fisher, 1469–1535, as Vice-chancellor, built Christ's and St John's Colleges, Cambridge. Bishop of Rochester. His love of truth brought about his death. **St Thomas More**, 1478–1535, the first commoner to be Lord Chancellor of England, suffered martyrdom also under Henry VIII. Patron of lawyers and those in public life.

Next Sunday's readings: Zec 12:10-11, 13:1. Ps 62:2-6.8-9. Gal 3:26-29. Lk 9:18-24. *Lect* I:870

June 2013 Psalter Week 4

23 Sunday **TWELFTH SUNDAY IN ORDINARY TIME**
Green ✠ HOURS Proper. Te Deum. Psalter Week 4
MASS Proper. Gloria. Creed. Preface: Sundays I–VIII
FIRST EVENING PRAYER of **Nativity of St John the Baptist**
Evening MASS of the Vigil of the solemnity Proper. Gloria. Creed. Preface: Proper

No Masses for the dead, except funeral Masses, are permitted today (see Lit. Note 7)

---

24 Monday **THE NATIVITY OF ST JOHN THE BAPTIST** Solemnity
White HOURS Proper. Te Deum. Complementary Psalms at Day Hour
MASS Proper. Gloria. Creed. Preface: Proper
EVENING PRAYER of St John the Baptist

No Masses for the dead, except funeral Masses, are permitted today (see Lit. Note 7)

---

25 Tuesday **12th Week in Ordinary Time**
Green HOURS Psalter Week 4. MASS of choice

---

26 Wednesday 12th Week in Ordinary Time
Green HOURS Psalter Week 4. MASS of choice

---

27 Thursday **12th Week in Ordinary Time**
Green HOURS Psalter Week 4. MASS of choice
White Optional memorial of **St Cyril of Alexandria, bishop and doctor of the Church**

---

28 Friday **12th Week in Ordinary Time**
St Irenaeus, bishop and martyr Memorial
Red HOURS of the memorial. Psalter Week 4.
MASS of the memorial. Preface: Common or of the Saint
FIRST EVENING PRAYER of **Ss Peter and Paul**
Evening MASS of the Vigil of the solemnity Proper. Gloria. Creed. Preface: Proper

---

29 Saturday **SS PETER AND PAUL, APOSTLES** Solemnity
Red HOURS Proper. Te Deum. Complementary Psalms at Day Hour
MASS Proper. Gloria. Creed. Preface: Proper
EVENING PRAYER of Ss Peter and Paul

No Masses for the dead, except funeral Masses, are permitted today (see Lit. Note 7)

June 2013   READINGS Sunday Cycle C   Weekday Cycle 1

TWELFTH WEEK IN ORDINARY TIME

23 Sunday   Zec 12:10-11, 13:1. Ps 62:2-6.8-9. Gal 3:26-29. Lk 9:18-24. *Lect* I:870

What does it mean to follow Christ? It implies leaving everything and not looking back. It means doing so now, not waiting until the time seems suitable to me. We pray to be shown the path of life.

Vigil of St John the Baptist: Jer 1:4-10. Ps 70:1-6, 15, 17. 1 Pt 1:8-12. Lk 1:5-17. *Lect* I:973 or II:1070

24 Monday   Is 49:1-6. Ps 138:1-3, 13-15. Acts 13:22-26. Lk 1:57-66, 80. *Lect* I:976 or II:1073

We rejoice at the coming of **St John the Baptist**, a man of self-denial, integrity of life and purpose, and an uncompromising prophetic voice. John means 'The Lord has shown favour'. This feast relates to the summer solstice, when the days begin to grow shorter, recalling John's words, 'He must increase, but I must decrease'.

25 Tuesday   Gn 13:2, 5-18. Ps 14:2-5. Mt 7:6, 12-14. *Lect* II:151

Abraham was one who did no wrong to his brother, but selflessly sought peace. His generosity is an example of treating others as you would like them to treat you.

26 Wednesday Gn 15:1-12, 17-18. Ps 104:1-4, 6-9. Mt 7:15-20. *Lect* II:153

The ritual sacrifices that mark the making of a covenant may seem strange to us. How much more wonderful is God's taking us to himself in an everlasting covenant of love. Let the hearts that seek the Lord rejoice.

27 Thursday   Gn 16:1-12, 15-16 (shorter form 16:6-12, 15-16)**. Ps 105:1-5. Mt 7:21-29.** *Lect* II:155

The birth of Ishmael and the prophecy of the great number of his descendants. **St Cyril**, 370–444, patriarch of Alexandria, fought against Nestorianism at the Council of Ephesus, 431, which proclaimed Mary, Mother of God.

28 Friday   Gn 17:1, 9-10, 15-22. Ps 127:1-5. Mt 8:1-4. *Lect* II:158

Circumcision is given as a sign of the covenant; and Abraham is to be the father of many peoples.

Vigil of Ss Peter and Paul: Acts 3:1-10. Ps 18:2-5. Gal 1:11-20. Jn 21:15-19. *Lect* I:979 or II:1079

Down and Connor Tomorrow is the anniversary of the episcopal ordination of Most Rev. Noel Treanor, 29 June 2008.

29 Saturday   Acts 12:1-11. Ps 33:2-9. 2 Tm 4:6-8, 17-18. Mt 16:13-19. *Lect* I:981 *or* II:1082

On the day traditionally considered in pagan Rome to be its foundation day by Romulus, we celebrate the twin founders of the Church in Rome. **St Peter** died by crucifixion and **St Paul** by beheading between 64–7.

Next Sunday's readings: 1 Kg 19:16, 19-21. Ps 15:1-2, 5, 7-11. Gal 5:1, 13-18. Lk 9:51-62. *Lect* I:872

NOTES FOR JULY 2013

THE POPE'S INTENTIONS

General – World Youth Day: That the World Youth Day taking place in Brazil may encourage all young Christians to become disciples and missionaries of the Gospel.

Mission – Asia: That throughout the Asian continent, doors may be opened to the messengers of the Gospel.

THE IRISH CALENDAR IN JULY

1st: St Oliver Plunkett from Irish nobility whose family supported King Charles I. Ordained in Rome in 1654 he became a professor of theology from 1654 through 1669. He was appointed Archbishop of Armagh in 1669. He was forced to conduct a covert ministry during the suppression of priests. He was arrested and tried at Dundalk in 1679 for conspiring against the state. It was seen that Oliver would never be convicted in Ireland, and he was moved to Newgate prison, London. St Oliver Plunkett was found guilty of high treason 'for promoting the Catholic faith', and was condemned to a gruesome death. He was martyred 1 July 1681 at Tyburn, by hanging, disembowelling, quartering and beheading. He was the last Catholic to die for his faith at Tyburn, and the first of the Irish martyrs to be beatified. His body was initially buried in two tin boxes next to five Jesuits who had died before; his head is in St Peter's Church at Drogheda, Ireland; most of his body is at Downside Abbey, England; and some relics are in Ireland.

6th: St Moninne of Killeavy was one of Ireland's early women saints. After instruction on the religious life, she founded a community which initially consisted of eight virgins and a widow with a baby at Sliabh Gullion, Co. Armagh. They lived an eremitical life, based on that of Elijah and St John the Baptist. Moninne died in 517 or 518.

7th: St Maelruain (Maolruain), bishop and abbot, founded the monastery of Tallaght, Co. Dublin in 774 which introduced a reform. Important liturgical and spiritual writings emerged from this movement known as the Célí Dé reform. He died in 792.

8th: St Kilian was born in the parish of Mullagh in the diocese of Kilmore. With eleven companions he left Ireland and became known as the apostle of Thuringia and Eastern Franconia. With Kolonat and Totnan he was put to death in 689. There is a very strong devotion to him in Würzburg, where his remains lie, and also throughout the Bavarian countryside.

24th: St Declan is considered to be one of the pre-Patrician saints. He was of noble blood. Colman, a local priest, baptised him. Later he went to Europe to continue his studies where he was ordained priest and possibly bishop. He settled in Ardmore and evangelised the Decies country.

23–28 July: WORLD YOUTH DAY

Pope Benedict XVI, in announcing the theme for the 27th World Youth Day said, 'This year's World Youth Day theme comes from Saint Paul's exhortation in his Letter to the Philippians: *"Rejoice in the Lord always"* (4:4). Joy is at the heart of Christian experience. At each World Youth Day we experience immense joy, the joy of communion, the joy of being Christian, the joy of faith. This is one of the marks of these gatherings. We can see the great attraction that joy exercises. In a world of sorrow and anxiety, joy is an important witness to the beauty and reliability of the Christian faith.

The Church's vocation is to bring joy to the world, a joy that is authentic and enduring, the joy proclaimed by the angels to the shepherds on the night Jesus was born (cf. *Lk* 2:10). Not only did God speak, not only did he accomplish great signs throughout the history of humankind, but he drew so near to us that he became one of us and lived our life completely. In these difficult times, so many young people all around you need to hear that the Christian message is a message of joy and hope!'

26 July: MEMORIAL OF SS JOACHIM AND ANNE

Joachim and Anne (or Anna), honoured as the parents of the Blessed Virgin Mary and grandparents of Jesus, are not named in the Bible. The earliest reference to their names is the second-century apocryphal Gospel of James. Their feasts were celebrated separately until joined together in the Calendar reform of 1969.

The death of Anne is celebrated in the Byzantine rite on 25 July, also the day the basilica at Constantinople was dedicated in her honour around the year 550. Her cult in the West began in the twelfth century, and in the following century her feast was placed on 26 July. Though suppressed for a short time from 1568, it was reintroduced to the Universal Calendar in 1584.

The feast of St Joachim was also included in the 1584 Calendar, on 20 March and in 1738 moved to the Sunday after the Octave of the Assumption and in 1913 changed to 16 August.

In art, the images of the marriage of Joachim and Anne and of Anne teaching Mary to read are popular.

The 7th Annual Grandparents Pilgrimage to Knock takes place on Sunday, 8 September 2013. It is organised by the Catholic Grandparents Association.

SECOND VATICAN COUNCIL – PRAYER OF THE COUNCIL FATHERS

We stand before you, Holy Spirit, conscious of our sinfulness, but aware that we gather in your name.
Come to us, remain with us, and enlighten our hearts.
Give us light and strength to know your will, to make it our own, and to live it in our lives.
Guide us by your wisdom, support us by your power, for you are God, sharing the glory of Father and Son.
You desire justice for all; enable us to uphold the rights of others; do not allow us to be misled by ignorance or corrupted by fear or favour.
Unite us to yourself in the bond of love and keep us faithful to all that is true.
As we gather in your name, may we temper justice with love, so that all our discussions and reflections may be pleasing to you, and earn the reward promised to good and faithful servants. Amen.
– This prayer, used before each meeting of commissions of the Second Vatican Council, is attributed to St Isidore of Seville (c. 560–636) and is included in the prayer for the opening of a synod in the Roman Pontifical (1596).

June 2013   Psalter Week 1

30 Sunday   **THIRTEENTH SUNDAY IN ORDINARY TIME**
Green ✠   HOURS Proper. Te Deum. Psalter Week 1
            MASS Proper. Gloria. Creed. Preface: Sundays I–VIII
No Masses for the dead, except funeral Masses, are permitted today (see Lit. Note 7)
The First Martyrs of the Holy Roman Church are not celebrated this year.
Ferns   **Dedication of the Cathedral** (see *Lit. Note 11*)

JULY 2013

1 Monday   **13th Week in Ordinary Time**
            St Oliver Plunkett, bishop and martyr   Memorial
Red   HOURS of the memorial. Psalter Week 1.
                 MASS of the memorial. Preface: Common or of the Saint
Armagh   **St Oliver Plunkett, bishop and martyr**   Feast
Meath   **St Oliver Plunkett, bishop and martyr**   Feast
Elphin   **Dedication of the Cathedral** (see *Lit. Note 11*)

---

2 Tuesday   **13th Week in Ordinary Time**
Green   HOURS Psalter Week 1. MASS of choice

---

3 Wednesday   ST THOMAS, APOSTLE   Feast
Red   HOURS Proper. Te Deum. Psalter Week 1 at Day Hour
                 MASS Proper. Gloria. Preface: Apostles I–II
No Masses for the dead, except funeral Masses, are permitted today (see Lit. Note 7)

---

4 Thursday   **13th Week in Ordinary Time**
Green   HOURS Psalter Week 1. MASS of choice
White   Optional memorial of **St Elizabeth of Portugal**

---

5 Friday   **13th Week in Ordinary Time**
Green   HOURS Psalter Week 1. MASS of choice
White   Optional memorial of **St Anthony Zaccaria, priest**

---

6 Saturday   **13th Week in Ordinary Time**
Green   HOURS Psalter Week 1. MASS of choice
Red   Optional memorial of **St Maria Goretti, virgin and martyr**
White   Optional memorial of **St Moninne of Killeavy, virgin**
White/Green   Saturday Mass of the **Blessed Virgin Mary**

June 2013 READINGS Sunday Cycle C Weekday Cycle 1

THIRTEENTH WEEK IN ORDINARY TIME

30 Sunday **1 Kg 19:16, 19-21. Ps 15:1-2, 5, 7-11. Gal 5:1, 13-18. Lk 9:51-62.** *Lect* I:872

The Scripture readings today all encourage us to practise fortitude. By it we will conquer our many fears and be able to face trials, persecutions and even death itself.

JULY 2013

1 Monday **Gn 18:16-33. Ps 102:1-4, 8-11. Mt 8:18-22.** *Lect* II:163

Abraham bargains with God to save the just among the sinners of Sodom. He trusts in a God who is compassion and love. Can the goodness of a few win mercy for all?
St Oliver Plunkett see *July notes*.

2 Tuesday **Gn 19:15-29. Ps 25:2-3, 9-12. Mt 8:23-27.** *Lect* I:165

A weakness of faith gives rise to fear. Jesus calls his disciples to greater faith. Lot's wife in her fear did not trust God's word.

3 Wednesday **Eph 2:19-22. Ps 116. Jn 20:24-29.** *Lect* II:1087

St Thomas is said to have preached the gospel in India where he was martyred. The faith that led him to know Christ in his wounds also sent him to the farthest places to preach Christ.

4 Thursday **Gn 22:1-19. Ps 114:1-6, 8-9. Mt 9:1-8.** *Lect* II:169

The sacrifice of our father Abraham. In being prepared to sacrifice his son Isaac, Abraham's faith is tested. He is proved loyal and faithful and is rewarded with the promise of many descendants who will become a great nation.
St Elizabeth of Portugal, 1271–1336, of the House of Aragon, had an unhappy marriage with the King of Portugal. She persevered in prayer and good works, and as a widow lived in poverty as a Franciscan tertiary.

5 Friday **Gn 23:1-4, 19, 24:1-8, 62-67. Ps 105:1-5. Mt 9:9-13.** *Lect* II:172

Isaac loved Rebekah and so was consoled for the loss of his mother. God's love for us is without end and is the cause of our joy and consolation. In Christ we see the fullness of that love.
St Anthony Zaccaria, 1502–39, was a medical doctor before becoming a priest in Milan. He founded the Barnabites.

6 Saturday **Gn 27:1-5, 15-29. Ps 134:1-6. Mt 9:14-17.** *Lect* II:175

The mysterious ways of God are seen in the supplanting of Esau by Jacob. 'The Lord does whatever he wills.' His ways are not our ways.
St Maria Goretti, 1890–1902, stabbed to death in defence of her virtue.
St Moninne see *July notes*.

Next Sunday's readings: Is 66:10-14. Ps 65:1-7, 16, 20. Gal 6:14-18. Lk 10:1-12, 17-20 (shorter form 10:1-9). *Lect* I:875

July 2013   Psalter Week 2

7 Sunday   **FOURTEENTH SUNDAY IN ORDINARY TIME**
Green ✠   HOURS Proper. Te Deum. Psalter Week 2
                     MASS Proper. Gloria. Creed. Preface: Sundays I–VIII
No Masses for the dead, except funeral Masses, are permitted today (see Lit. Note 7)
St Maelruain, bishop and abbot is not celebrated this year.

---

8 Monday   **14th Week in Ordinary Time**
Green   HOURS Psalter Week 2. MASS of choice
Red   Optional memorial of **St Kilian, bishop and martyr**

---

9 Tuesday   **14th Week in Ordinary Time**
Green   HOURS Psalter Week 2. MASS of choice
Red   Optional memorial of **Ss Augustine Zhao Rong, priest, and Companions, martyrs**

---

10 Wednesday 14th Week in Ordinary Time
Green   HOURS Psalter Week 2. MASS of choice

---

11 Thursday   ST BENEDICT, ABBOT, PATRON OF EUROPE   Feast
White   HOURS Proper. Te Deum. Psalter Week 2 at Day Hour
                     MASS Proper. Gloria. Preface: Saint
No Masses for the dead, except funeral Masses, are permitted today (see Lit. Note 7)

---

12 Friday   **14th Week in Ordinary Time**
Green   HOURS Psalter Week 2. MASS of choice

---

13 Saturday   **14th Week in Ordinary Time**
Green   HOURS Psalter Week 2. MASS of choice
White   Optional memorial of **St Henry**
White/Green   Saturday Mass of the **Blessed Virgin Mary**

July 2013   READINGS Sunday Cycle C   Weekday Cycle 1

FOURTEENTH WEEK IN ORDINARY TIME

7 Sunday   Is 66:10-14. Ps 65:1-7, 16, 20. Gal 6:14-18. Lk 10:1-12, 17-20 (shorter form 10:1-9). *Lect* I:875

Jesus is the 'Prince of Peace'. Peace is one of the fruits of the Holy Spirit. Christians are to share that peace with others. The earthly peace we seek is the image of that peace of Christ. We have no option but to be peace makers.

8 Monday   Gn 28:10-22. Ps 90:1-4, 14-15. Mt 9:18-26. *Lect* II:178

God confirms the blessing given by Isaac to Jacob. God's faithfulness to his promise is shown in the protection that is to be given to Jacob.
St Kilian see *July notes*.

9 Tuesday   Gn 32:23-33. Ps 16:1-3, 6-8, 15. Mt 9:32-38. *Lect* II:180

The new name of Israel expresses a new mission for the wily Jacob. Father of a new nation, he will be specially protected by God, and God's own people will be reminded always of their struggle with God and their mission in the whole plan of God's salvation.
Ss Augustine Zhao Rong and Companions. St Augustine Tchao, born 1746, converted to Christianity, was ordained priest and martyred in 1815. The memorial celebrates 119 companions, martyred in China over several centuries but especially in the Boxer Risings.

10 Wednesday Gn 41:55-57, 42:5-7, 17-24. Ps 32:2-3, 10-11, 18-19. Mt 10:1-7. *Lect* II:182

The story of Joseph and his brothers has led to the situation where the brothers begin to repent. God's goodness in preserving them in time of famine is a further sign of his providential protection.

11 Thursday   Prov 2:1-9. Ps 33:2-11. Mt 19:27-29. *Lect* II:1095
St Benedict, c. 480–547, after living as a hermit at Subiaco, founded the monastery of Monte Cassino. His Rule, observed by Benedictines and Cistercians, is distinguished by its wisdom and balance and those who lived by it did much to shape the Europe of today. Named patron of Europe in 1964.

12 Friday   Gn 46:1-7, 28-30. Ps 36:3-4, 18-19, 27-28, 39-40. Mt 10:16-23. *Lect* II:187

The final purposes of God will be worked out when he makes of Israel a great people in Egypt. They are destined to return to Canaan.

13 Saturday   Gn 49:29-33, 50:15-26. Ps 104:1-4, 6-7. Mt 10:24-33. *Lect* II:189

The Church's liturgy has retained certain elements of the worship of the Old Covenant as integral and irreplaceable. She has adopted them as her own: notably, reading the Old Testament, praying the psalms and above all, recalling the saving events which have their fulfillment in the mystery of Christ – promise and covenant, Exodus and Passover, kingdom and Temple, exile and return (see *CCC*, 1093).
St Henry, 973–1024, Duke of Bavaria and later Emperor, a just ruler, humble man of prayer, and reformer of the Church.

Next Sunday's readings: Deut 30:10-14. Ps 68:14, 17, 30-31, 33-34, 36-37 *or* **18:8-11. Col 1:15-20. Lk 10:25-37.** *Lect* I:878

July 2013 Psalter Week 3

14 Sunday **FIFTEENTH SUNDAY IN ORDINARY TIME**
Green ✠ HOURS Proper. Te Deum. Psalter Week 3
MASS Proper. Gloria. Creed. Preface: Sundays I–VIII
No Masses for the dead, except funeral Masses, are permitted today (see Lit. Note 7)
St Camillus de Lellis, priest is not celebrated this year.

---

15 Monday **15th Week in Ordinary Time**
St Bonaventure, bishop and doctor of the Church
Memorial
White HOURS of the memorial. Psalter Week 3
MASS of the memorial. Preface: Common or of the Saint

---

16 Tuesday **15th Week in Ordinary Time**
Green HOURS Psalter Week 3. MASS of choice
White Optional memorial of **Our Lady of Mount Carmel**

---

17 Wednesday **15th Week in Ordinary Time**
Green HOURS Psalter Week 3. MASS of choice

---

18 Thursday **15th Week in Ordinary Time**
Green HOURS Psalter Week 3. MASS of choice

---

19 Friday **15th Week in Ordinary Time**
Green HOURS Psalter Week 3. MASS of choice

---

20 Saturday **15th Week in Ordinary Time**
Green HOURS Psalter Week 3. MASS of choice
Red Optional memorial of **St Apollinaris, bishop and martyr**
White/Green Saturday Mass of the **Blessed Virgin Mary**
Armagh **Dedication of the Cathedral** (see *Lit. Note 11*)

July 2013 READINGS Sunday Cycle C Weekday Cycle 1

FIFTEENTH WEEK IN ORDINARY TIME

14 Sunday   Deut 30:10-14. Ps 68:14, 17, 30-31, 33-34, 36-37 or 18:8-11. Col 1:15-20. Lk 10:25-37. *Lect* I:878

The great virtue of charity is put before us today. It is the virtue by which we love God above all things for his own sake, and our neighbour as ourselves for the love of God. This is the new commandment of Jesus. He tells us to love one another as he has loved us. The story of the Good Samaritan is to show us that this is a virtue well within our reach.

15 Monday   Ex 1:8-14, 22. Ps 123. Mt 10:34-11:1. *Lect* II:192

The people of Israel are oppressed by Pharaoh. Christ warns his disciples that their fate will be to suffer opposition. In all our difficulties, our help is in the name of the Lord.

St Bonaventure, 1221–74, born in Tuscany, Minister General of the Franciscans, Cardinal Archbishop of Albano, theologian of the Council of Lyons.

16 Tuesday   Ex 2:1-15. Ps 68:3, 14, 30-31, 33-34. Mt 11:20-24. *Lect* II:194

St Matthew's Gospel sees in Christ the new Israel and the new Moses. Like Israel Christ was baptised through the water and tested in the desert. Like Israel's great lawgiver, Moses, he gave the new law on the Mount.

Our Lady of Mount Carmel: Zec 2:14-17. Ps Lk 1:46-55. Mt 12:46-50. *Lect* II:1103

The Carmelite communities inherit the early hermits' devotions to Elijah and his solitary prayer, and to Mary under this title of Mount Carmel.

17 Wednesday Ex 3:1-6, 9-12. Ps 102:1-4, 6-7. Mt 11:25-27. *Lect* II:196

God reveals himself to Moses and gives him a mission. Jesus is to bring a great revelation of the Father to all who are open to receive his word.

18 Thursday   Ex 3:13-20. Ps 104:1, 5, 8-9, 24-27. Mt 11:28-30. *Lect* II:198

Moses protests his ability to carry out God's tasks for him. He is given Aaron as a helper. No task that God gives us is impossible to bear – his burden is light.

19 Friday   Ex 11:10-12,14. Ps 115:12-13, 15-18. Mt 12:1-8. *Lect* II:200

Familiarity with the Passover ritual is a good background for deeper appreciation of the meaning of the Mass in the Christian life.

20 Saturday   Ex 12:37-42. Ps 135:1, 10-15, 23-24. Mt 12:14-21. *Lect* II:202

'Night devoid of all dark, O night dispelling sleep and teaching us the vigilance of angels, O night the demons tremble at, night of all nights in all the year desired. Night of the church's bridal, night of new birth in baptism, night when the Devil slept and was stripped, night when the heir took the heiress to enjoy their inheritance' (Asterius of Amasia, fourth century).

St Apollinarius in the second century preached the gospel in the region of Ravenna. He was bishop of Classis where he suffered martyrdom.

Next Sunday's readings: Gn 18:1-10. Ps 14:2-5. Col 1:24-28. Lk 10:38-42. *Lect* I:882

July 2013   Psalter Week 4

21 Sunday   **SIXTEENTH SUNDAY IN ORDINARY TIME**
Green ✠   HOURS Proper. Te Deum. Psalter Week 4
                 MASS Proper. Gloria. Creed. Preface: Sundays I–VIII
No Masses for the dead, except funeral Masses, are permitted today (see Lit. Note 7)
St Lawrence of Brindisi, priest and doctor of the Church is not celebrated this year.
Dromore   **Dedication of the Cathedral** (see *Lit. Note 11*)

---

22 Monday   **16th Week in Ordinary Time**
                 St Mary Magdalene   Memorial
White   HOURS of the memorial. Psalter Week 4 at Day Hour
                 MASS of the memorial. Preface: Common or of the Saint

---

23 Tuesday   ST BRIDGET OF SWEDEN, RELIGIOUS, PATRON OF EUROPE
                                                                          Feast
White   HOURS Proper. Te Deum. Psalter Week 4 at Day Hour
                 MASS Proper. Gloria. Preface: Saints I or Virgins and Religious
No Masses for the dead, except funeral Masses, are permitted today (see Lit. Note 7)

---

24 Wednesday 16th Week in Ordinary Time
Green   HOURS Psalter Week 4. MASS of choice
White   Optional memorial of **St Sharbel Makhlūf, priest**
White   Optional memorial of **St Declan, bishop**
Waterford and
Lismore   **St Declan, bishop**   Feast

---

25 Thursday   ST JAMES, APOSTLE   Feast
Red   HOURS Proper. Te Deum. Psalter Week 4 at Day Hour
                 MASS Proper. Gloria. Preface: Apostles I–II
No Masses for the dead, except funeral Masses, are permitted today (see Lit. Note 7)

---

26 Friday   **16th Week in Ordinary Time**
                 Ss Joachim and Anne, parents of the Blessed Virgin
                 Mary   Memorial
White   HOURS Proper of the memorial. Psalter Week 4 at Day Hour
                 MASS of the memorial. Preface: Common or of the Saints

---

27 Saturday   **16th Week in Ordinary Time**
Green   HOURS Psalter Week 4. MASS of choice
White/Green   Saturday Mass of the **Blessed Virgin Mary**

July 2013 READINGS Sunday Cycle C Weekday Cycle 1
SIXTEENTH WEEK IN ORDINARY TIME
21 Sunday   Gn 18:1-10. Ps 14:2-5. Col 1:24-28. Lk 10:38-42.
Lect I:882

Hospitality has a special place in the life of God's people. He always rewards kindness done to him. The welcome we give to him should be characterised by listening in faith. 'For some have entertained angels unaware.' There is a need to make space in our lives for listening to the Word, a time in each day for Scripture reading.

22 Monday   Song 3:1-4 *or* 2 Cor. 5:14-17. Ps 62:2-6, 8-9. Jn 20:1-2, 11-18. *Lect* II:1108

St Mary Magdalen stood by the Cross of Jesus; with two other women she discovered the empty tomb; she was granted an appearance of the Risen Lord early the same day, from which incident she has been described as 'the apostle to the apostles'. The Gospels give no warrant for identifying her with the 'woman who was a sinner' who anointed Christ's feet (*Lk* 7:37) or with Mary the sister of Martha who also anointed him (*Jn* 12:3).

23 Tuesday   Gal 2:19-20. Ps 33:2-11. Jn 15:1-8. *Lect.* II:1111

St Bridget was born in Sweden in 1303. She brought up eight children, and after the death of her husband dedicated herself to an ascetical life. Later she founded the Bridgettine Order and lived in Rome. She wrote many works about her mystical experiences. She died in Rome in 1373. She was declared a Patron of Europe in 2000.

24 Wednesday Ex 16:1-5, 9-15. Ps 77:18-19, 23-28. Mt 13:1-9. *Lect* II:209

The Lord gave them bread from heaven, mere mortals ate the bread of angels. The Eucharist is the nourishment for the Christian life; we must prepare worthily to receive the food of life.

St Sharbel Makhlūf became a monk at the monastery of St Maron at Annaya and was ordained in 1859. He became a hermit from 1875 until his death in 1898. He was much sought after for counsel and blessing and had a great personal devotion to the Blessed Sacrament.

St Declan see *July notes*.

Waterford and Lismore Tomorrow is the anniversary of the episcopal ordination of Most Rev. William Lee, 25 July 1993.

Clogher Tomorrow is the anniversary of the episcopal ordination of Most Rev. Liam MacDaid, 25 July 2010.

25 Thursday   2 Cor 4:7-15. Ps 125. Mt 20:20-28. *Lect* II:1113

St James, son of Zebedee and brother of John, called the Greater. He was put to death by Herod Agrippa about the year 44, being the first of the Apostles to die for Christ. His shrine is at Compostella in Spain.

26 Friday   Ex 20:1-17. Ps 18:8-11. Mt 13:18-23. *Lect* II:213

Moses is called up to the mountain as God manifests himself in terrifying splendour. Jesus reveals the mysteries of the kingdom to his disciples in parables.

Ss Joachim and Anne. Traditionally named parents of the Blessed Virgin Mary and grandparents of the Lord. St Anne is patron of Canada, women in labour, miners, cabinet-makers and home-makers.

27 Saturday   Ex 24:3-8. Ps 49:1-2, 5-6, 14-15. Mt 13:24-30. *Lect* II:216

God reveals himself as a caring God, active in the lives of his people. God is powerful and he protects, defends and leads his people. God is compassionate and loving, faithful and kind, a God of integrity and justice.

Next Sunday's readings: Gn 18:20-32. Ps 137:1-3, 6-8. Col 2:12-14. Lk 11:1-13. *Lect* I:884

NOTES FOR AUGUST 2013

THE POPE'S INTENTIONS

General – Parents and Teachers: That parents and teachers may help the new generation to grow in upright conscience and life.

Mission – Africa: That the local Churches in Africa, faithful to the Gospel proclamation, may promote the building of peace and justice.

THE IRISH CALENDAR IN AUGUST

9th: St Nathy is said to have been born in the barony of Leyny, Co. Sligo. He made a foundation in Achrony, where many students gathered to learn from him. He is buried in Achadh Cain.

9th: St Felim was born in the sixth century in Breifne. He was a hermit near Kilmore, Co. Cavan where he later founded a monastery. He is patron of Kilmore diocese.

12th: St Muiredach is regarded as the founder of the church at Killala. He may also be the founder and patron of the monastery of Inishmurray off the Sligo coast.

12th: St Attracta lived in the sixth or seventh century. Local tradition remembers her great healing powers. Her convents were famous for hospitality and charity to the poor.

12th: St Lelia (Liadain) had a church at Kileely, near Thomand Bridge. She is said to have been baptised by St Patrick.

13th: St Fachtna (also called Fachanan) founder of the monastery of Ross Carbery (Ross Ailithir). He died around 600. His monastery became the principal monastery of west Cork and later had a famous scripture school.

17th Our Lady of Knock. The story of Knock began on the 21 August 1879 when Our Lady, St Joseph and St John the Evangelist appeared at the south gable of Knock Parish Church. This miraculous apparition was witnessed by fifteen people, young and old. Knock is an internationally recognised Marian Shrine and was visited by Blessed John Paul II as part of his 1979 papal pilgrimage to Ireland. The date of the memorial is within the annual novena conducted at the Shrine.

23rd: St Eugene (Eoghan) lived in the sixth century and was said to have been taken by pirates to Britain. On obtaining his freedom he went to study at Candida Casa. Returning to Ireland he made a foundation at Kilnamanagh in the Wicklow hills, but his principal foundation was at Ardstraw (Ard Sratha), Co. Tyrone.

30th: St Fiacre was an Irishman who went abroad to seek a hermitage. He passed through Normandy and eventually met Faro, who was a great patron of Irish pilgrims at Meaux. Fiachre was given a hermitage near Breuil and there he stayed until his death around 670.

31st: St Aidan of Lindisfarne was of Irish descent and was a monk of Iona. When Oswald, the exiled king of Northumbria who had fled for refuge to Iona, returned to his throne in 634, he invited Aidan to come to reconvert his people. Aidan made his headquarters at Lindisfarne. With the aid of the king as interpreter he was very successful in his mission. He died in 651.

2 August: THE INDULGENCE OF ST MARY OF THE PORTIUNCULA

On 2 August, or on another day determined by the Ordinary for the convenience of the people, a plenary indulgence may be acquired in parish churches. The practices prescribed for the obtaining of the indulgence are a devout visit to the church and the recitation there of the Our Father and Creed, and in addition a sacramental confession, Holy Communion, and prayer for the intentions of the Supreme Pontiff. This indulgence may be acquired only once. The visit may be made from noon the previous day until midnight of the day itself.

MORNING PRAYER AND EVENING PRAYER

'By the venerable tradition of the universal Church, lauds as morning prayer and vespers as evening prayer are the two hinges on which the daily office turns; hence they are to be considered as the chief hours and celebrated as such' (SC 89, see 100).

As is clear from many of the elements that make it up, morning prayer is intended and arranged to sanctify the morning. St Basil the Great gives an excellent description of this character in these words: 'It is said in the morning in order that the first stirrings of our mind and will may be consecrated to God and that we may take nothing in hand until we have been gladdened by the thought of God, as it is written: "I was mindful of God and was glad" (Ps 77:4 [Jerome's translation from Hebrew]), or set our bodies to any task before we do what has been said: "I will pray to you, Lord, you will hear my voice in the morning; I will stand before you in the morning and gaze on you" (Ps 5:4-5)' (*Reg. fusius tractatae* 37).

Celebrated as it is, as the light of a new day is dawning, this hour also recalls the resurrection of the Lord Jesus, the true light enlightening all people (see Jn 1:9) and 'the sun of justice' (Mal 4:2), 'rising from on high' (Lk 1:78). Hence, we can well understand the advice of St Cyprian: 'There should be prayer in the morning so that the resurrection of the Lord may thus be celebrated' (*De or. dom.* 35).

When evening approaches and the day is already far spent, evening prayer is celebrated in order that 'we may give thanks for what has been given us, or what we have done well, during the day' (St Basil). We also recall the redemption through the prayer we send up 'like incense in the Lord's sight', and in which 'the raising up of our hands' becomes 'an evening sacrifice' (see Ps 141:2). This sacrifice 'may also be interpreted more spiritually as the true evening sacrifice that our Saviour the Lord entrusted to the apostles at supper on the evening when he instituted the sacred mysteries of the Church or of the evening sacrifice of the next day, the sacrifice, that is, which, raising his hands, he offered to the Father at the end of the ages for the salvation of the whole world' (John Cassian, *De inst. coenob.* 3,3). Again, in order to fix our hope on the light that knows no setting, 'we pray and make petition for the light to come down on us anew; we implore the coming of Christ who will bring the grace of eternal light' (St Cyprian, *op. cit.* 35). Finally, at this hour we join with the Churches of the East in calling upon the 'joy-giving light of that holy glory, born of the immortal, heavenly Father, the holy and blessed Jesus Christ; now that we have come to the setting of the sun and have seen the evening star, we sing in praise of God, Father, Son, and Holy Spirit ...'

Morning prayer and evening prayer are therefore to be accorded the highest importance as the prayer of the Christian community. Their public or communal celebration should be encouraged, especially in the case of those who live in community. Indeed, the recitation of these hours should be recommended also to individual members of the faithful unable to take part in a celebration in common.

– *General Introduction of the Liturgy of the Hours*, 37–40

July 2013 Psalter Week 1

28 Sunday **SEVENTEENTH SUNDAY IN ORDINARY TIME**
Green ✠ HOURS Proper. Te Deum. Psalter Week 1
MASS Proper. Gloria. Creed. Preface: Sundays I–VIII
No Masses for the dead, except funeral Masses, are permitted today (see Lit. Note 7)

---

29 Monday **17th Week in Ordinary Time**
 St Martha Memorial
White HOURS of the memorial. Psalter Week 1
MASS of the memorial. Preface: Common or of the Saint

---

30 Tuesday **17th Week in Ordinary Time**
Green HOURS Psalter Week 1. MASS of choice
White Optional memorial of **St Peter Chrysologus, bishop and doctor of the Church**

---

31 Wednesday **17th Week in Ordinary Time**
 St Ignatius of Loyola, priest Memorial
White HOURS of the memorial. Psalter Week 1
MASS of the memorial. Preface: Common or of the Saint

AUGUST 2013

1 Thursday **17th Week in Ordinary Time**
 St Alphonsus Liguori, bishop and doctor of the Church
Memorial
White HOURS of the memorial. Psalter Week 1
MASS of the memorial. Preface: Common or of the Saint

---

2 Friday **17th Week in Ordinary Time**
Green HOURS Psalter Week 1. MASS of choice
White Optional memorial of **St Eusebius of Vercelli, bishop**
White Optional memorial of **St Peter Julian Eymard, priest**
The **Indulgence of St Mary of the Portiuncula** may be gained by visiting the Parish Church. See *August notes*

---

3 Saturday **17th Week in Ordinary Time**
Green HOURS Psalter Week 1. Mass of choice
White/Green Saturday Mass of the **Blessed Virgin Mary**

Next Sunday's readings: Eccl (Qo) 1:2, 2:21-23. Ps 89:3-6, 12-14, 17 *or* 94:1-2, 6-9. Col 3:1-5, 9-11. Lk 12:13-21. *Lect* I:888

July 2013   READINGS Sunday Cycle C   Weekday Cycle 1
SEVENTEENTH WEEK IN ORDINARY TIME
28 Sunday   Gn 18:20-32. Ps 137:1-3, 6-8. Col 2:12-14. Lk 11:1-13. Lect I:884

We are creatures who are not our own beginning or last end. Christ is glorified by what we ask the Father in his name. Because of God's love for us we can ask for anything.

29 Monday   1 Jn 4:7-16. Ps 33:2-11. Jn 11:19-27 or Lk 10:38-42. Lect II:1117

St Martha, sister of Lazarus and Mary, is a woman of faith who made her profession of faith in Christ as the Son of God, and in the resurrection. In welcoming a guest we welcome Christ: we show our Christian spirit of service; and we ready ourselves to be welcomed as guests in the Kingdom of God. Patron of innkeepers, cooks and dieticians.

30 Tuesday   Ex 33:7-11, 34:5-9, 28. Ps 102:6-13. Mt 13:36-43. Lect II:220

The Lord reveals himself as a God of tenderness and compassion. Moses speaks with God, face to face, on behalf of the people.

St Peter Chrysologus, died c. 450, bishop of Ravenna, famous for his preaching.

31 Wednesday Ex 34:29-35. Ps 98: 5-7, 9. Mt 13:44-46. Lect II:223

Moses comes down the mountain and his face reflects the holiness of God.

St Ignatius of Loyola, 1491–1556, from the north of Spain, founded the Society of Jesus. By the time of his death, the society had spread widely and had over one thousand members. His great theme was the service of God and God's greater glory. The experience of his conversion led to his writing of the Spiritual Exercises.

AUGUST 2013
1 Thursday   Ex 40:16-21, 34-38. Ps 83:3-6, 8, 11. Mt 13:47-53. Lect II:225

The cloud covered the Tent of Meeting and the glory of the Lord filled the tabernacle. How lovely is your dwelling place, Lord, God of Hosts. In the Sunday meeting Christ is present to the assembly, in his word and in Eucharist.

St Alphonsus Liguori, 1696–1787, founder of the Redemptorist Congregation, taught much on moral theology and the spiritual life. He is remembered as a popular preacher and influential writer of theology.

2 Friday   Lev 23:1, 4-11, 15-16, 27, 34-37. Ps 80:3-6, 10-11. Mt 13:54-58. Lect II:227

Jewish festivals: Passover, celebrates the Exodus event. At Pentecost, seven weeks later, is celebrated Shavuot, God's gift of the Torah as a guide to life. Jewish New Year is Rosh Hashanah which begins sunset 4 September 2013 (5774); a period of penance concluding with the feast of Yom Kippur or Day of Atonement. 13 September 2013; Sukkot, the feast of tents, 18 September 2013, a harvest celebration of God's generous gifts of nature and our creation. Hanukkah, Feast of Lights, first day begins 28 November 2013.

St Eusebius of Vercelli and the zealous Saint Hilary of Poitiers laboured to suppress Arianism in the West.

St Peter Julian Eymard, 1811–68, a fervent disciple of the Eucharistic Mystery, established the Blessed Sacrament Fathers and, with the help of Marguerite Guillot, the Servants of the Blessed Sacrament.

3 Saturday   Lev 25:1, 8-17. Ps 66:2-3, 5, 7-8. Mt 14:1-12. Lect II:229

Let none of you wrong his neighbour in the year of Jubilee. A year of renewal in which past debts are annulled.

August 2013   Psalter Week 2

4 Sunday   **EIGHTEENTH SUNDAY IN ORDINARY TIME**
Green ✠   HOURS Proper. Te Deum. Psalter Week 2
                 MASS Proper. Gloria. Creed. Preface: Sundays I–VIII
No Masses for the dead, except funeral Masses, are permitted today (see Lit. Note 7)
St John Mary Vianney, priest is not celebrated this year.

---

5 Monday   **18th Week in Ordinary Time**
Green   HOURS Psalter Week 2. MASS of choice
White   Optional memorial of **The Dedication of the Basilica of St Mary Major**

---

6 Tuesday   THE TRANSFIGURATION OF THE LORD   Feast
White   HOURS Proper. Te Deum. Psalter Week 2 at Day Hour
                 MASS Proper. Gloria. Preface: Proper
No Masses for the dead, except funeral Masses, are permitted today (see Lit. Note 7)

---

7 Wednesday   **18th Week in Ordinary Time**
Green   HOURS Psalter Week 2. MASS of choice
Red   Optional memorial of **Ss Sixtus II, pope, and Companions, martyrs**
White   Optional memorial of **St Cajetan, priest**

---

8 Thursday   **18th Week in Ordinary Time**
                   St Dominic, priest   Memorial
White   HOURS of the memorial. Psalter Week 2
                 MASS of the memorial. Preface: Common or of the Saint

---

9 Friday   ST TERESA BENEDICTA OF THE CROSS (Edith Stein)
                  VIRGIN AND MARTYR, PATRON OF EUROPE   Feast
Red   HOURS Proper. Te Deum. Psalter Week 2 at Day Hour
                 MASS Proper. Gloria. Preface: Martyrs I–II
No Masses for the dead, except funeral Masses, are permitted today (see Lit. Note 7)
St Nathy, bishop and **St Felim, bishop** are not celebrated this year.
Achonry   **St Nathy, bishop**   Feast
Kilmore   **St Felim, bishop**   Feast

---

10 Saturday   ST LAWRENCE, DEACON AND MARTYR   Feast
Red   HOURS Proper. Te Deum. Psalter Week 2 at Day Hour
                MASS Proper. Gloria. Creed. Preface: Martyrs I–II
No Masses for the dead, except funeral Masses, are permitted today (see Lit. Note 7)

Next Sunday's readings: Wis 18:6-9. Ps 32:1, 12, 18-20, 22. Heb 11:1-2, 8-19 (shorter form 11:1-2, 8-12)**. Lk 12:32-48** (shorter form 12:35-40)**.** *Lect* I:891

August 2013 READINGS Sunday Cycle C Weekday Cycle 1

EIGHTEENTH WEEK IN ORDINARY TIME

4 Sunday **Eccl (Qo) 1:2, 2:21-23. Ps 89:3-6, 12-14, 17 or 94:1-2, 6-9. Col 3:1-5, 9-11. Lk 12:13-21.** Lect I:888

'The economy of law and grace turns men's hearts away from avarice and envy. It initiates them into desire for the Sovereign Good; it instructs them in the desires of the Holy Spirit who satisfies man's heart. The God of the promises always warned man against seduction by what from the beginning has seemed "good for food ... a delight to the eyes ... to be desired to make one wise"' (CCC, 2541).

5 Monday **Num 11:4-15. Ps 80:12-17. Mt 14:13-21.** Lect II:232

'A better knowledge of the Jewish people's faith and religious life as professed and lived even now can help our better understanding of certain aspects of Christian liturgy. The relationship between Jewish liturgy and Christian liturgy, but also their differences in content, are particularly evident in the great feasts of the liturgical year, such as Passover' (CCC, 1096).

St Mary Major: Apoc 21:1-5. Ps Jdt 13:18-19. Lk 11:27-28. Lect II:1129
The basilica was built by Pope Sixtus III after the Council of Ephesus (431). It is the first church in the West named in honour of the Mother of God.

6 Tuesday **Dn 7:9-10, 13-14. or 2 Pt 1:16-19. Ps. 96:1-2, 5-6, 9. Lk 9:28-36.** Lect I:989 or II:1131

The Transfiguration. The cross requires the exodus of Jesus, his death, resurrection and glorification. The disciples have to realise that he must depart, just as they are now prepared for his going up to Jerusalem to die.

7 Wednesday **Num 13:1-2, 25–14:1, 26-29, 34-35. Ps 105:6-7, 13-14, 21-23. Mt 15:21-28.** Lect II:238

The Israelites' continuing lack of faith in God is seen as they give way to human fears. They forgot the great deeds of the past.
St Sixtus II, pope, and his four deacon companions were put to death in 258.
St Cajetan, 1480–1547, founded the Theatines to renew sacramental life in the Church.

8 Thursday **Num 20:1-13. Ps 94:1-2, 6-9. Mt 16:13-23.** Lect II:241

'Hail the rock who saves us!' The people lose faith at Meribah and water is given from the rock. Peter publicly professes his faith in Christ and is hailed as the rock on which the Church is to be built.
St Dominic, 1170–1221, a Spaniard who founded the Order of Preachers (Dominicans) to counteract the Albigensian heresy.

9 Friday **Hos 2:16-17, 21-22. Ps 44:11-12, 14-17. Mt 25:1-13.** Lect II:1518 and 1524

St Teresa Benedicta of the Cross (Edith Stein), born 1891 at Breslaw (now Wroclaw, Poland), the youngest of seven children of a Jewish family. A brilliant student, she gained her doctorate in philosophy at twenty-five. Became a Catholic in 1922 and a Carmelite nun. Both Jewish and Catholic, she fled to Holland when the Nazis came to power but she was captured and sent to Auschwitz where she died in its gas chamber on 9 August 1942.
St Nathy see August notes.
St Felim see August notes.

10 Saturday **2 Cor 9:6-10. Ps 111:1-2, 5-9. Jn 12:24-26.** Lect II:1141

St Lawrence, died 258, is seen as the cheerful giver since he was one of the seven deacons of the Roman Church in charge of the material needs of the faithful. Gifted with a sense of humour, he met his death cheerfully on a gridiron. From earliest times seen not only as a patron saint of the poor, but also of cooks.

August 2013   Psalter Week 3

11 Sunday   **NINETEENTH SUNDAY IN ORDINARY TIME**
Green ✠   HOURS Proper. Te Deum. Psalter Week 3
                MASS Proper. Gloria. Creed. Preface: Sundays I–VIII
No Masses for the dead, except funeral Masses, are permitted today (see Lit. Note 7)
St Clare, virgin is not celebrated this year.

---

12 Monday	**19th Week in Ordinary Time**
Green	HOURS Psalter Week 3. MASS of choice
White	Optional memorial of **St Jane Frances de Chantal, religious**
White	Optional memorial of **St Lelia, virgin**
White	Optional memorial of **St Attracta, virgin**
Achonry	**St Attracta, virgin** Feast
Killala	**St Muredach, bishop** Feast
Cloyne	**Dedication of the Cathedral** (see *Lit. Note 11*)
Killala	**Dedication of the Cathedral** (see *Lit. Note 11*)

---

13 Tuesday	**19th Week in Ordinary Time**
Green	HOURS Psalter Week 3. MASS of choice
Red	Optional memorial of **Ss Pontian, pope, and Hippolytus, priest, martyrs**
White	Optional memorial of **St Fachtna, bishop**
Ross	**St Fachtna, bishop** Feast

---

14 Wednesday   **19th Week in Ordinary Time**
                  St Maximilian Kolbe, priest and martyr   Memorial
Red   HOURS of the memorial. Psalter Week 3
                  MASS of the memorial. Preface: Common or of the Saint
                  FIRST EVENING PRAYER of the **Assumption**

---

15 Thursday   **THE ASSUMPTION OF THE BLESSED VIRGIN MARY**
                                                                   Solemnity
White ✠   HOURS Proper. Complementary Psalms at Day Hour
                 MASS Proper. Gloria. Creed. Preface: Proper
                 EVENING PRAYER of the Assumption
No Masses for the dead, not even funeral Masses, are permitted today (see Lit. Note 7)
Galway   **Dedication of the Cathedral** (see *Lit. Note 11*)

---

16 Friday	**19th Week in Ordinary Time**
Green	HOURS Psalter Week 3. MASS of choice
White	Optional memorial of **St Stephen of Hungary**

---

17 Saturday   **19th Week in Ordinary Time**
                      Our Lady of Knock   Memorial
White   HOURS of the memorial. Psalter Week 3
                    MASS of the memorial. Preface: Blessed Virgin Mary

August 2013   READINGS Sunday Cycle C   Weekday Cycle 1
NINETEENTH WEEK IN ORDINARY TIME

11 Sunday   **Wis 18:6-9. Ps 32:1, 12, 18-20, 22. Heb 11:1-2, 8-19** (shorter form 11:1-2, 8-12)**. Lk 12:32-48** (shorter form 12:35-40)**.** Lect I:891

Christ calls us to continual vigilance. To be always watchful that we are not led into temptation. He taught us to pray that we may not be put to the test. But above all we are to be concerned about our final perseverance.

12 Monday   **Deut 10:12-22. Ps 147:12-15, 19-20. Mt 17:22-27.** Lect II:247

Look for justice for the poor. Give hospitality to strangers.
St Jane Frances de Chantal, 1572–1641, at the age of twenty married Baron de Chantal but after nine years she was left a widow with four children. Her friendship with St Francis de Sales led to the foundation of the Congregation of the Visitation.
St Muredach see *August notes.*
St Attracta see *August notes.*
St Lelia see *August notes.*

13 Tuesday   **Deut 31:1-8. Ps Deut 32:3-4, 7-9. Mt 18:1-5, 10, 12-14.** Lect II:249

'Be strong; stand firm.' Words of encouragement from Moses to the new leader, Joshua.
St Pontian became bishop of Rome in 230 but was exiled in Sardinia where he abdicated during persecution in 235. **St Hippolytus** was a Roman priest. Both died from ill-treatment and are honoured as martyrs.
St Fachtna see *August notes.*

14 Wednesday Deut 34:1-12. Ps 65:1-3, 5, 16-17. Mt 18:15-20. Lect II:251

Jesus illustrates his teaching on forgiveness with the parable about the unjust servant.
St Maximilian Kolbe, 1894–1941, a Conventual Franciscan who worked in the apostolate of the press in Poland and Japan, and died in Auschwitz.
Elphin Tomorrow is the anniversary of the episcopal ordination of Most Rev. Christopher Jones, 15 August 1994.
Vigil of the Assumption of the BVM: 1 Chr 15:3-4,15-16, 16:1-2. Ps 131:6-7, 9-10, 13-14. 1 Cor 15:54-57. Lk 11:27-28. Lect I:992 or II:1146

15 Thursday   **Apoc 11:19, 12:1-6, 10. Ps 44:10-12, 16. 1 Cor 15:20-26. Lk 1:39-56.** Lect I:994 or II:1148

'The **Assumption of Mary** honours the fullness of blessedness that was her destiny, the glorification of her immaculate soul and virginal body that completely conformed her to the risen Christ. This is a celebration that offers to the Church and to all humanity an exemplar and a consoling message, teaching us the fulfilment of our highest hopes. Their own future glorification is happily in store for all those whom Christ has made his own brothers and sisters by taking on their flesh and blood' (*Marialis Cultus*). Patronal Day of France, India, Malta, Paraguay.

16 Friday   **Jos 24:1-13. Ps 135:1-3, 16-18, 21-22, 24. Mt 19:3-12.** Lect II: 256

It is right to give God thanks and praise for all his wonderful works.
St Stephen of Hungary, 975–1038, first king of Hungary and its patron saint, worked for the conversion of his people to Christianity.

17 Saturday   **Our Lady of Knock: Common of the Blessed Virgin Mary** Lect II:1421–49

Next Sunday's readings: Jer 38:4-6, 8-10. Ps 39:2-4, 18. Heb 12:1-4. Lk 12:49-53. Lect I:895

August 2013   Psalter Week 4

18 Sunday   **TWENTIETH SUNDAY IN ORDINARY TIME**
Green ✠   HOURS Proper. Te Deum. Psalter Week 4
            MASS Proper. Gloria. Creed. Preface: Sundays I–VIII
No Masses for the dead, except funeral Masses, are permitted today (see Lit. Note 7)
Tuam   **Dedication of the Cathedral** (see *Lit. Note 11*)

---

19 Monday   **20th Week in Ordinary Time**
Green   HOURS Psalter Week 4. MASS of choice
White   Optional memorial of **St John Eudes, priest**

---

20 Tuesday   **20th Week in Ordinary Time**
             St Bernard, abbot and doctor of the Church   Memorial
White   HOURS of the memorial. Psalter Week 4
            MASS of the memorial. Preface: Common or of the Saint

---

21 Wednesday **20th Week in Ordinary Time**
                 St Pius X, pope   Memorial
White   HOURS of the memorial. Psalter Week 4
                 MASS of the memorial. Preface: Common or of the Saint

---

22 Thursday   **20th Week in Ordinary Time**
              The Queenship of the Blessed Virgin Mary   Memorial
White   HOURS of the memorial. Psalter Week 4
            MASS of the memorial. Preface: Blessed Virgin Mary
Cork   **Dedication of the Cathedral** (see *Lit. Note 11*)
Kerry   **Dedication of the Cathedral** (see *Lit. Note 11*)

---

23 Friday   **20th Week in Ordinary Time**
Green   HOURS Psalter Week 4. MASS of choice
White   Optional memorial of **St Rose of Lima, virgin**
White   Optional memorial of **St Eugene, bishop**
Derry   **St Eugene, bishop**   Feast

---

24 Saturday   ST BARTHOLOMEW, APOSTLE   Feast
Red   HOURS Proper. Te Deum. Psalter Week 4 at Day Hour
                MASS Proper. Gloria. Preface: Apostles I–II
No Masses for the dead, except funeral Masses, are permitted today (see Lit. Note 7)

Next Sunday's readings: Is 66:18-21. Ps 116. Heb 12:5-7, 11-13. Lk 13:22-30. *Lect* I:898

August 2013 READINGS Sunday Cycle C Weekday Cycle 1

TWENTIETH WEEK IN ORDINARY TIME

18 Sunday Jer 38:4-6, 8-10. Ps 39:2-4, 18. Heb 12:1-4. Lk 12:49-53. *Lect* I:895

Christ promises his followers the same cross as he himself bore. They must meet rejection, ridicule, ostracism from family and society, and martyrdom. The saints who have gone before us encourage us to leave all for the Gospel's sake.

19 Monday Jg 2:11-19. Ps 105:34-37, 39-40, 43-44. Mt 19:16-22. *Lect* II:261

The Lord's anger flamed out against Israel because of infidelity. Despite the quality of leadership given them, they still turned away to other gods.

St John Eudes, 1601–80, from Normandy, France, spent a fruitful twenty years with the French Oratory, then left to found a congregation to improve the standards of the clergy through seminaries. He founded also the Sisters of Our Lady of Charity and Refuge. He was a powerful preacher and among the first to promote devotion to the Sacred Heart.

20 Tuesday Jg 6:11-24. Ps 84:9, 11-14. Mt 19:23-30. *Lect* II:263

Time after time God has rescued his people but they dared to defy him. The vocation of Gideon is to bring peace.

St Bernard, b. 1090, d. August 20, 1153, became a Cistercian monk at Citeaux in 1113 and was chosen abbot of Clairvaux in 1115. His writings reveal a solid grasp of biblical studies, spiritual theology, and philosophy. Patron of Gibralter and beekeepers.

21 Wednesday Jg 9:6-15. Ps 20:2-7. Mt 20:1-16. *Lect* II:266

Jotham tells the story of the trees seeking a king to warn the people that a king will be either useless or dangerous. Jesus tells a story to illustrate the generosity of God who rewards even the latecomers.

St Pius X, 1835–1914, Cardinal Patriarch of Venice, then Pope from 1903. Encouraged pastoral liturgy and sacramental practice, especially of frequent communion, to which he admitted young children.

22 Thursday Is 9:1-6. Ps 112:1-8. Lk 1:26-38. *Lect* II:1160

The Queenship of Mary. During the Middle Ages Mary was venerated as queen of the angels and saints. Pope Pius XII prescribed the feast for the universal Church at the close of Marian Year of 1955. It is placed on this date to stress the connection of Mary's queenship with the Assumption.

23 Friday Ruth 1:1, 3-6, 14-16, 22. Ps 145:5-10. Mt 22:34-40. *Lect* II:271

'Your people shall be my people.' Ruth the Moabitess, after the death of her husband, a man originally from Bethlehem, returns to his country with her mother-in-law, Naomi.

St Rose of Lima, 1586–1617, Dominican tertiary and recluse, helped the poor and marginalised. Seen as originator of social service in Peru.

St Eugene see *August notes*.

24 Saturday Apoc 21:9-14. Ps 144:10-13, 17-18. Jn 1:45-51. *Lect* II:1164

St Bartholomew's name occurs in the Synoptic Gospels only in the list of apostles. He is probably to be identified with Nathanael of Cana, whom Philip brings to our Lord. Preached the Gospel in India. Patron saint of plasterers, tanners and leather workers.

August 2013 Psalter Week 1

25 Sunday **TWENTY-FIRST SUNDAY IN ORDINARY TIME**
Green ✠ HOURS Proper. Te Deum. Psalter Week 1
MASS Proper. Gloria. Creed. Preface: Sundays I–VIII
No Masses for the dead, except funeral Masses, are permitted today (see Lit. Note 7)
St Louis of France and **St Joseph Calasanz, priest** are not celebrated this year.

---

26 Monday **21st Week in Ordinary Time**
Green HOURS Psalter Week 1. MASS of choice

---

27 Tuesday **21st Week in Ordinary Time**
St Monica Memorial
White HOURS of the memorial. Psalter Week 1
MASS of the memorial. Preface: Common or of the Saint.

---

28 Wednesday **21st Week in Ordinary Time**
St Augustine, bishop and doctor of the Church
Memorial
White HOURS of the memorial. Psalter Week 1
MASS of the memorial. Preface: Common or of the Saint

---

29 Thursday **21st Week in Ordinary Time**
The Passion of St John the Baptist Memorial
Red HOURS Proper of the memorial. Psalter Week 1 at Day Hour
MASS of the memorial. Preface: Proper

---

30 Friday **21st Week in Ordinary Time**
Green HOURS Psalter Week 1. MASS of choice
White Optional memorial of **St Fiacre, monk**
Meath **Dedication of the Cathedral** (see *Lit. Note 11*)

---

31 Saturday **21st Week in Ordinary Time**
Green HOURS Psalter Week 1. MASS of choice
White Optional memorial of **St Aidan of Lindisfarne, bishop and missionary**
White/Green Saturday Mass of the **Blessed Virgin Mary**

August 2013   READINGS Sunday Cycle C   Weekday Cycle 1

TWENTY-FIRST WEEK IN ORDINARY TIME

25 Sunday   Is 66:18-21. Ps 116. Heb 12:5-7, 11-13. Lk 13:22-30. Lect I:898

The universality of salvation is the message from all the readings on this day. Salvation does not belong to any special race or culture but to those who accept Christ. It is the desire of God that all should be saved. Some who are regarded as last will be saved while the first called may be last.

26 Monday   1 Th 1:1-5, 8-10. Ps 149:1-6, 9. Mt 23:13-22. Lect II:276

God loves us and has called us to be his people.

27 Tuesday   1 Th 2:1-8. Ps 138:1-3, 4-6. Mt 23:23-26. Lect II:278

As a mother looking after the welfare of her children so has Paul been with the Thessalonians. His only desire was that the gospel of Christ might grow among them.

St Monica, 332–87, converted her pagan husband, Patricius, to the faith, and by her prayers and tears brought her son St Augustine to Christianity and a moral life. Patron saint of mothers.

28 Wednesday 1 Th 2:9-13. Ps 138:7-12. Mt 23:27-32. Lect II:280

There is a contrast between Paul's single-minded work for the Gospel, and the Pharisees who are condemned for their hypocrisy.

St Augustine, 354–430. Bishop of Hippo, where he lived with a community until his death. His theological influence has been most significant in the Church, especially on the understanding of God's grace. Patron of theologians.

Killaloe Tomorrow is the anniversary of the episcopal ordination of Most Rev. Kieran O'Reilly, 29 August 2010.

29 Thursday   Jer 1:17-19. Ps 70:1-6, 15, 17. Mk 6:17-29. Lect II:1175

The Mass Preface lists the favours shown to **St John the Baptist** and the vocation given him. He is found worthy of the martyr's death, his last and greatest act of witness to Christ.

30 Friday   1 Th 4:1-8. Ps 96:1-2, 5-6, 10-12. Mt 25:1-13. Lect II:284

Paul calls for an improvement in the community's sexual ethics. Jesus reiterates his message of watchfulness.

St Fiacre see August notes.

31 Saturday   1 Th 4:9-11. Ps 97:1, 7-9. Mt 25:14-30. Lect II:286

Faithfulness in small things is the lesson of the parable of the talents. We all have the talent to love. Paul reminds us: let us make progress.

St Aidan see August notes.

Next Sunday's readings: Eccles (Sir) 3:17-20, 28-29. Ps 67:4-7, 10-11. Heb 12:18-19, 22-24. Lk 14:1, 7-14. Lect I:900

NOTES FOR SEPTEMBER 2013

THE POPE'S INTENTIONS

General – Silence: That the men and women of our time, often overwhelmed by noise, may rediscover the value of silence and learn to listen to the voice of God and their brothers and sisters.

Mission – Persecuted Christians: That Christians who suffer persecution in many parts of the world may be prophets of the love of Christ by their testimony.

THE IRISH CALENDAR IN SEPTEMBER

4th: St Mac Nissi. Oengus Mac Nissi took his name from his mother Cnes or Ness. It is claimed that Patrick baptised him and taught him the psalms. He chose the district of Connor for his hermitage, but later became bishop of his clan. He died early in the sixth century.

9th: St Ciaran was born in Roscommon around 512. He came to Clonmacnois in January 545 where he founded a monastery which was to become one of the most renowned in Europe. He died at the age of thirty-three while the monastery was still being built.

12th: St Ailbe is sometimes claimed as one of the pre-Patrician saints, but the annals note his death in 528. A tradition held that he went to Rome and was ordained bishop by the Pope. He founded the monastery of Emly which became very important in Munster. A ninth-century Rule bears his name.

23rd: St Eunan (Adomnan) was born in Donegal around 624 and died in 704. He became a monk in Iona and was chosen abbot there in 679. One of his writings is the Life of Colum Cille.

25th: St Finbarr came to Loch Irce (Gougane Barra) and lived there as a hermit. When disciples gathered round him he moved to Cork at the mouth of the Lee where he founded a monastery which became a famous centre of learning.

THE SUNDAY EUCHARIST

It is true that, in itself, the Sunday Eucharist is no different from the Eucharist celebrated on other days, nor can it be separated from liturgical and sacramental life as a whole. By its very nature, the Eucharist is an epiphany of the Church; and this is most powerfully expressed when the diocesan community gathers in prayer with its Pastor: 'The Church appears with special clarity when the holy People of God, all of them, are actively and fully sharing in the same liturgical celebrations – especially when it is the same Eucharist – sharing one prayer at one altar, at which the Bishop is presiding, surrounded by his presbyters and his ministers' (SC 41). This relationship with the Bishop and with the entire Church community is inherent in every Eucharistic celebration, even when the Bishop does not preside, regardless of the day of the week on which it is celebrated. The mention of the Bishop in the Eucharistic Prayer is the indication of this.

But because of its special solemnity and the obligatory presence of the community, and because it is celebrated 'on the day when Christ conquered death and gave us a share in his immortal life', the Sunday Eucharist expresses with greater emphasis its inherent ecclesial dimension. It becomes the paradigm for other Eucharistic celebrations. Each community, gathering all its members for the 'breaking of the bread', becomes the place where the mystery of the Church is concretely made present. In celebrating the Eucharist, the community opens itself to communion with the universal Church, imploring the Father to 'remember the Church throughout the world' and make her grow in the unity of all the faithful with the Pope and with the Pastors of the particular Churches, until love is brought to perfection.

Therefore, the *dies Domini* is also the *dies Ecclesiae*. This is why on the pastoral level the community aspect of the Sunday celebration should be particularly stressed. As I have noted elsewhere, among the many activities of a parish, 'none is as vital or as community-forming as the Sunday celebration of the Lord's Day and his Eucharist'. Mindful of this, the Second Vatican Council recalled that efforts must be made to ensure that there is 'within the parish, a lively sense of community, in the first place through the community celebration of Sunday Mass' (SC 42). Subsequent liturgical directives made the same point, asking that on Sundays and holy days the Eucharistic celebrations held normally in other churches and chapels be coordinated with the celebration in the parish church, in order 'to foster the sense of the Church community, which is nourished and expressed in a particular way by the community celebration on Sunday, whether around the Bishop, especially in the Cathedral, or in the parish assembly, in which the pastor represents the Bishop'(*Euch. mysterium*).

The Sunday assembly is the privileged place of unity: it is the setting for the celebration of the *sacramentum unitatis* which profoundly marks the Church as a people gathered 'by' and 'in' the unity of the Father, of the Son and of the Holy Spirit (St Cyprian, LG 4, SC 26). For Christian families, the Sunday assembly is one of the most outstanding expressions of their identity and their 'ministry' as 'domestic churches', when parents share with their children at the one Table of the word and of the Bread of Life. We do well to recall in this regard that it is first of all the parents who must teach their children to participate in Sunday Mass; they are assisted in this by catechists, who are to see to it that initiation into the Mass is made a part of the formation imparted to the children entrusted to their care, explaining the important reasons behind the obligatory nature of the precept. When circumstances suggest it, the celebration of Masses for Children, in keeping with the provisions of the liturgical norms, can also help in this regard.

At Sunday Masses in parishes, insofar as parishes are 'Eucharistic communities', it is normal to find different groups, movements, associations and even the smaller religious communities present in the parish. This allows everyone to experience in common what they share most deeply, beyond the particular spiritual paths which, by discernment of Church authority, legitimately distinguish them. This is why on Sunday, the day of gathering, small group Masses are not to be encouraged: it is not only a question of ensuring that parish assemblies are not without the necessary ministry of priests, but also of ensuring that the life and unity of the Church community are fully safeguarded and promoted. Authorisation of possible and clearly restricted exceptions to this general guideline will depend upon the wise discernment of the Pastors of the particular Churches, in view of special needs in the area of formation and pastoral care, and keeping in mind the good of individuals or groups – especially the benefits which such exceptions may bring to the entire Christian community.

– Pope John Paul II, *Dies Domini, Keeping the Lord's Day Holy* 34–6 (1998)

SEPTEMBER 2013   Psalter Week 2

1 Sunday   **TWENTY-SECOND SUNDAY IN ORDINARY TIME**
Green ✠   HOURS Proper. Te Deum. Psalter Week 2
                  MASS Proper. Gloria. Creed. Preface: Sundays I–VIII
No Masses for the dead, except funeral Masses, are permitted today (see Lit. Note 7)

---

2 Monday   **22nd Week in Ordinary Time**
Green   HOURS Psalter Week 2. MASS of choice

---

3 Tuesday   **22nd Week in Ordinary Time**
                   St Gregory the Great, pope and doctor of the Church
                                                                       Memorial
White   HOURS of the memorial. Psalter Week 2
                  MASS of the memorial. Preface: Common or of the Saint

---

4 Wednesday   **22nd Week in Ordinary Time**
Green   HOURS Psalter Week 2. MASS of choice
White   Optional memorial of **St Mac Nissi, bishop**
Connor   **St Mac Nissi, bishop**   Feast
Down   **St Mac Nissi, bishop**   Memorial

---

5 Thursday   **22nd Week in Ordinary Time**
Green   HOURS Psalter Week 2. MASS of choice

---

6 Friday   **22nd Week in Ordinary Time**
Green   HOURS Psalter Week 2. MASS of choice

---

7 Saturday   **22nd Week in Ordinary Time**
Green   HOURS Psalter Week 2. MASS of choice
White/Green   Saturday Mass of the **Blessed Virgin Mary**

SEPTEMBER 2013   READINGS Sunday Cycle C   Weekday Cycle 1

TWENTY-SECOND WEEK IN ORDINARY TIME

1 Sunday   Eccles (Sir) 3:17-20, 28-29. Ps 67:4-7, 10-11. Heb 12:18-19, 22-24. Lk 14:1, 7-14. *Lect* I:900

Humility is opposed to a pride that shows no respect for others, but tends to dominate, to exercise power for its own sake, to be unconcerned for the rights of others. It is a virtue which sees service of others as the meaning of authority.

Clogher Tomorrow is the anniversary of the episcopal ordination of Most Rev. Joseph Duffy, 2 September 1979.

2 Monday   1 Th 4:13-18. Ps 95:1, 3-5, 11-13. Lk 4:16-30. *Lect* II:288

Paul says that physical death is no barrier to sharing in the victory of the risen Lord. We are to encourage one another to prepare in hope for the return of the Lord.

3 Tuesday   1 Th 5:1-6, 9-11. Ps 26:1, 4, 13-14. Lk 4:31-37. *Lect* II:291

We are children of the day and no longer live as in the night. Speculation about the time and place of death can be useless. We should so live as to be always ready for the coming of the Lord. Affirmation of each other will strengthen us in the faith.

St Gregory the Great, 540–604. A Roman noble who was Prefect of the City before becoming a monk. As Pope he established a pattern for the papacy in years to come. He sent missions to Lombardy, Sardinia, and England. Patron of musicians.

4 Wednesday   Col 1:1-8. Ps 51:10-11. Lk 4:38-44. *Lect* II:293

St Paul writes to the Colossians to counteract heretical tendencies. He begins by praising their genuine charity, something that is not based on feelings or mood. The truth of the Gospel is shown by its universal application. The Good News must be proclaimed to all places.

St Mac Nissi see *September notes*.

5 Thursday   Col 1:9-14. Ps 97:2-6. Lk 5:1-11. *Lect* II:295

We come to God in prayer to discover his will and to request the courage to carry it out. Gratitude for the gift of salvation should be part of our prayer also.

6 Friday   Col 1:15-20. Ps 99:2-5. Lk 5:33-39. *Lect* II:297

There is a serious obligation to observe Friday as a penitential day. We recommend that each person should choose some form of penance for Fridays, in memory, as was Friday abstinence, of the passion and death of our Lord (Irish Bishops 1983).

7 Saturday   Col 1:21-23. Ps 53:3-4, 6, 8. Lk 6:1-5. *Lect* II:299

The harsh interpretation of the Sabbath commandment is criticised by Jesus. The weekly observance of Christians helps them to persevere and stand firm on the solid base of the faith as St Paul describes it.

Next Sunday's readings: Wis 9:13-18. Ps 89:3-6, 12-14, 17. Phm 9-10, 12-17. Lk 14:25-33. *Lect* I:903

September 2013 Psalter Week 3

8 Sunday	**TWENTY-THIRD SUNDAY IN ORDINARY TIME**
Green ✠	HOURS Proper. Te Deum. Psalter Week 3
	MASS Proper. Gloria. Creed. Preface: Sundays I–VIII

No Masses for the dead, except funeral Masses, are permitted today (see Lit. Note 7)
The Nativity of the Blessed Virgin Mary is not celebrated this year.

---

9 Monday	**23rd Week in Ordinary Time**	
	St Ciaran, abbot	Memorial
White	HOURS of the memorial. Psalter Week 3	
	MASS of the memorial. Preface: Common or of the Saint	
Clonmacnois	**St Ciaran, abbot**	Feast

---

10 Tuesday	**23rd Week in Ordinary Time**
Green	HOURS Psalter Week 3. MASS of choice

---

11 Wednesday **23rd Week in Ordinary Time**
Green   HOURS Psalter Week 3. MASS of choice

---

12 Thursday	**23rd Week in Ordinary Time**	
Green	HOURS Psalter Week 3. MASS of choice	
White	Optional memorial of **The Most Holy Name of Mary**	
White	Optional memorial of **St Ailbe, bishop**	
Cashel and Emly	**St Ailbe, bishop**	Feast
Kilmore	**Dedication of the Cathedral** (see *Lit. Note 11*)	

---

13 Friday	**23rd Week in Ordinary Time**
	St John Chrysostom, bishop and doctor of the Church
White	HOURS of the memorial. Psalter Week 3
	MASS of the memorial. Preface: Common or of the Saint

---

14 Saturday	THE EXALTATION OF THE HOLY CROSS	Feast
Red	HOURS Proper. Te Deum. Psalter Week 3 at Day Hour	
	MASS Proper. Gloria. Preface: Proper or Passion I	

No Masses for the dead, except funeral Masses, are permitted today (see Lit. Note 7)

Next Sunday's readings: Ex 32:7-11, 13-14. Ps 50:3-4, 12-13, 17, 19. 1 Tm 1:12-17. Lk 15:1-32 (shorter form 15:1-10). *Lect* I:906

September 2013   READINGS Sunday Cycle C   Weekday Cycle 1
TWENTY-THIRD WEEK IN ORDINARY TIME
8 Sunday   Wis 9:13-18. Ps 89:3-6, 12-14, 17. Phm 9-10, 12-17. Lk 14:25-33. *Lect* I:903
Detachment means a striving for liberation through self-denial. True wisdom means not being oppressed by our human nature. We must study how to meet the demands of discipleship of Christ.

9 Monday   Col 1:24-2:3. Ps 61:6-7, 9. Lk 6:6-11. *Lect* II:300
Paul believes that being called to ministry is to be associated with Christ in his sufferings. His task is to preach the secret of God that the gentiles too are to share in union with Christ, to achieve salvation and the glory of heaven.
St Ciaran see *September notes.*
Kerry Tomorrow is the anniversary of the episcopal ordination of Most Rev. William Murphy, 10 September 1995.

10 Tuesday   Col 2:6-15. Ps 144:1-2, 8-11. Lk 6:12-19. *Lect* II:302
The whole meaning of our salvation is rooted in Christ, not in any other philosophy. We are saved from our sins not by any action other than that of entering into the very death of Christ.

11 Wednesday Col 3:1-11. Ps 144:2-3, 10-13. Lk 6:20-26. *Lect* II:304
'The Church's love for the poor … is a part of her constant tradition.' This love is inspired by the Gospel of the Beatitudes, of the poverty of Jesus, and of his concern for the poor. Love for the poor is even one of the motives for the duty of working so as to "be able to give to those in need". It extends not only to material poverty but also to the many forms of cultural and religious poverty' (*CCC*, 2444).

12 Thursday   Col 3:12-17. Ps 150:1-6. Lk 6:27-38. *Lect* II:306
Christian community life is described for the Colossians. Christ who is the source of unity, peace, and harmony calls them to live lives of humility, meekness, patience, forgiveness, and, above all, charity. Music has a large part to play in instruction and mutual upbuilding.
The Holy Name of Mary: Gal 4:4-7 *or* **Eph 1:3-6, 11-12. Ps Lk 1:46-55. Lk 1:39-47.** *Lect* II:1438,1432,1444
St Ailbe see *September notes.*
Tuam Tomorrow is the anniversary of the episcopal ordination of Most Rev. Michael Neary, 13 September 1992.

13 Friday   1 Tm 1:1-2, 12-14. Ps 15:1-2, 5, 7-8, 11. Lk 6:39-42. *Lect* II:308
Why, Jesus asks, do we tend to dwell on the small defects of others while our own failures are much worse? It is his mercy and love that will help us to show the same compassion of heart.
St John Chrysostom, 347–407, one of the four great Greek Doctors, the 'Golden-mouthed' preacher, was Archbishop of Constantinople. He incurred much opposition and died in exile. Patron saint of preachers.

14 Saturday   Num 21:4-9. Ps 77:1-2, 34-38. Phil 2:6-11. Jn 3:13-17. *Lect* I:996 or II:1186
The Exaltation of the Holy Cross. The discovery of the True Cross is dated to 14 September 320. On 13 September 335 the churches on Calvary were dedicated and the cross that St Helena discovered was venerated there the next day. The annual commemoration of that event has been celebrated since, in praise of the redemption won for us by Christ.

September 2013   Psalter Week 4

15 Sunday   **TWENTY-FOURTH SUNDAY IN ORDINARY TIME**
Green ✠   HOURS Proper. Te Deum. Psalter Week 4
     MASS Proper. Gloria. Creed. Preface: Sundays I–VIII
No Masses for the dead, except funeral Masses, are permitted today (see Lit. Note 7)
Our Lady of Sorrows is not celebrated this year.

---

16 Monday   **24th Week in Ordinary Time**
     Ss Cornelius, pope, and Cyprian, bishop, martyrs
                                                            Memorial
Red   HOURS of the memorial. Psalter Week 4
     MASS of the memorial. Preface: Common or of the Saint

---

17 Tuesday   **24th Week in Ordinary Time**
Green   HOURS Psalter Week 4. MASS of choice
White   Optional memorial of **St Robert Bellarmine, bishop and doctor of the Church**

---

18 Wednesday   **24th Week in Ordinary Time**
Green   HOURS Psalter Week 4. MASS of choice

---

19 Thursday   **24th Week in Ordinary Time**
Green   HOURS Psalter Week 4. MASS of choice
Red   Optional memorial of **St Januarius, bishop and martyr**

---

20 Friday   **24th Week in Ordinary Time**
     Ss Andrew Kim Tae-gŏn, priest, Paul Chŏng Ha-sang, and Companions, martyrs   Memorial
Red   HOURS of the memorial. Psalter Week 4
     MASS of the memorial. Preface: Common or of the Saint

---

21 Saturday   ST MATTHEW, APOSTLE AND EVANGELIST   Feast
Red   HOURS Proper. Te Deum. Psalter Week 4 at Day Hour
     MASS Proper. Gloria. Preface: Apostles I–II
No Masses for the dead, except funeral Masses, are permitted today (see Lit. Note 7)

Next Sunday's readings: Am 8:4-7. Ps 112:1-2, 4-8. 1 Tm 2:1-8. Lk **16:1-13** (shorter form 16:10-13). *Lect* I:910

September 2013 READINGS Sunday Cycle C Weekday Cycle 1

TWENTY-FOURTH WEEK IN ORDINARY TIME

15 Sunday **Ex 32:7-11, 13-14. Ps 50:3-4, 12-13, 17, 19. 1 Tm 1:12-17. Lk 15:1-32** (shorter form 15:1-10). *Lect* I:906
Jesus gives three parables about the question of those who have wandered away and were lost and how the communities must rejoice when they return and are found.

16 Monday **1 Tm 2:1-8. Ps 27:2, 7-9. Lk 7:1-10.** *Lect* II:312
Paul gives instructions for the good ordering of the liturgical assembly and prayer meetings of the community. He sees himself as apostle, herald and teacher.
St Cornelius became Pope in 251 and died in exile at Civitavecchia in 253. Patron for cattle and domestic animals.
St Cyprian, 210–58, bishop of Carthage, teacher and preacher, martyred.
Dublin Tomorrow is the anniversary of the episcopal ordination of Most Rev. Fiachra Ó Ceallaigh OFM, 17 September 1994.

17 Tuesday **1 Tm 3:1-13. Ps 100:1-3, 5, 6. Lk 7:11-17.** *Lect* II:314
The Letter to Timothy has called for a community of intercession for all. Now it addresses the need for high standards in the ministerial offices of the Church. Those of impeccable character only should be chosen.
St Robert Bellarmine, 1542–1621, Jesuit, Cardinal Bishop of Capua, involved in theological controversies of the time. Patron of catechists.

18 Wednesday 1 Tm 3:14-16. Ps 110:1-6. Lk 7:31-35. *Lect* II:316
'Belief in the true Incarnation of the Son of God is the distinctive sign of Christian faith: He was manifested in the flesh' (*CCC*, 463).
Dromore Tomorrow is the anniversary of the episcopal ordination of Most Rev. John McAreavey, 19 September 1999.

19 Thursday **1 Tm 4:12-16. Ps 110:7-10. Lk 7:36-50.** *Lect* II:318
When Christ was taken up in glory after his glorious resurrection the Holy Spirit showed forth in a special way the divinity of Christ. Before this his contemporaries had difficulty in accepting him.
St Januarius, bishop of Benevento, was martyred at Naples in 305, with six companions.

20 Friday **1 Tm 6:2-12. Ps 48:6-10, 17-20. Lk 8:1-3.** *Lect* II:320
'The love of money is the root of all evils' and can bring people away from faith and do damage to their souls. But the person of faith avoids all that and aims to be saintly and religious. Each has to fight the good fight of faith.
St Andrew Kim Tae-gŏn, the first Korean priest, **St Paul Chŏng Ha-sang**, a catechist, and 101 others were martyred during the persecutions of the Church in Korea, 1839–67.
Galway Tomorrow is the anniversary of the episcopal ordination of Most Rev. Martin Drennan, 21 September 1997.
Dublin Tomorrow is the anniversary of the episcopal ordination of Most Rev. Raymond Field, 21 September 1997.

21 Saturday **Eph 4:1-7, 11-13. Ps 18:2-5. Mt 9:9-13.** *Lect* II:1198
St Matthew, the tax collector, may also be identified with Levi, son of Alphaeus, in Mk 2:13. He is said to have been a missionary in Persia and Ethiopia. Patron of accountants, book-keepers, tax-collectors, customs officers and security guards.
Kildare and Leighlin Tomorrow is the anniversary of the episcopal ordination of Most Rev. James Moriarty, 22 September 1991.

September 2013 Psalter Week 1

22 Sunday — **TWENTY-FIFTH SUNDAY IN ORDINARY TIME**
Green ✠ — HOURS Proper. Te Deum. Psalter Week 1
MASS Proper. Gloria. Creed. Preface: Sundays I–VIII
No Masses for the dead, except funeral Masses, are permitted today (see Lit. Note 7)
Clogher — **Dedication of the Cathedral** (see *Lit. Note 11*)

---

23 Monday — **25th Week in Ordinary Time**
St Pius of Pietrelcina (Padre Pio), priest Memorial
White — HOURS of the memorial. Psalter Week 1
MASS of the memorial. Preface: Common or of the Saint
Raphoe — **St Eunan (Adomnan) abbot** Feast

---

24 Tuesday — **25th Week in Ordinary Time**
Green — HOURS Psalter Week 1. MASS of choice

---

25 Wednesday — **25th Week in Ordinary Time**
Green — HOURS Psalter Week 1. MASS of choice
White — Optional memorial of **St Finbarr, bishop**
Cork — **St Finbarr, bishop** Feast

---

26 Thursday — **25th Week in Ordinary Time**
Green — HOURS Psalter Week 1. MASS of choice
Red — Optional memorial of **Ss Cosmas and Damian, martyrs**

---

27 Friday — **25th Week in Ordinary Time**
St Vincent de Paul, priest Memorial
White — HOURS of the memorial. Psalter Week 1
MASS of the memorial. Preface: Common or of the Saint

---

28 Saturday — **25th Week in Ordinary Time**
Green — HOURS Psalter Week 1. MASS of choice
Red — Optional memorial of **St Wenceslaus, martyr**
Red — Optional memorial of **Ss Lawrence Ruiz and Companions, martyrs**
White/Green — Saturday Mass of the **Blessed Virgin Mary**

September 2013   READINGS Sunday Cycle C   Weekday Cycle 1
TWENTY-FIFTH WEEK IN ORDINARY TIME

22 Sunday   Am 8:4-7. Ps 112:1-2, 4-8. 1 Tm 2:1-8. Lk 16:1-13
(shorter form 16:10-13). *Lect* I:910
Christ does not approve of the dishonesty of the steward but notes how attentive to profit-making so many are, while Christians are apathetic about true values.
Tuam Tomorrow is the anniversary of the episcopal ordination of Most Rev. Joseph Cassidy, 23 September 1979.

23 Monday   Ezra 1:1-6. Ps 125. Lk 8:16-18. *Lect* II:325
Jerusalem and the Temple were destroyed by the Babylonian armies and the real exile began in 587–6 BC. Jeremiah had prophesied throughout the exile that there would be a return to a glorious future. Cyrus, king of Persia, conquered Babylon in 539 and encouraged the exiles to return home and rebuild the temple.
St Pius of Pietrelcina (Padre Pio), died 23 September 1968. Capuchin friar, stigmatist, confessor, friend of all who suffer.
St Eunan see *September notes.*

24 Tuesday   Ezra 6:7-8, 12, 14-20. Ps 121:1-5. Lk 8:19-21. *Lect* II:327
'Semitic languages in Jesus' time did not have a precise vocabulary for a wide range of family relationships. Rather they reflected a tribal background, where members of the same tribe, clan, or family were considered brothers and sisters, no matter what their precise relationship.' The Greek terms used in the Gospel may have been influenced by early Christian references phrased in Aramaic or Hebrew (cf. R.E. Brown SS, *101 Questions and Answers on the Bible*, Paulist Press, 2003).

25 Wednesday Ezra 9:5-9. Ps Tob 13:2, 4, 6-8. Lk 9:1-6. *Lect* II:329
The joy of the return from Exile and the building of the Second Temple are memories of God's favour to his people.
St Finbarr see *September notes.*

26 Thursday   Hg 1:1-8. Ps 149:1-6, 9. Lk 9:7-9. *Lect* II:331
The age of salvation, with the coming of the Lord and the setting up of his kingdom, is conditional on the rebuilding of the Temple.
Ss Cosmas and Damian, early martyrs in Syria, patrons of physicians. They are known as the Anargyri (the holy moneyless ones) in the East, since they never took money for their medical services.

27 Friday   Hg 1:15-2:9. Ps 42:1-4. Lk 9:18-22. *Lect* II:333
The Temple signals the fulfilment of Israel's hopes.
St Vincent de Paul, 1580–1660, founded the Congregation of the Mission (the Vincentians) and the Daughters of Charity (1633), the first sisters to work outside their convents in active service. He is the patron of all charitable works.

28 Saturday   Zec 2:5-9, 14-15. Ps Jer 31:10-13. Lk 9:43-45. *Lect* II:335
The disciples find the foretelling of Christ's death puzzling. They will come to realise that through the Paschal Mystery many nations will join the Lord and he will dwell among us his people.
St Wenceslaus, 905–25, Prince of Bohemia, killed by his brother. Patron of brewers.
St Lawrence Ruiz and Companions. During the period 1633–7 these sixteen martyrs shed their blood out of love for Christ in the city of Nagasaki, Japan.

Next Sunday's readings: Am 6:1, 4-7. Ps 145:6-10. 1 Tm 6:11-16. Lk 16:19-31. *Lect* I:914

NOTES FOR OCTOBER 2013

THE POPE'S INTENTIONS

General – People who feel crushed by life: That those who feel weary from the heaviness of life, and even long for its end, may sense the closeness of God's love.

Mission – World Missions Day: That the celebration of World Missions Day may make all Christians aware that they are not only recipients but also proclaimers of the Word of God.

THE IRISH CALENDAR IN OCTOBER

3rd: Bl. Columba Marmion. Joseph, his baptismal name, was born in Dublin in 1858 and ordained priest in Rome in 1881. He served as curate in Dundrum Parish and then as professor in Holy Cross College, Clonliffe, before entering the Abbey of Maredsous, Belgium, in 1886. Elected as Abbot, he received his abbatial blessing on 3 October 1909. He died on 30 January 1923. His trilogy, *Christ, the Life of the Soul*, *Christ, in His Mysteries* and *Christ, the Life of the Monk* have been some of the most influential spiritual writings of the twentieth century, nourishing the lives of generations of seminarians, priests, religious sisters and monks. His writings, letters and retreats fulfilled his aim in life: to bring people to God and to bring God to people. He was beatified in Rome on 1 September 2000.

9th: Bl. John Henry Newman was beatified by Pope Benedict XVI at Cofton Park, Birmingham on 19 September 2010. The memorial of the new Blessed is 9 October, the anniversary of his reception into the Catholic Church on 9 October 1845. The Church in Ireland is deeply aware of Blessed John Henry's gentle scholarship, deep human wisdom and profound love for the Lord. It also recalls his connections with Ireland. Though his project on the establishment of the Catholic University of Ireland was not a great success, his reflection on education was written in part when he lived in Dublin and has remained a vital contribution to an understanding of Christian education. Invited to Ireland in 1850, he became Rector of the Catholic University of Ireland in 1854 until his resignation in 1858.

11th: St Canice was born in Co. Derry around 527 and died in 603. Though his people were poor he studied at Clonard under Finnian and at Glasnevin under Mobhi. A deep friendship developed between himself and Columba, with whom he worked for a time in Scotland, where he set up a number of churches. In Ireland his principal foundation was in Aghaboe in Ossory, but this was replaced centuries later by his church in Kilkenny.

16th: St Gall was a monk of Bangor and set out with Columbanus for the Continent. When Columbanus was exiled from France, Gall accompanied him to Bregenz on Lake Constance. When Columbanus crossed into Italy, Gall remained in Switzerland. He lived in a hermitage, which later became the monastery of St Gallen. He died around 630.

25th (Cloyne, Cork and Ross): Bl. Thaddeus MacCarthy was born in 1455. His appointment as Bishop of Ross was opposed and Innocent VIII then appointed him bishop of Cork and Cloyne. He set out as a humble pilgrim to Rome where he was confirmed as bishop of Cork and Cloyne. On his return journey in 1492 he died at Ivrea in Italy.

27th: St Otteran, a descendant of Conall Gulban, is usually identified with Odhran who preceded Columba in Iona. His death is recorded in 548 and his grave was greatly revered in Iona. He was chosen by the Vikings as patron of the city of Waterford in 1096 and later patron of the diocese.

29th: St Colman hailed from Kilmacduagh, Co. Clare, in the seventh century. After studying in Aran, where he founded two churches on Inis Mhór, he returned to make a foundation at Kilmacduagh.

31st (Cloyne): Bl. Dominic Collins was born around 1566 in the city of Youghal, Co. Cork. In 1598, after a military career, he entered the Society of Jesus as a Brother. He returned to Ireland in 1601, but on 17 June 1602 he was captured by the English who tried in vain to make him abjure his faith. Condemned to death, he was hanged in his native city on 31 October 1602.

WORLD MISSION SUNDAY 2013 – THEME: GROWING IN FAITH

October is Mission Month. 'This month must be regarded in all countries as the Month of Universal Mission. The penultimate Sunday, proclaimed as World Mission Day, is the high point of the month.' (Congregation of Rites 1926)

Since its founding in 1926, World Mission Sunday has been entrusted to the Society for the Propagation of the Faith, founded by Pauline Marie Jaricot.

'World Mission Day, which seeks to heighten awareness of the missions, as well as to collect funds for them, is an important date in the life of the Church, because it teaches how to give: as an offering made to God, *in* the Eucharistic celebration and *for* all the missions of the world.' (*Redemptoris Missio* 81)

The celebration of Mission Month this year has a very special meaning as we come to the end of the Year of Faith. 'Faith is a gift that is given to us to be shared. It is a talent received so that it may bear fruit. It is a light that must never be hidden. It is the most important gift that has been given to us in our lives and which we cannot keep to ourselves.' (Pope Benedict XVI)

Each Mission Sunday we celebrate that we are growing in faith with the younger Churches throughout the world as we offer them our prayers and material support. Our entire Mission Sunday collection is made available to the Universal Solidarity Fund to be distributed to as many as 1,100 young Churches, and to help train novices and seminarians.

World Missions, Ireland – the work of the Pontifical Mission Societies, is the vehicle of this communion, bringing the prayers, solidarity and financial help of the Church in Ireland to Christian communities in other parts of the world, especially those in greatest need.

The theme *Growing in Faith* has a particular resonance this year for the Pontifical Society for Missionary Children as it celebrates its 170th anniversary. Ten years after Bishop Charles de Forbin-Janson founded the society in France in 1843, it had come to Ireland. The Society holds its National Day of Prayer on the second Friday of October. This Society promotes the unique concept of Children helping Children, by challenging children to share with and pray for children in poorer countries.

Mission Alive (Irish Missionary Union) also has a programme arranged for parish groups and secondary schools for Mission Month.

'I thank the Pontifical Mission Societies, instruments for cooperation in the universal mission of the Church across the world,' wrote Pope Benedict XVI for Mission Sunday 2012. 'Through their action, the proclamation of the Gospel not only bears witness to Christ but also becomes an intervention on behalf of one's neighbour, justice for the poorest, the possibility of education in the most remote villages, medical aid in isolated places, emancipation from poverty, the rehabilitation of the marginalised, support for the development of peoples, overcoming ethnic divisions, and respect for life in all its stages.'

www.wmi.ie

September 2013 Psalter Week 2

29 Sunday **TWENTY-SIXTH SUNDAY IN ORDINARY TIME**
Green ✠ HOURS Proper. Te Deum. Psalter Week 2
MASS Proper. Gloria. Creed. Preface: Sundays I–VIII
No Masses for the dead, except funeral Masses, are permitted today (see Lit. Note 7)
Ss Michael, Gabriel and Raphael, archangels are not celebrated this year.

---

30 Monday	**26th Week in Ordinary Time**
	St Jerome, priest and doctor of the Church Memorial
White	HOURS of the memorial. Psalter Week 2
	MASS of the memorial. Preface: Common or of the Saint

OCTOBER 2013

1 Tuesday **26th Week in Ordinary Time**
St Thérèse of the Child Jesus, virgin and doctor of the Church Memorial
White HOURS of the memorial. Psalter Week 2
MASS of the memorial. Preface: Common or of the Saint

---

2 Wednesday **26th Week in Ordinary Time**
The Guardian Angels Memorial
White HOURS Proper of the memorial. Psalter Week 2 at Day Hour
MASS of the memorial. Preface: Angels

---

3 Thursday **26th Week in Ordinary Time**
Green HOURS Psalter Week 2. MASS of choice
White Optional memorial of **Bl. Columba Marmion, priest**

---

4 Friday **26th Week in Ordinary Time**
St Francis of Assisi Memorial
White HOURS of the memorial. Psalter Week 2
MASS of the memorial. Preface: Common or of the Saint

---

5 Saturday **26th Week in Ordinary Time**
Green HOURS Psalter Week 2. MASS of choice
White/Green Saturday Mass of the **Blessed Virgin Mary**

September 2013 READINGS Sunday Cycle C Weekday Cycle 1

TWENTY-SIXTH WEEK IN ORDINARY TIME

29 Sunday **Am 6:1, 4-7. Ps 145:6-10. 1 Tm 6:11-16. Lk 16:19-31.** *Lect* I:914

The gap between the haves and the have-nots is condemned by Amos. Wealth and pleasure sought without reference to any responsibilities merits condemnation in this life and in the life to come.

30 Monday **Zec 8:1-8. Ps 101:16-21, 29, 22-23. Lk 9:46-50.** *Lect* II:337

The hope of the messianic age supports the people. But they cannot postpone until then a correct way of living. They must live now by the covenant.

St Jerome, 340–420, translated the Bible into Latin, known as the Vulgate, and wrote commentaries on scripture. Patron of librarians.

Raphoe Tomorrow is the anniversary of the episcopal ordination of Most Rev. Philip Boyce, OCD, 1 October 1995.

OCTOBER 2013

1 Tuesday **Zec 8:20-23. Ps 86. Lk 9:51-56.** *Lect* II:339

James and John want revenge with fire and brimstone, but Jesus has another way.

Thérèse of Lisieux. Marie François Thérèse Martin died at the Carmel in Lisieux on 30 September 1897. She was declared a Doctor of the Church by Pope John Paul II in 1997. Patron of missions, florists, aviators, and France.

Killaloe Tomorrow is the anniversary of the episcopal ordination of Most Rev. William Walsh, 2 October 1994.

2 Wednesday **Ex 23:20-23. Ps 90:1-6, 10-11. Mt 18:1-5, 10.** *Lect* II:1212

The Guardian Angels Catholic tradition has recognised that not only individual people have guardian angels but also homes, cities, and states.

3 Thursday **Neh 8:1-12. Ps 18:8-11. Lk 10:1-12.** *Lect* II:343

The assembled people are in tears as they renew their covenant with God. 'Whenever the Church, gathered by the Holy Spirit for liturgical celebration, announces and proclaims the word of God, it has the experience of being a new people in whom the covenant made in the past is fulfilled' (Lectionary, 7).

Bl. Columba Marmion see *October notes*.

4 Friday **Bar 1:15-22. Ps 78:1-5, 8-9. Lk 10:13-16.** *Lect* 346

Israel in exile is punished because of her sins in abandoning the Law given to Moses. This psalm of penitence is her confession of guilt.

5 Saturday **Bar 4:5-12, 27-29. Ps 68:33-37. Lk 10:17-24.** *Lect* II:348

'Jesus confesses the Father, acknowledges and blesses him because he has hidden the mysteries of the Kingdom from those who think themselves learned and revealed them to infants, the poor of the Beatitudes' (*CCC*, 2603).

Next Sunday's readings: Hab 1:2-3, 2:2-4. Ps 94:1-2, 6-9. 2 Tm 1:6-8, 13-14. Lk 17:5-10. *Lect* I:917

October 2013 Psalter Week 3

6 Sunday **TWENTY-SEVENTH SUNDAY IN ORDINARY TIME**
Day for Life
Green ✠ HOURS Proper. Te Deum. Psalter Week 3
MASS Proper. Gloria. Creed. Preface: Sundays I–VIII
No Masses for the dead, except funeral Masses, are permitted today (see Lit. Note 7)
St Bruno, priest is not celebrated this year.

---

7 Monday **27th Week in Ordinary Time**
 Our Lady of the Rosary Memorial
White HOURS of the memorial. Psalter Week 3 at Day Hour
 MASS of the memorial. Preface: Blessed Virgin Mary

---

8 Tuesday **27th Week in Ordinary Time**
Green HOURS Psalter Week 3. MASS of choice
Ossory **Dedication of the Cathedral** (see *Lit. Note 11*)

---

9 Wednesday **27th Week in Ordinary Time**
Green HOURS Psalter Week 3. MASS of choice
White Optional memorial of **Bl. John Henry Newman, priest**
Red Optional memorial of **Ss Denis, bishop, and Companions, martyrs**
White Optional memorial of **St John Leonardi, priest**

---

10 Thursday **27th Week in Ordinary Time**
Green HOURS Psalter Week 3. MASS of choice

---

11 Friday **27th Week in Ordinary Time**
Green HOURS Psalter Week 3. MASS of choice
White Optional memorial of **St Canice, abbot**
Kilkenny City **St Canice, abbot** Feast

---

12 Saturday **27th Week in Ordinary Time**
Green HOURS Psalter Week 3. MASS of choice
White/Green Saturday Mass of the **Blessed Virgin Mary**

October 2013 READINGS Sunday Cycle C Weekday Cycle 1

TWENTY-SEVENTH WEEK IN ORDINARY TIME

6 Sunday **Hab 1:2-3, 2:2-4. Ps 94:1-2, 6-9. 2 Tm 1:6-8, 13-14. Lk 17:5-10.** *Lect* I:917

The prophet Habakkuk is surrounded by a people of violence, strife and greed. How is he to live in such a world? He is counselled to have patient faith, to remain faithful despite the apparent hopelessness. Christ's disciples should realise the gift of faith is given to them for perseverance.

7 Monday **Acts 1:12-14. Ps Lk 1:46-55. Lk 1:26-38.** *Lect* II:1217

Our Lady of the Rosary. 'Today's celebration urges all to meditate on the mysteries of Christ, following the example of the Blessed Virgin Mary who was in a special manner associated with the incarnation, passion and glorious resurrection of the Son of God' (*Divine Office*).

8 Tuesday **Jon 3:1-10. Ps 129:1-4, 7-8. Lk 10:38-42.** *Lect* II:353

Jonah preached repentance. The people of Nineveh renounced their evil behaviour, and God relented.

9 Wednesday **Jon 4:1-11. Ps 85:3-6, 9-10. Lk 11:1-4.** *Lect* II:355

Jonah in his ill-humour is told by God to have a sense of proportion. The lives of the people of Nineveh are of more account than the dead plant. We must forgive others.

St Denis and his companions, **Rusticus** and **Eleutherius** were beheaded and thrown into the Seine in 258 and later buried at Montmartre. Their finest tribute is the abbey church of Saint-Denis where the kings of France are buried. Denis, the first Bishop of Paris, is one of the patrons of France.

St John Leonardi, 1541–1609, supported the reforms of Trent, published a Catechism and helped to found the Propagation of the Faith in Rome.

Bl. John Henry Newman see *October notes*.

10 Thursday **Mal 3:13-20. Ps 1. Lk 11:5-13.** *Lect* II:357

We are asked to make a choice of God's way or the way of sinners. The choice is ours but God's judgement awaits us. The way of the wicked leads to doom, 'but for you who fear, the sun of righteousness will shine out with healing in its rays'.

11 Friday **Jl 1:13-15, 2:1-2. Ps 9:2-3, 6, 16, 8-9. Lk 11:15-26.** *Lect* II:359

God will judge with justice. That judgement, because it is so searching, is to be feared. The work of the devil is to create a false security in our lives.

St Canice see *October notes*.

12 Saturday **Jl 4:12-21. Ps 96:1-2, 5-6, 11-12. Lk 11:27-28.** *Lect* II:362

The word of God goes forth and does not return empty. It calls for repentance; for judgement is near. Happy are those who hear the word of God and keep it.

Next Sunday's readings: 2 Kg 5:14-17. Ps 97:1-4. 2 Tm 2:8-13. Lk 17:11-19. *Lect* I:919

October 2013 Psalter Week 4

13 Sunday **TWENTY-EIGHTH SUNDAY IN ORDINARY TIME**
Green ✠ HOURS Proper. Te Deum. Psalter Week 4
MASS Proper. Gloria. Creed. Preface: Sundays I–VIII
No Masses for the dead, except funeral Masses, are permitted today (see Lit. Note 7)

---

14 Monday **28th Week in Ordinary Time**
Green HOURS Psalter Week 4. MASS of choice
Red Optional memorial of **St Callistus I, pope and martyr**
Down and
Connor **Dedication of the Cathedral** (see *Lit. Note 11*)

---

15 Tuesday **28th Week in Ordinary Time**
St Teresa of Avila, virgin and doctor of the Church
Memorial
White HOURS of the memorial. Psalter Week 4
MASS of the memorial. Preface: Common or of the Saint

---

16 Wednesday **28th Week in Ordinary Time**
Green HOURS Psalter Week 4. MASS of choice
White Optional memorial of **St Hedwig, religious**
White Optional memorial of **St Margaret Mary Alacoque, virgin**
White Optional memorial of **St Gall, abbot and missionary**

---

17 Thursday **28th Week in Ordinary Time**
St Ignatius of Antioch, bishop and martyr Memorial
Red HOURS of the memorial. Psalter Week 4
MASS of the memorial. Preface: Common or of the Saint

---

18 Friday ST LUKE, EVANGELIST Feast
Red HOURS proper. Te Deum. Psalter Week 4 at Day Hour
MASS Proper. Gloria. Preface: Apostles II
No Masses for the dead, except funeral Masses, are permitted today (see Lit. Note 7)

---

19 Saturday **28th Week in Ordinary Time**
Green HOURS Psalter Week 4. MASS of choice
Red Optional memorial of **Ss John de Brébeuf, Isaac Jogues,**
priests, and Companions, martyrs
White Optional memorial of **St Paul of the Cross, priest**
White/Green Saturday Mass of the **Blessed Virgin Mary**

October 2013 READINGS Sunday Cycle C Weekday Cycle 1
TWENTY-EIGHTH WEEK IN ORDINARY TIME
13 Sunday **2 Kg 5:14-17. Ps 97:1-4. 2 Tm 2:8-13. Lk 17:11-19.** *Lect* I:919

In the readings, cleansing from leprosy is seen as a sign of Messianic salvation and gratitude in response to the gifts of faith and salvation is advocated.

14 Monday **Rm 1:1-7. Ps 97:1-4. Lk 11:29-32.** *Lect* II:364
The Letter to the Romans gives a synthesis of Paul's theology, but not it all. The main themes headlined at the beginning are: God's free choice of his people, the relationship of faith to justification, salvation through Christ's death and resurrection, and the new covenant as fulfilment of the old.
St Callistus I, after a life of slavery and imprisonment for criminal offences, was freed and became a deacon in charge of catacombs that bear his name. He became Pope in 217, opposed by Hippolytus. Died at the hands of a mob in 222.

15 Tuesday **Rm 1:16-25. Ps 18:2-5. Lk 11:37-41.** *Lect* II:366
Faith relies on God's promises, his faithfulness to them and on his power to carry them out. The gospel reveals the power of God to make people righteous.
St Teresa of Avila, 1515–82, established Carmelite convents under a reformed rule, and wrote much on prayer and the spiritual life. Patron of lace-makers and headache sufferers.

16 Wednesday Rm 2:1-11. Ps 61:2-3, 6-7, 9. Lk 11:42-46. *Lect* II:368
Jews in possessing the Law are not immune from God's wrath. God shows no partiality and will condemn Jew and Gentile alike. But there will be glory, honour, and peace for all who do good.
St Gall see *October notes*.
St Hedwig, 1174–1243, wife of the Duke of Silesia, mother of seven children, some of whom caused her trouble, devoted herself to charitable works.
St Margaret Mary, 1647–90, visionary and ascetic, revived devotion to the Sacred Heart of Jesus, and was exemplary in her patience and trust.

17 Thursday **Rm 3:21-30. Ps 129:1-6. Lk 11:47-54.** *Lect* II:370
Paul is clear that grace means a gift that is given absolutely freely. God takes the initiative in making us agreeable to him, only then can there be the human response.
St Ignatius, bishop of Antioch, died a martyr at Rome c.107. He urged Christians to unity in and through the Eucharist and around their local bishop.

18 Friday **2 Tm 4:10-17. Ps 144:10-13, 17-18. Lk 10:1-9.** *Lect* II:1233
St Luke was a physician from a Gentile Christian milieu. He was with St Paul on his second missionary journey and during his imprisonment in Rome. After Paul's death he is reputed to have worked in Greece. Patron of butchers, book-binders, doctors and surgeons, artists, glassworkers.

19 Saturday **Rm 4:13, 16-18. Ps 104:6-9, 42-43. Lk 12:8-12.** *Lect* II:374
Faith is the basic requirement for salvation for all, not just for the descendants of Abraham. The promises were offered in response to faith, not as a reward for keeping the Law. Their fulfilment in Christ is accessible through faith.
St Paul of the Cross, 1694–1775, founded the Passionists in Rome, preaching on the Passion of Christ and tending the sick, the dying and the lapsed.
Ss John de Brébeuf and Isaac Jogues, with their six Jesuit companions, were slain by Huron and Iroquois Indians in 1647/8.
Next Sunday's readings: Ex 17:8-13. Ps 120. 2 Tm 3:14-4:2. Lk 18:1-8. *Lect* I:922

October 2013 Psalter Week 1

20 Sunday **TWENTY-NINTH SUNDAY IN ORDINARY TIME**
World Mission Sunday: Growing in Faith
Green ✠ HOURS Proper. Te Deum. Psalter Week 1
MASS Proper. Gloria. Creed. Preface: Sundays I–VIII
No Masses for the dead, except funeral Masses, are permitted today (see Lit. Note 7)

---

21 Monday **29th Week in Ordinary Time**
Green HOURS Psalter Week 1. MASS of choice

---

22 Tuesday **29th Week in Ordinary Time**
Green HOURS Psalter Week 1. MASS of choice

---

23 Wednesday 29th Week in Ordinary Time
Green HOURS Psalter Week 1. MASS of choice
White Optional memorial of **St John of Capistrano, priest**

---

24 Thursday **29th Week in Ordinary Time**
Green HOURS Psalter Week 1. MASS of choice
White Optional memorial of **St Anthony Mary Claret, bishop**

---

25 Friday **29th Week in Ordinary Time**
Green HOURS Psalter Week 1. MASS of choice
Cork and Ross **Bl. Thaddeus MacCarthy, bishop** Memorial
Cloyne **Bl. Thaddeus MacCarthy, bishop** Memorial
Waterford and
Lismore **Dedication of the Cathedral** (see *Lit. Note 11*)

---

26 Saturday **29th Week in Ordinary Time**
Green HOURS Psalter Week 1. MASS of choice
White/Green Saturday Mass of the **Blessed Virgin Mary**

October 2013 READINGS Sunday Cycle C   Weekday Cycle 1
TWENTY-NINTH WEEK IN ORDINARY TIME

20 Sunday   **Ex 17:8-13. Ps 120. 2 Tm 3:14-4:2. Lk 18:1-8.** *Lect* I:922

World Mission Sunday: *Growing in Faith.* 'Faith is a gift that is given to us to be shared. It is a talent received so that it may bear fruit. It is a light that must never be hidden. It is the most important gift that has been given to us in our lives and which we cannot keep to ourselves.' (Pope Benedict XVI)

21 Monday   **Rm 4:20-25. Ps Lk 1:69-75. Lk 12:13-21.** *Lect* II:376
Abraham's faith in God's promise never wavered. It is a model for ours. We place our faith in the mighty saviour who would free us from our sins.

22 Tuesday   **Rm 5:12, 15, 17-21. Ps 39:7-10, 17. Lk 12:35-38.** *Lect* II:378
Jesus Christ restores life to those who have inherited death through another man. The power of grace is greater than the inclination to sin.

23 Wednesday Rm 6:12-18. Ps 123. Lk 12:39-48. *Lect* II:380
We are still subject to natural human inclinations that can lead to sin. But Christ has freed us from evil so as to restore us to God.
St John of Capistrano, 1386–1456, studied civil and canon law and joined the Franciscan Order. A faithful servant of four popes, he attended the Council of Florence, went to Jerusalem as apostolic emissary, and, in 1451, set out on a preaching tour through the German provinces and Poland. In a battle at Belgrade he contracted fever and died there. Patron saint of jurists and military chaplains.

24 Thursday   **Rm 6:19-23. Ps 1:1-4, 6. Lk 12:49-53.** *Lect* II:382
The sinner earns death as the wages of sin. The Christian has been given new life, has been sanctified, but has to live out this holiness in practice, and grow in sanctity.
St Anthony Mary Claret, 1807–70, founded the Claretians in Spain for missionary work. Archbishop of Santiago, Cuba, then returned as chaplain to the Queen of Spain, and built schools and museums, before being exiled with the monarchy.

25 Friday   **Rm 7:18-25. Ps 118:66, 68, 76-77, 93-94. Lk 12:54-59.** *Lect* II:384
The powerful force of sin is such that the Christian can be torn between what is known to be the right thing and the attraction of sin. Personal responsibility for evil and good still remain, but the Spirit can transform the body into the likeness of the Risen Christ in a new life of uprightness and holiness.
Bl. Thaddeus McCarthy see *October notes.*

26 Saturday   **Rm 8:1-11. Ps 23:1-6. Lk 13:1-9.** *Lect* II:386
The Christian is enabled to live for God by the vitalising power of the Holy Spirit. Through this power the follower of Christ will bring forth much fruit.

Next Sunday's readings: Eccles (Sir) 35:12-14, 16-19. Ps 32:2-3, 17-19, 23. 2 Tm 4:6-8, 16-18. Lk 18:9-14 *Lect* I:925.

NOTES FOR NOVEMBER 2013

THE POPE'S INTENTIONS

General – Priests experiencing difficulties: That priests experiencing difficulties may be comforted in their sufferings, sustained in their doubts and confirmed in their fidelity.

Mission – Churches of Latin America: That the Churches of Latin America may send missionaries to other Churches as a fruit of the continental mission.

THE IRISH CALENDAR IN NOVEMBER

3rd: St Malachy was born near Armagh in 1094. He introduced the Cistercians and the Canons Regular into Ireland. He died at Clairvaux, in 1148.

6th: All Saints of Ireland. 'In the communion of saints, many and varied spiritualities have been developed throughout the history of the Churches ... The different schools of Christian spirituality share in the living tradition of prayer and are essential guides for the faithful. In their rich diversity they are refractions of the one pure light of the Holy Spirit' (CCC, 2684).

7th: St Willibrord was born in Northumbria in 658. He entered the Benedictine order and was sent to study. After ordination he was sent with eleven companions to evangelise Frisia. He established a mission at Utrecht and in 695 was ordained archbishop of Utrecht by Pope Sergius I. He founded a monastery at Echternach in Luxembourg in 700, where he died in 739.

14th: St Laurence O'Toole became a monk and abbot of Glendalough. He was made Archbishop of Dublin in 1162. He returned to Ireland after the Third Lateran Council as papal legate in 1179. He died at Eu in Normandy seeking to make peace between Henry II and the Irish rulers in 1180.

23rd: St Columban (also known as Columbanus) was born around 543. He became a monk of Bangor and later principal teacher there. In 591, desiring to 'go on pilgrimage for Christ', he set out with twelve companions and came to Burgundy. He established monasteries at Annegray, Luxeuil and Fontaine according to the severe Irish rule. Later he founded Bregenz in Austria and his greatest foundation at Bobbio, near Genoa, where he died in 615. He is remembered as one of the greatest of the Irish missionary monks.

25th: St Colman was born around 530, probably in West Cork. A bard by profession, he is reputed to have been influenced by St Brendan to become a priest. His apostolate was to East Cork and his main foundation was at Cloyne.

27th: St Fergal (Virgil) lived first in France and then in Bavaria, where he founded the monastery of Chiemsee. He was appointed bishop of Salzburg around 754 and died in 784 leaving a reputation for learning and holiness.

2 November: ALL SOULS
Norms for Indulgences at the Commemoration of All Souls

1. From 12 o'clock noon on 1 November until midnight on 2 November, all who have confessed, received Holy Communion and prayed for the Pope's intentions

(one Our Father and Hail Mary, or any other prayer of one's choice) can gain one plenary indulgence by visiting a church or oratory, and there reciting one Our Father and the Apostle's Creed.
This indulgence is applicable only to the souls of the departed.
Confession may be made at any time within the week preceding or the week following 1 November.
Holy Communion may be received on any day from 1 November to 8 November.

2. The faithful who visit a cemetery and pray for the dead may gain a plenary indulgence applicable only to the Holy Souls on the usual conditions once per day from 1 to 8 November. The conditions mentioned above apply also for this.

FAITH IN THE RESURRECTION OF THE DEAD

Belief in the resurrection of the dead is an essential part of Christian revelation. It implies a particular understanding of the ineluctable mystery of death.

Death is the end of earthy life, but 'not of our existence' (St Ambrose), since the soul is immortal. 'Our lives are measured by time, in the course of which we change, grow old and, as with all living beings on earth, death seems like the normal end of life' (CCC 1007). Seen from the perspective of the faith, 'death is the end of man's earthly pilgrimage, of the time of grace and mercy which God offers him so as to work out his earthly life in keeping with the divine plan, and to decide his ultimate destiny' (CCC 1013).

In one light death can seem natural, in another it can be seen as 'the wages of sin' (Rm 6:23). Authentically interpreting the meaning of Scripture (cf. Jn 2:17; 3:3; 3:19; Wis 1:13; Rm 5:12; 6:23), the Church teaches that 'death entered the world on account of man's sin' (CCC 1008).

Jesus, the Son of God, 'born of a woman and subject to the law' (Gal 4:4) underwent death which is part of the human condition; despite his anguish in the face of death (Mk 14:33-34; Heb 5:7-8), 'he accepted it in an act of complete and free submission to his Father's will. The obedience of Jesus has transformed the curse of death into a blessing' (CCC 1009).

Death is the passage to the fullness of true life. The Church, subverting the logic of this world, calls the Christian's day of death his *dies natalis*, the day of his heavenly birth, where 'there will be no more death, and no more mourning or sadness [for] the world of the past has gone' (Rv 21:4). Death is the prolongation, in a new way, of life as the Liturgy says: 'For your faithful, O Lord, life has changed not ended; while our earthly dwelling is destroyed, a new and eternal dwelling is prepared for us in Heaven' (*Missal*, Preface).

The death of a Christian is an event of grace, having, as it does, a positive value and significance in Christ and through Christ. Scripture teaches that: 'Life to me, of course, life is Christ, but then death would bring me something more' (Phil 1:21); here is a saying you can rely on: if we have died with him, then we shall live with him' (2 Tm 2:11).

According to the faith of the Church, 'to die in Christ' begins at Baptism. In Baptism, the Lord's disciples sacramentally die in Christ so as to live a new life. If the disciples die in the grace of Christ, physical death seals that 'dying with Christ', and consummates it by incorporating them fully and definitively into Christ the Redeemer.

The Church's prayer of suffrage for the souls of the faithful departed implores eternal life not only for the disciples of Christ who have died in his peace, but for the dead whose faith is known to God (see *Eucharistic Prayer IV*).

– Congregation for Divine Worship and the Discipline of the Sacraments, *Directory on Popular Piety and the Liturgy, principles and guidelines*, 249–50

October 2013 Psalter Week 2

27 Sunday **THIRTIETH SUNDAY IN ORDINARY TIME**
Green ✠ HOURS Proper. Te Deum. Psalter Week 2
MASS Proper. Gloria. Creed. Preface: Sundays I–VIII
No Masses for the dead, except funeral Masses, are permitted today (see Lit. Note 7)
St Otteran, monk is not celebrated this year.
Waterford **St Otteran, monk** This year as Solemnity

---

28 Monday SS SIMON AND JUDE, APOSTLES Feast
Red HOURS Proper. Te Deum. Psalter Week 2 at Day Hour
MASS Proper. Gloria. Preface: Apostles I–II
No Masses for the dead, except funeral Masses, are permitted today (see Lit. Note 7)

---

29 Tuesday **30th Week in Ordinary Time**
Green HOURS Psalter Week 2. MASS of choice
White Optional memorial of **St Colman, bishop**
Kilmacduagh **St Colman, bishop** Feast

---

30 Wednesday 30th Week in Ordinary Time
Green HOURS Psalter Week 2. MASS of choice

---

31 Thursday **30th Week in Ordinary Time**
Green HOURS Psalter Week 2. MASS of choice
Cloyne **Bl. Dominic Collins, martyr**
FIRST EVENING PRAYER of **All Saints**

NOVEMBER 2013

1 Friday **ALL SAINTS** Solemnity
White ✠ HOURS Proper. Te Deum. Complementary Psalms at Day Hour
MASS Proper Gloria. Creed. Preface: Proper
EVENING PRAYER of All Saints
Night Prayer 2 of Sunday
No other celebrations, not even funeral Masses, are permitted today (see Lit. Note 7)
Achonry **Dedication of the Cathedral** (see *Lit. Note 11*)

---

2 Saturday **THE COMMEMORATION OF ALL THE FAITHFUL DEPARTED**
(All Souls Day)
Violet/Black HOURS from the Office for the Dead
MASS Proper for the Dead. Preface: Proper
FIRST EVENING PRAYER of **Sunday**
All priests may celebrate three Masses today, for only one of which may a stipend be taken. The other Masses have the intention for all the faithful departed and for the intentions of the Pope.
No other celebrations are permitted today. See November Notes on **Indulgences**.

October 2013 READINGS Sunday Cycle C Weekday Cycle 1

THIRTIETH WEEK IN ORDINARY TIME

27 Sunday   Eccles (Sir) 35:12-14, 16-19. Ps 32:2-3, 17-19, 23. 2 Tm 4:6-8, 16-18. Lk 18:9-14 *Lect* I:925.
The Pharisee came before God trusting in his own virtue which was genuine enough. The tax-collector knew that he was a sinner and threw himself on God's mercy. The Pharisee sang his own praises, the tax-collector sang the mercies of the Lord.
St Otteran see *October notes*.

28 Monday   Eph 2:19-22. Ps 18:2-5. Lk 6:12-19. *Lect* II:1242
Ss Simon and Jude. The teaching of the apostles is the living gospel for all to hear. Their authority comes from their fidelity to Christ and his message. St Jude is patron saint of hopeless causes.

29 Tuesday   Rm 8:18-25. Ps 125. Lk 13:18-21. *Lect* II: 390
'At the very heart of Christianity is the conviction that suffering and glory are intimately related. There can be no glory without suffering. The reason for this is sin, which introduced distortion and alienation and corruption into the world. These cannot be removed without the pain of a correcting reversal of the world's direction. Paul speaks of this pain and suffering here, but he wants to begin on a positive note by stressing the coming glory as of surpassing value' (E.H. Maly, N.T. Message no. 9, Veritas).
St Colman see *October notes*.

30 Wednesday Rm 8:26-30. Ps 12:4-6. Lk 13:22-30. *Lect* II:392
The final destiny of Christians who put their faith in Christ is eternal glory. But it is the Spirit who gives the grace to each to make progress. God's purpose and plan are behind all that happens to Christians.

31 Thursday   Rm 8:31-39. Ps 108:21-22, 26-27, 30-31. Lk 13:31-35. *Lect* II:394
Paul expresses his total confidence in the presence and power of the Lord. Nothing can come between him and the love of Christ.
Bl. Dominic Collins see *October notes*.

NOVEMBER 2013

1 Friday   Apoc 7:2-4, 9-14. Ps 23:1-6. 1 Jn 3:1-3. Mt 5:1-12. *Lect* I:999 or II:1244
All Saints. 'The ultimate object of veneration of the Saints is the glory of God and the sanctification of man by conforming one's life fully to the divine will and by imitating the virtue of those who were pre-eminent disciples of the Lord. Catechesis and other forms of doctrinal instruction should therefore make known to the faithful that our relationship with the Saints must be seen in the light of the faith and should not obscure the *cultus latriae* due to God the Father through Christ in the Holy Spirit, but intensify it' (*Directory on Popular Piety and the Liturgy*, 212).

2 Saturday   Is 25:6-9. Ps 26:1, 4, 7-9, 13-14. Rm 5:5-11. Lk 7:11-17. *Lect* I:1002 or Readings are chosen from Masses for the Dead. *Lect* III:849–90
All Souls. 'Indeed, the Church in its pilgrim members, from the very earliest days of the Christian religion, has honoured with great respect the memory of the dead; and "because it is a holy and a wholesome thought to pray for the dead that they may be loosed from their sins" (2 *Mac* 12, 46) she offers her suffrages for them. These consist, primarily, in the celebration of the holy sacrifice of the Eucharist, and in other pious exercises, such as prayers for the dead, alms deeds, works of mercy, and the application of indulgences to the souls of the faithful departed' (*Directory on Popular Piety and the Liturgy*, 251).

Next Sunday's readings: Wis 11:22-12:2. Ps 144:1-2, 8-11, 13-14. 2 Th 1:11-2:2. Lk 19:1-10. *Lect* I:928

November 2013 Psalter Week 3

3 Sunday **THIRTY-FIRST SUNDAY IN ORDINARY TIME**
Green ✠ HOURS Proper. Te Deum. Psalter Week 3
MASS Proper. Gloria. Creed. Preface: Sundays I–VIII
No Masses for the dead, except funeral Masses, are permitted today (see Lit. Note 7)
St Malachy, bishop is not celebrated this year.
Armagh **St Malachy, bishop** This year as Solemnity

---

4 Monday **31st Week in Ordinary Time**
St Charles Borromeo, bishop Memorial
White HOURS of the memorial. Psalter Week 3
MASS of the memorial. Preface: Common or of the Saint

---

5 Tuesday **31st Week in Ordinary Time**
Green HOURS Psalter Week 3. MASS of choice

---

6 Wednesday ALL THE SAINTS OF IRELAND Feast
White HOURS Proper (Divine Office, p. 460*)
Te Deum. Psalter Week 3 at Day Hour
MASS Proper. Gloria. Preface: Proper
No Masses for the dead, except funeral Masses, are permitted today (see Lit. Note 7)

---

7 Thursday **31st Week in Ordinary Time**
Green HOURS Psalter Week 3. MASS of choice
White Optional memorial of **St Willibrord, bishop and missionary**

---

8 Friday **31st Week in Ordinary Time**
Green HOURS Psalter Week 3. MASS of choice

---

9 Saturday THE DEDICATION OF THE LATERAN BASILICA Feast
White HOURS Proper. Te Deum. Psalter Week 3 at Day Hour
MASS Proper. Gloria. Preface: Proper
No Masses for the dead, except funeral Masses, are permitted today (see Lit. Note 7)

November 2013   READINGS Sunday Cycle C   Weekday Cycle 1

THIRTY-FIRST WEEK IN ORDINARY TIME

3 Sunday   **Wis 11:22-12:2. Ps 144:1-2, 8-11, 13-14. 2 Th 1:11-2:2. Lk 19:1-10.** *Lect* I:928

The story of Zacchaeus shows Jesus bringing to life the understanding that God is merciful to all, and spares all things because all things are his. Jesus teaches by his treatment of Zacchaeus that God's compassion is wider than ours, his judgements more merciful than ours can be.
St Malachy see *November notes.*

4 Monday   **Rm 11:19-36. Ps 68:30-31, 33-34, 36-37. Lk 14:12-14.** *Lect* II:400

Who could ever know the mind of the Lord? We are asked to look at the depths of God's mercy, his wisdom and knowledge. Our generosity should emulate that of God.
St Charles Borromeo, 1538–84, Cardinal Archbishop of Milan at the age of twenty-one, worked for reform in his diocese, drafting the Catechism of the Council of Trent. Patron saint of catechists and seminarians.

5 Tuesday   **Rm 12:5-16. Ps 130. Lk 14:15-24.** *Lect* II:402

Mutual love binds all Christians together as one body. Each member works for the good of all.

6 Wednesday   **Heb 11:2, 12:1-4, 15, 13:1 *or* Eccles (Sir) 44:1-15. Ps 125. Lk 6:20-26.** National Proper
All the Saints of Ireland see *November notes.*

7 Thursday   **Rm 14:7-12. Ps 26:1, 4, 13-14. Lk 15:1-10.** *Lect* II:406

We live and die as the Lord's servants and his property: we are the Lord's. He does not wish the death of the sinner, but goes out to seek the lost. There is always rejoicing over the repentant sinner.
St Willibrord see *November notes.*

8 Friday   **Rm 15:14-21. Ps 97:1-4. Lk 16:1-8.** *Lect* II:408

Paul speaks of his vocation as apostle to the Gentiles. His first words were always to the Jews, but he was rejected by them. Luke's Gospel addresses the pressing problem of how a Christian is to deal with money.
Galway Tomorrow is the anniversary of the episcopal ordination of Most Rev. Eamonn Casey, 9 November 1969

9 Saturday   **Ez 47:1-2, 8-9, 12 *or* 1 Cor 3:9-11, 16-17. Ps 45:2-3, 5-6, 8-9. Jn 2:13-22.** *Lect* I:1006 (or II:1250)

The **Church of St John on the Lateran** in Rome is 'Mother and Head of all the churches of the City and the World'. It is the cathedral church of the Bishop of Rome, and was called 'St John' after the two monasteries once attached, dedicated to St John the Divine and St John the Baptist. It is however dedicated to the Most Holy Saviour.

Next Sunday's readings: 2 Mac 7:1-2, 9-14. Ps 16:1, 5-6, 8, 15. 2 Th 2:16-3:5. Lk 20:27-38 (shorter form 20:27, 34-38)**.** *Lect* I:930

November 2013   Psalter Week 4

10 Sunday   **THIRTY-SECOND SUNDAY IN ORDINARY TIME**
Green ✠   HOURS Proper. Te Deum. Psalter Week 4
                    MASS Proper. Gloria. Creed. Preface: Sundays I–VIII
No Masses for the dead, except funeral Masses, are permitted today (see Lit. Note 7)
St Leo the Great, pope and doctor of the Church is not celebrated this year.

---

11 Monday   **32nd Week in Ordinary Time**
                    St Martin of Tours, bishop   Memorial
White   HOURS of the memorial. Psalter Week 4 at Day Hour
                    MASS of the memorial. Preface: Common or of the Saint
Restorative Justice Week begins today.

---

12 Tuesday   **32nd Week in Ordinary Time**
                    St Josaphat, bishop and martyr   Memorial
Red   HOURS of the memorial. Psalter Week 4
                    MASS of the memorial. Preface: Common or of the Saint

---

13 Wednesday **32nd Week in Ordinary Time**
Green   HOURS Psalter Week 4. MASS of choice

---

14 Thursday   **32nd Week in Ordinary Time**
Green   HOURS Psalter Week 4. MASS of choice
White   Optional memorial of **St Laurence O'Toole, bishop**
Dublin   **St Laurence O'Toole, bishop**   Feast

---

15 Friday   **32nd Week in Ordinary Time**
Green   HOURS Psalter Week 4. MASS of choice
White   Optional memorial of **St Albert the Great, bishop and doctor of the Church**

---

16 Saturday   **32nd Week in Ordinary Time**
Green   HOURS Psalter Week 4. MASS of choice
White   Optional memorial of **St Margaret of Scotland**
White   Optional memorial of **St Gertrude, virgin**
White/Green   Saturday Mass of the **Blessed Virgin Mary**

November 2013   READINGS Sunday Cycle C   Weekday Cycle 1

THIRTY-SECOND WEEK IN ORDINARY TIME

10 Sunday   2 Mac 7:1-2, 9-14. Ps 16:1, 5-6, 8, 15. 2 Th 2:16-3:5. Lk 20:27-38 (shorter form 20:27, 34-38). *Lect* I:930

These final Sundays of the year highlight the resurrection of the dead and the life of the world to come.

11 Monday   Wis 1:1-7. Ps 138:1-10. Lk 17:1-6. *Lect* II:412

St Martin of Tours, 335–97, Bishop of Tours, apostle of rural Gaul, founder of monasteries. Patron of France, soldiers, beggars and inn-keepers.

12 Tuesday   Wis 2:23-3:9. Ps 33:2-3, 16-19. Lk 17:7-10. *Lect* II:414

'God did not bring death, and he does not delight in the death of the living … It was through the devil's envy that death entered the world' (*CCC*, 413).

St Josaphat, 1580–1623, Bishop of Polotz, worked for the reunion of Ukranian Catholics; his murder by those who opposed it brought about many conversions.

13 Wednesday Wis 6:1-11. Ps 81:3-4, 6-7. Lk 17:11-19. *Lect* II:416

Rulers who acquire true wisdom will show concern for the poor and weak, the oppressed and alienated.

14 Thursday   Wis 7:22-8:1. Ps 118:89-91, 130, 135, 175. Lk 17:20-25. *Lect* II:418

In praise of Wisdom, its nature and origin. This Wisdom, close to God, with his power and creating with him, anticipates the theology of the Spirit of New Testament times. A perfect number of twenty-one attributes are given to describe Wisdom.

St Laurence O'Toole see *November notes*.

15 Friday   Wis 13:1-9. Ps 18:2-5. Lk 17:26-37. *Lect* II:420

Idolatry in whatever form is to be condemned. The study of nature should lead us to acknowledge the transcendent God, universal Creator. The beauty of the world is a work of art reflecting the beauty of its creator.

St Albert the Great, 1206–80, Dominican theologian who taught in Cologne, was called the 'Universal Teacher' for the vast range of his interests. Patron of scientists.

16 Saturday   Wis 18:14-16, 19:6-9. Ps 104:2-3, 36-37, 42-43. Lk 18:1-8. *Lect* II:422

On the night of the Exodus the Word of God is seen as the agent of God's power in the deaths of the first-born and the journey across the Red Sea. At his Second Coming the Word will again stand in judgement.

St Margaret, 1045–93, wife of Malcolm III, King of Scotland, helped by her example and influence the work of reform in the Church.

St Gertrude, 1256–1302, a Benedictine nun, from the age of five she cultivated devotion to the Sacred Heart and advocated frequent Communion.

Next Sunday's readings: Mal 3:19-20. Ps 95:5-9. 2 Th 3:7-12. Lk 21:5-19. *Lect* I:934

November 2013

Psalter Week 1

17 Sunday **THIRTY-THIRD SUNDAY IN ORDINARY TIME**
Green ✠ HOURS Proper. Te Deum. Psalter Week 1
MASS Proper. Gloria. Creed. Preface: Sundays I–VIII
No Masses for the dead, except funeral Masses, are permitted today (see Lit. Note 7)
St Elizabeth of Hungary, religious is not celebrated this year.

---

18 Monday **33rd Week in Ordinary Time**
Green HOURS Psalter Week 1. MASS of choice
White Optional memorial of **The Dedication of the Basilicas of Ss Peter and Paul**
Killaloe **Dedication of the Cathedral** (see *Lit. Note 11*)

---

19 Tuesday **33rd Week in Ordinary Time**
Green HOURS Psalter Week 1. MASS of choice

---

20 Wednesday **33rd Week in Ordinary Time**
Green HOURS Psalter Week 1. MASS of choice

---

21 Thursday **33rd Week in Ordinary Time**
 The Presentation of the Blessed Virgin Mary Memorial
White HOURS of the memorial. Psalter Week 1
MASS of the memorial. Preface: Blessed Virgin Mary

---

22 Friday **33rd Week in Ordinary Time**
 St Cecilia, virgin and martyr Memorial
Red HOURS of the memorial. Psalter Week 1
MASS of the memorial. Preface: Common or of the Saint

---

23 Saturday **33rd Week in Ordinary Time**
 St Columban, abbot and missionary Memorial
White HOURS of the memorial. Psalter Week 1
MASS of the memorial. Preface: Common or of the Saint

November 2013   READINGS Sunday Cycle C   Weekday Cycle 1

THIRTY-THIRD WEEK IN ORDINARY TIME

17 Sunday   Mal 3:19-20. Ps 95:5-9. 2 Th 3:7-12. Lk 21:5-19. Lect I:934

Christians are called to patience and endurance in all of life's circumstances. We have no reason to expect that things will get better and better, or that the building up of the Kingdom of God will proceed without opposition. All we are assured of is that God will work his purposes out and that good will triumph.

18 Monday   1 Mac 1:10-15, 41-43, 54-57, 62-64. Ps 118:53, 61, 134, 150, 155, 158. Lk 18:35-43. Lect II:425

Antiochus Epiphanes began a forcible repression of Judaism. He imposed gentile practices on the Jews who before this had the Mosaic Law as their civil Law. This had the result of producing resistance from those who remained faithful to the Law.
Dedication of the Basilicas of Ss Peter and Paul: Acts 28:11-16, 30-31. Ps 97:1-6. Mt 14:22-33. Lect II:1269

19 Tuesday   2 Mac 6:18-31. Ps 3:2-7. Lk 19:1-10. Lect II:427

Eleazar spurned the unlawful sacrifice and remained faithful to the Law. His witness through death showed the importance of that obedience. His conscience did not allow him to cooperate in what might have been a scandal to the weak.

20 Wednesday 2 Mac 7:1, 20-31. Ps 16:1, 5-6, 8, 15. Lk 19:11-28. Lect II:429

A mother and her seven sons are ordered by the king to disobey the law.

21 Thursday   Zec 2:14-17. Ps Lk 1:46-55. Mt 12:46-50. Lect II:1271

The feast of the **Presentation of the Blessed Virgin Mary** originated in the East and was included on the General Calendar in the sixteenth century. It celebrates Mary in her grace-filled life, wholly given over to the Holy Spirit.

22 Friday   1 Mac 4:36-37, 52-59. Ps 1 Chr 29:10-12. Lk 19:45-48. Lect II:435

Judas proposed to cleanse and dedicate the Temple sanctuary. The annual Jewish festival of lights called Hanukkah is the commemoration of this rededication and is celebrated in December.
St Cecilia, third-century Roman martyr. Patron of music and musicians.

23 Saturday   1 Mac 6:1-13. Ps 9:2-4, 6, 16, 19. Lk 20:27-40. Lect II:437

The death of Antiochus Epiphanes is seen as a punishment for his pillaging of the Temple of God in Jerusalem.
St Columban see November notes.

Next Sunday's readings: 2 Sm 5:1-3. Ps 121:1-5. Col 1:12-20. Lk 23:35-43. Lect I:936

November 2013 Psalter Week 2

24 Sunday — **OUR LORD JESUS CHRIST, KING OF THE UNIVERSE**
Solemnity
White ✠   HOURS Proper. Te Deum. Psalter 1 at Day Hour
MASS Proper (*RM* p. 371). Gloria. Creed. Preface: Proper
No other celebrations, not even funeral Masses, are permitted today (see Lit. Note 7)
Ss Andrew Dũng-Lạc, priest, and Companions, martyrs are not celebrated this year.

---

25 Monday — **34th Week in Ordinary Time**
Green   HOURS Psalter Week 2. MASS of choice
Red   Optional memorial of **St Catherine of Alexandria, virgin and martyr**
White   Optional memorial of **St Colman, bishop**
Cloyne   **St Colman, bishop**   Feast

---

26 Tuesday — **34th Week in Ordinary Time**
Green   HOURS Psalter Week 2. MASS of choice

---

27 Wednesday — **34th Week in Ordinary Time**
Green   HOURS Psalter Week 2. MASS of choice
White   Optional Memorial of **St Fergal, bishop and missionary**

---

28 Thursday — **34th Week in Ordinary Time**
Green   HOURS Psalter Week 2. MASS of choice

---

29 Friday — **34th Week in Ordinary Time**
Green   HOURS Psalter Week 2. MASS of choice
Kildare and Leighlin   **Dedication of the Cathedral** (see *Lit. Note 11*)

---

30 Saturday — ST ANDREW, APOSTLE   Feast
Red   HOURS Proper. Te Deum. Psalter Week 2 at Day Hour
MASS Proper. Gloria. Preface: Apostles I–II
FIRST EVENING PRAYER of **Advent**
No Masses for the dead, except funeral Masses, are permitted today (see Lit. Note 7)

November 2013 READINGS Sunday Cycle C   Weekday Cycle 1
LAST WEEK IN ORDINARY TIME

24 Sunday **2 Sm 5:1-3. Ps 121:1-5. Col 1:12-20. Lk 23:35-43.** Lect I:936
Christ, King of the Universe. We celebrate Christ as a crucified King. Through his cross he has won a holy nation and a royal people. In his kingdom he has reconciled all things to himself and through himself. He is the true shepherd-king who leads his people to peace.

25 Monday **Dn 1:1-6, 8-20. Ps Dn 3:52-56. Lk 21:1-4.** Lect II:439
In these days leading into Advent, the theme of the end times predominates in the liturgy. The Book of Daniel encourages faithfulness to the practice of the faith, despite the material allurements of the world and different forms of persecution.
St Catherine was martyred in 310 at Alexandria. Her body is venerated at the monastery on Mount Sinai.
St Colman see *November notes*.

26 Tuesday **Dn 2:31-45. Ps Dn 3:57-61. Lk 21:5-11.** Lect II:442
'The Last Judgement will come when Christ returns in glory. Only the Father knows the day and the hour, only he determines the moment of its coming. Then through his Son Jesus Christ he will pronounce the final word on all history. We shall know the ultimate meaning of the whole work of creation and of the entire economy of salvation, and understand the marvellous ways by which his Providence led everything towards its final end. The Last Judgement will reveal that God's justice triumphs over all the injustices committed by his creatures and that God's love is stronger than death' (*CCC*, 1040).

27 Wednesday Dn 5:1-6, 13-14, 16-17, 23-28. Ps Dn 3:62-67. Lk 21:12-19. Lect II:444
Belshazzar's Feast. 'You have been weighed in the balance and found wanting.' God punishes those who, instead of glorifying him in whose hands lies their fate, worship other gods and celebrate sacrilegious feasts.
St Fergal, see *November notes*.

28 Thursday **Dn 6:12-28. Ps Dn 3:68-74. Lk 21:20-28.** Lect II:447
Daniel is thrown into the lion pit but comes out unhurt. The king acknowledges the living God, who saves, sets free, and works signs and wonders. With great signs and wonders the Son of Man will come in great glory.

29 Friday **Dn 7:2-14. Ps Dn 3:75-81. Lk 21:29-33.** Lect II:449
Again the four kingdoms of Babylon, Persia, Greece and Rome are represented by four beasts. After them will come the messianic king whose kingdom will be everlasting.

30 Saturday **Rm 10:9-18. Ps 18:2-5. Mt 4:18-22.** Lect II:1279
St Andrew from Bethsaida was a disciple of St John the Baptist when he was called by Jesus. He in turn brought his brother Peter to Jesus. He is said to have suffered martyrdom on this date by crucifixion, but the tradition of an X-shaped cross is much later. Patron of Scotland, Russia and fishermen.

Next Sunday's readings: Is 2:1-5. Ps 121:1-2, 4-5, 6-9. Rm 13:11-14. Mt 24:37-44. Lect I:3

DECEMBER 2013

1 Sunday ✠	**FIRST SUNDAY OF ADVENT**	
	READINGS: Is 2:1-5. Ps 121:1-2, 4-5, 6-9. Rm 13:11-14. Mt 24:37-44.	
2 Monday	**1st Week of Advent**	
3 Tuesday	**1st Week of Advent**	
	St Francis Xavier, priest	Memorial
4 Wednesday	**1st Week of Advent**	
	St John Damascene, priest and doctor of the Church	Opt. Mem.
5 Thursday	**1st Week of Advent**	
6 Friday	**1st Week of Advent**	
	St Nicholas, bishop	Opt. Mem.
	Galway: St Nicholas, bishop	Feast
7 Saturday	**1st Week of Advent**	
	St Ambrose, bishop and doctor of the Church	Memorial
8 Sunday ✠	**SECOND SUNDAY OF ADVENT**	
	READINGS: Is 11:1-10. Ps 71:1-2, 7-8, 12-13, 17. Rm 15:4-9. Mt 3:1-12.	
9 Monday	**THE IMMACULATE CONCEPTION OF THE BLESSED VIRGIN MARY**	Solemnity
	READINGS: Gn 3:9-15, 20. Ps 97:1-4. Eph 1:3-6, 11-12. Lk 1:26-38.	
10 Tuesday	**2nd Week of Advent**	
11 Wednesday	**2nd Week of Advent**	
	St Damasus I, pope	Opt. Mem.
12 Thursday	**2nd Week of Advent**	
	Our Lady of Guadalupe	Opt. Mem.
	St Finnian, bishop	Opt. Mem.
	Meath: St Finnian, bishop	Feast
13 Friday	**2nd Week of Advent**	
	St Lucy, virgin and martyr	Memorial
14 Saturday	**2nd Week of Advent**	
	St John of the Cross, priest and doctor of the Church	Memorial
15 Sunday ✠	**THIRD SUNDAY OF ADVENT**	
	READINGS: Is 35:1-6, 10. Ps 145:6-10. Jas 5:7-10. Mt 11:2-11.	
16 Monday	**3rd Week of Advent**	
17 Tuesday	**3rd Week of Advent**	
18 Wednesday	**3rd Week of Advent**	
	Memorial may be made of **St Flannan, bishop**	Opt. Mem.
	Killaloe: St Flannan, bishop	Feast
19 Thursday	**3rd Week of Advent**	
20 Friday	**3rd Week of Advent**	
	Memorial may be made of **St Fachanan, bishop**	Opt. Mem.
	Kilfenora: St Fachanan, bishop	Feast
21 Saturday	**3rd Week of Advent**	
	Memorial may be made of **St Peter Canisius, priest and doctor of the Church**	Opt. Mem.

22 Sunday ✠	**FOURTH SUNDAY OF ADVENT**	

READINGS: Is 7:10-14. Ps 23:1-6. Rm 1:1-7. Mt 1:18-24.

23 Monday   **4th Week of Advent**
Memorial may be made of **St John of Kanty, priest**

24 Tuesday   **4th Week of Advent**

25 Wednesday ✠ **THE NATIVITY OF THE LORD (CHRISTMAS)**   Solemnity
READINGS: Vigil:Is 62:1-5. Ps 88:4-5, 16-17, 27, 29. Acts 13:16-17, 22-25. Mt 1:1-25 (shorter form 1:18-25).
Midnight Mass: Is 9:1-7. Ps 95:1-3, 11-13. Ti 2:11-14. Lk 2:1-14.
Dawn Mass: Is 62:11-12. Ps 96:1, 6, 11-12. Ti 3:4-7. Lk 2:15-20.
Mass during the Day: Is 52:7-10. Ps 97:1-6. Heb 1:1-6. Jn 1:1-18 (shorter form 1:1-5, 9-14).

26 Thursday   **St Stephen, first martyr**   Feast
27 Friday   **St John, apostle and evangelist**   Feast
St Fergal see *November notes*.
28 Saturday   **The Holy Innocents, martyrs**   Feast

29 Sunday ✠ **THE HOLY FAMILY OF JESUS, MARY AND JOSEPH**
   Feast
READINGS: Eccles (Sir) 3:2-6, 12-14. Ps 127:1-5. Col 3:12-21 (shorter form 3:12-17). Mt 2:13-15, 19-23.

30 Monday   **6th Day in the Octave of Christmas**
31 Tuesday   **7th Day in the Octave of Christmas**
Memorial may be made of **St Sylvester I, pope**   Opt. Mem.

Obituary List

July 2011 — Diocese

2	Fleming, Laurence (PE), Ballyadams, Co. Laois	Kildare & Leighlin
9	Kennedy, Conor (CSSp), Laval House, 121 Victoria Ave, Toronto, Ontario M4E352, Canada	
10	Fahey, Patrick (SSC), St Columban's, Dalgan Park, Navan, Co. Meath	
12	Madden, Noel (PP), Donnycarney	Dublin
13	Connors, Kevin (SSC), St Columban's, Dalgan Park, Navan, Co. Meath	
19	Creaton, Patrick (SSC), St Columban's, Dalgan Park, Navan, Co. Meath	
19	Cummins, Norbert (OCD), Aliva, Morehampton Road, Dublin 4	
19	Fogarty, James (AP), Clonoulty, Cashel, Co. Tipperary	Cashel & Emly
21	Drumgoole, Joseph (PP), Grange Park	Dublin
22	O'Brien, Michael (Canon), Buttevant, Co. Cork	Cloyne
23	O'Reilly, Andrew (OCarm), Carmelite Priory, Moate, Co. Westmeath	
25	Clune, Anthony (CM), St Paul's, Sybil Hill, Raheny, Dublin 5	
26	Ward, Eugene (Edward) (OCarm), Gort Muire, Ballinteer, Dublin 16	
31	Coughlan, Leonard (OFM Cap), Capuchin Friary, Church Street, Dublin 7	

August 2011

4	Byrne, Martin (OMI), Caixa Postal, 1177 Goiania-go, Brazil	
4	Foley, James C. (CSSp), Marian House, Kimmage Manor, Dublin 12	
8	Lehane, Aidan P. (CSSp), Templeogue College, Templeville Road, Dublin 6W	
9	McMyler, Francis (PE), Louisburgh, Co. Mayo	Tuam
10	Keogh, Henry, Oughterard, Co. Galway	Galway, Kilmacduagh & Kilfenora
12	Duffy, Austin (Mgr), 23 Glenroe Park, Dungiven, Co. Derry	Derry
19	Cullen, Joseph (OP), 47 Leeson Park, Dublin 6	
20	Ross, Cyril (OP), 47 Leeson Park, Dublin 6	
23	Quinn, Francis (OCD), The Abbey, Loughrea, Co. Galway	

August 2011 (continued)	**Diocese**

27	Keane, Michael (PE), Claremorris, Co. Mayo	Tuam
28	Lane, Thomas (CM), All Hallows College, Drumcondra, Dublin 9	
30	Rodgers, Manus, Silvermines, Co. Tipperary	Killaloe

September 2011

2	Hanahoe, Thomas (SSC), St Columban's, Dalgan Park, Navan, Co. Meath	
8	Colleran, Gabriel (PP), Templeogue	Dublin
10	Cribbin, John (OMI), Igreja Sao José, Rua Salustiano Silva 27, Magalhaes Bastos, Brazil	
11	Mannion, Thomas (Canon, PP), The Parochial House, Claremorris, Co. Mayo	Tuam
13	Delaney, John (OMI), House of Retreat, Tyrconnell Road, Inchicore, Dublin 8	
15	Connell, Roy (Former Chaplain Beaumont Hospital)	Dublin
19	Raymond, Bernard (Bennie) (SMA), Blackrock Road, Cork	
20	Clenaghan, Gerard (OMI), House of Retreat, Tyrconnell Road, Inchicore, Dublin 8	
24	Fitzgerald, Shane (SVD), 3 Pembroke Road, Ballsbridge, Dublin 4	
28	Murray, Patrick (Canon), Athlone	Elphin

October 2011

1	Halliden, Donal (SSC), St Columban's, Dalgan Park, Navan, Co. Meath	
3	O'Byrne, John (Simon) (OFM), Franciscan Friary, Killiney, Co. Dublin	
5	Nolan, Patrick (CSSp), c/o Holy Spirit Provincialate, Temple Park, Richmond Ave South, Dublin 6	
8	McKeown, Hugh (SMA), Dromantine, Newry, Co. Down	
9	O'Leary, Michael (Mgr), St John's Parish Centre, Castle Street, Tralee, Co. Kerry	Kerry
12	Gaffney, Liam, Derrylin, Co. Fermanagh	Kilmore
17	Browne, David, Ardpatrick, Co. Limerick	Limerick
19	O'Loughlin, Padhraic (SSC), St Columban's, Dalgan Park, Navan, Co. Meath	
20	McCarthy, Sylvius (OFM Cap), Capuchin Friary, Cork	
21	Woods, Thomas (CM), St Paul's, Sybil Hill, Raheny, Dublin 5	
26	O'Mahony, John (MSC), Woodview House, Mt Merrion Avenue, Blackrock, Co. Dublin	
30	Kernan, Niall (SM), Honiara, Solomon Islands	

November 2011
4	McGlinchey, James, Nazareth House, Fahan, Co. Donegal	Derry
14	Canning, Gerald (CC), Naul	Dublin
22	Ryan, Brendan (OP), Arima, Trinidad & Tobago	
28	Cantwell, Brendan (PP), Castledermot	Dublin
28	Kenny, Peter (IC), East Africa	
29	Heffernan, Columba (OSA), Hammersmith, London	
29	Ó Sabhaois, Tomás (Canon, PE), Avila Nursing Home, Convent Hill, Bessbrook, Newry, Co. Down BT35 7AW	Armagh
29	Walsh, John (OSA), Abbeyside, Co. Waterford	

December 2011
2	O'Donnell, Shaun (SSC), St Columban's, Dalgan Park, Navan, Co. Meath	
4	Cunningham, Joseph (Canon), Our Lady's Nursing Home, 68 Ardnava Road, Belfast	Down & Connor
9	O'Callaghan, John, Drimoleague, Co. Cork	Cork & Ross
9	Walsh, Patrick (MSC), Western Road, Cork	
19	Dunne, Christopher (OMI), Rushmere, 32 Allanson Road, Rhosonsea Conwy, North Wales	
19	Moore, Brian (Provincial) (CM), St Paul's, Sybil Hill, Raheny, Dublin 5	
23	McCarthy, Sean (SMA), Blackrock Road, Cork	
23	McHugh, Sean, Bohernasup, Ballina	Killala
25	✠ Finnegan, Thomas A. (Most Rev.), Retired Bishop of Killala, Carrowmore Lacken, Ballina	Elphin/Killala
26	Herlihy, Ronan (OFM Cap), Capuchin Friary, Cork	
27	O'Donnell, Columba (OSA), Abbeyside, Co. Waterford	
28	Cleere, Martin (PP), Windgap, Co. Kilkenny	Ossory
31	Purcell, Edmond (CSSp), Rockwell College, Cashel, Co. Tipperary	
31	Tierney, Mark (OSB), Glenstal Abbey, Limerick	

January 2012
2	McAuley, John (SJ), Milltown Park, Dublin 6	
4	Lynch, Dominic (PE), Banagher, Co. Offaly	Ardagh & Clonmacnois
13	FitzGerald, John (SJ), 35 Lower Leeson Street, Dublin 2	
14	Murphy, Malachy (Canon), Our Lady's Nursing Home, 68 Ardnava Road, Belfast	Down & Connor

| **January 2012 (continued)** | **Diocese** |

14 O'Sullivan, Liam (CSSp), Marian House,
   Kimmage Manor, Dublin 12
15 Pierse, Tom, 32 Knockmoyle Estate, Tralee, Co. Kerry   Kerry

18 Bergin, Francis, Shinrone, Co. Offaly   Killaloe
18 Scully, Patrick (SSC), St Columban's,
   Dalgan Park, Navan, Co. Meath
19 McInerney, Thomas (OP), St Mary's, Tallaght, Dublin 24
19 O'Brien, John, Danville, Bennettsbridge Road,
   Kilkenny   Ossory
22 O'Beirne, James (PE), Moate, Co. Westmeath   Ardagh &
   Clonmacnois
24 Corcoran, Patrick (SM), Chanel College, Coolock, Dublin 5
26 Graham, Edward (CSSp), Laval House, 121 Victoria Park Avenue,
   Toronto, Ontario M4E3S2, Canada
29 Battelle, John Patrick (Canon, PP), 14 Pine Valley,
   Grange Road, Rathfarnham   Dublin
29 O'Brien, Patrick (MI), Chaplain, St Luke's Hospital,
   St Camillus, South Hill Avenue, Blackrock, Co. Dublin
31 McPadden, Charles, Glangevlin, Co. Cavan   Kilmore

February 2012

 1 Walsh, Vincent (SSC), St Columban's, Dalgan Park,
   Navan, Co. Meath
 4 Lavery, Patrick (SJ), Clongowes Wood College, Clane
 7 Lawlor, Seán (CSsR), Mt St Alphonsus, Limerick
 9 O'Donnell, Patrick (CSsR), Clonard Monastery, Belfast
10 Whelan, Patrick (SMA), Claregalway, Co. Galway
15 Cahill, Michael (SMA), Blackrock Road, Cork
16 Clifford, Diarmaid (Leo) (OFM), Franciscan Friary,
   New York, USA
21 Cremins, Richard (SJ), 35 Lower Leeson Street, Dublin 2
28 Hegarty, Walter (OP), St Mary's, The Claddagh, Galway
29 Forrester, Gerard, Our Lady's Nursing Home,
   68 Ardava Road, Belfast   Down &
   Connor

March 2012

 1 Callanan, John (PE), Cairnhill Nursing Home,
   Foxrock, Co. Dublin   Waterford &
   Lismore
 2 Forde, Robert, 6 Cairn Court, Fermoy, Co. Cork   Cloyne
 4 Flanagan, Desmond (OCarm), Terenure College,
   Terenure, Dublin 6W

	March 2012 (continued)	**Diocese**
7	Tormey, James (CC), Ballybrack	Dublin
9	Curry, William (SSC), St Columban's, Dalgan Park, Navan, Co. Meath	
10	O'Donoghue, John Sean (CSSp), Marian House, Kimmage Manor, Dublin 12	
11	Haran, Casimir (CP), Holy Cross Retreat, 432 Crumlin Road, Ardoyne, Belfast BT14 7GE	
13	Sweetman, John, Riverchapel, Gorey, Co. Wexford	Ferns
19	Hopkins, Francis (AP), St Anne's Presbytery, Convent Hill, Co. Waterford	Waterford & Lismore
24	Beecher, Paul (Canon, PE), Bramleigh Lodge Nursing Home, Cahir, Co. Tipperary	Waterford & Lismore
25	Gilhooly, Peter (SPS, CC), Kilmurray, Co. Roscommon	
26	O'Connell, Denis (OMI), House of Retreat, Tyrconnell Road, Inchicore, Dublin 8	
30	Healy, Dermot (Der) (SMA), Blackrock Road, Cork	

April 2012

2	Stanley, James (CSsR, PC), Marianella, 75 Orwell Road, Rathgar, Dublin 6	
5	Murray, Senan Patrick (CSSp), Catholic Church, Askeaton, Co. Limerick	
7	Carrigg, Noel Flannan (MI), St Camillus, Killucan, Co. Westmeath	
10	Healy, Patrick (SSC), St Columban's, Dalgan Park, Navan, Co. Meath	
12	McKenna, Patrick (MI), St Camillus, Killucan, Co. Westmeath	
14	Spillane, Edmund (IC), Nursing Home	
21	McPartlan, Peter, Ballintemple, Co. Cavan	Kilmore
30	O'Sullivan, John L. (CSSp), Marian House, Kimmage Manor, Dublin 12	

May 2012

4	Coffey, John (MSC), 65 Terenure Rd West, Dublin 6W	
4	Kelly, Patrick (SJ), Milltown Park, Dublin 6	
7	Brereton, Joseph (SJ), Clongowes Wood College, Clane	
7	Connolly, Finbarr (CSsR), St Joseph's Monastery, Dundalk	
11	McDonnell, Thomas (PP), Naas, Sallins, Two-Mile House, Co. Kildare	Kildare & Leighlin

	May 2012 (continued)	**Diocese**
24	Candon, Cyprian (OP), St Saviour's, Dorset Street, Dublin 1	
25	Dunne, Sean A. (SSC), St Columban's, Dalgan Park, Navan, Co. Meath	

June 2012

12	Ward, Andrew (OSCO), Mellifont Abbey, Collon, Co. Louth	
14	Doona, Jeremiah (MHM), 50 Orwell Park, Rathgar, Dublin 6	
18	McHugh, Dominic (Canon), 79 Castle Street, Ballymoney, Co. Antrim	Down & Connor
19	Nealon, Edward (CSSp), Holy Spirit Missionaries, Ardbraccan, Navan, Co. Meath	
20	Corbally, James (MSC), Woodview House, Mt Merrion Ave, Blackrock, Co. Dublin	

July 2012

1	Byrne, John Joseph (CSSp), Templeogue College, Templeville Road, Dublin 6W	
5	Cronin, Anthony, Island Road, Newmarket, Co. Cork	Cloyne
6	Brennan, Stan (OFM), Franciscan Friary, Boxbury, South Africa	
8	Kennedy, Edmund, Youghalarra, Co. Tipperary	
10	Deane, Philip (OFM), Franciscan Friary, Cork	
16	Murray, Francis, 42 Knockmoyle Road, Omagh, Co. Tyrone, BT79 7TB	Derry
22	Gaffney, Peter (OP), St Mary's, The Claddagh, Galway	

Award Winning Printers

Fine Lithographic Printers

Specialising in promotional literature and marketing material

Fully automated Heidelberg CTP system

State of the art Heidelberg printing presses

Operating 24 hours a day, 5 days a week

High quality and competitive prices

Over 30 years of excellence

Unit B14 Ballycoolin Business Park Blanchardstown Dublin 15
T. +353 1 829 3450 F. +353 1 829 3451 E. print@hudsonkilleen.ie
W. www.hudsonkilleen.ie

RPD Limited is proud to have been a sponsor of IEC2012.

50th INTERNATIONAL EUCHARISTIC CONGRESS

*Specialists in Church Envelopes,
Memorial Cards, School Calendars,
Mass Cards, Christmas & Easter Cards.*

*Unit 25/26 Tolka Valley Business Park,
Ballyboggan Rd., Glasnevin, Dublin 11.
Phone: (+353) 1- 8603088,
Email: emmet@rpd.ie,
Web: www.rpd.ie*

RPD LIMITED

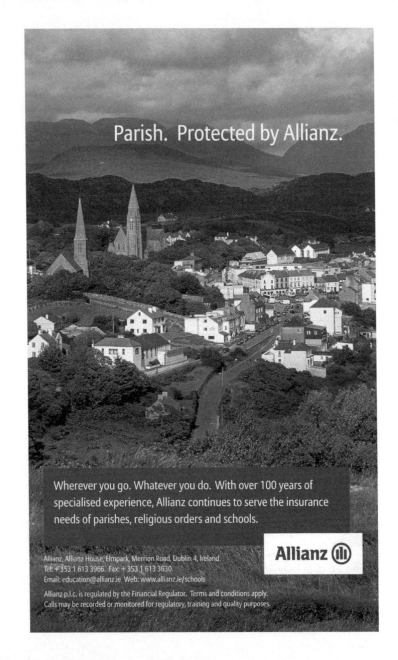

MASON HAYES & CURRAN

Many Minds On Your Charity Matters

Mason Hayes & Curran has the largest charity law team in Ireland. We have extensive experience in serving the specific needs of public benefit entities, such as charity and not-for-profit clients, based on practical insight, legal knowledge and relevant experience.

Clients of Mason Hayes & Curran are active in all areas including:

- Education
- Healthcare
- Housing
- Relief of poverty
- Environmental
- Advocacy
- Religious
- Overseas aid

For further information, please contact:

Edward Gleeson
Partner
t +353 1 614 2438
e egleeson@mhc.ie

Kevin Hoy
Partner
t +353 1 614 5812
e khoy@mhc.ie

MHC.ie

Dublin, London & New York

MAKE A DEGRE OF DIFFEENCE!
Mature applicants welcome

ALL HALLOWS COLEGE
Drumcondra, Dublin 9

UNDERGRADUATE PROGRAMMES

BA in Theology & Philosophy
BA in Theology & English Literature
BA in Theology & Psychology
Part-time Adult Learning BA (ALBA)

POSTGRADUATE PROGRAMMES

MA in Applied Christian Spirituality *(full- and part-time)*
MA in Ecology and Religion *(part-time over two years)*
MA in Leadership & Pastoral Care *(full- and part-time)*
MA in Management: Community & Voluntary Services *(full- & part-time)*
MA in Social Justice & Public Policy *(part-time over two years)*
MA in Supervisory Practice *(full-time over one year)*
Research Masters and Doctoral Degrees

**Academic Services Unit, All Hallows College,
Drumcondra, Dublin 9.
T: +353 1 837 3745   E: asu@allhallows.ie**

All Hallows College is a college of Dublin City University
All degrees are validated and accredited by DCU

Church Brass Refurbished

Polished and Lacquered

Also: Items Manufactured

Contact:

**MICHAEL J. SHANLEY
Cloonturk, Dromod,
Co. Leitrim
Telephone: 071-9638296 • 087-4135775**

THE NATIONAL BIBLE SOCIETY OF IRELAND
And Bestseller Bookshop

The widest possible effective distribution of the Holy Scriptures

'Bestseller', the Society's bookshop, will meet all your needs for religious books and special orders with discounts for members. Mail order welcome. All major credit cards accepted.

Special grants available for Scripture Resources for parish initiatives. Training courses are also available. Individuals and parishes may support the work by becoming members of the Society.

BRIATHAR DÉ NOCHTAITHE DO CHÁCH
GOD'S WORD OPEN FOR ALL

Contact: Ms. Judith Wilkinson, Chief Executive
41 Dawson Street, Dublin 2
Tel (01) 677 3272 • Fax (01) 671 0040
Email nbsi@natbibsoc.iol.ie
Website www.biblesociety.ie
Charity No. CHY1592

Serving all Irish Churches with the Holy Scriptures
Under the patronage of Most Rev Diarmuid Martin, Archbishop of Dublin,
and other church leaders

www.veritas.ie

Need something proofed, designed or simply printed?

THINK **VERITAS**

Booklets
Brochures
Fliers
Leaflets
Annual Reports

Catalogues
Prayer Cards
Bookmarks
Business Stationery

For anything you are thinking of publishing,

THINK **VERITAS**

For more information, contact
publications@veritas.ie

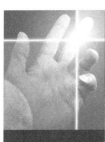

study theology by distance learning

Degree, diploma and certificate programmes

The Priory Institute, established in the Dominican tradition, is a centre for theological studies.

The Institute offers a variety of academic programmes, specialising in distance education.

Certificate, Diploma, Higher Certificate and Degree Programmes

(also open to those studying without academic credit)

Major Awards

Bachelor of Arts (Hons) in Theology (4 Years; NFQ Level 8)
Bachelor of Arts in Theology (3 Years; NFQ Level 7)
Higher Certificate in Theology (2 Years; NFQ level 7)

Minor Awards

Diploma in Theology (1 Year; NFQ level 7)
Diploma in Philosophy (1 Year; NFQ level 7)
Diploma in Scripture (1 Year; NFQ level 7)
Certificate in Theology (1 Year; NFQ level 6)
(*NFQ = National Framework of Qualifications)

All programmes are validated by the Institute of Technology Tallaght, Dublin

Study theology in your own home
For further information call 01 404 8124
enquiries@prioryinstitute.com
www.prioryinstitute.com

THE PRIORY INSTITUTE Tallaght Village, Dublin 24

Desmond Wisley Ecclesiastical Supplies

Ballinamore, Co. Leitrim. **Phone:** 071 9645921
Fax: 071 9645238 **Email:** wisley@eircom.net
Dessie Mobile: 087 2317921
Aileen Mobile: 087 2408559

SPECIALS AT WISLEY'S

MASS HOSTS

LOW GLUTEN ALTAR BREAD
Can be consumed by people who suffer from gluten sensitivity.
35mm or 13/8"
with single cross design in White
(50 Per Jar)

€9.00

Why not get an **ALTAR CLOTH** made to your own measurements with plenty of designs to choose from.

PRIEST'S HOSTS
70mm or 23/4" with double sided single cross design in white and stopped edges prevent crumbling.
(50 per sealed roll)

€4.00

Buy 10 jars or 10 boxes get 1 free!

JAR OF 1000
€12.00

BOX OF 1,000
(10 ROLLS OF 100) **€11.50**

35mm or 13/8" with double sided single cross design in White. These have carefully moulded sealed edges which prevent crumbling. (10 rolls in a sealed box, 1,000 in total)
Hosts also Available in 29mm & 38mm

Official wine of the 2012 Eucharistic Congress.

ALTAR WINE

Our Altar Wine has been approved by Ecclesiastical Authority and follows the indications of the Holy Congregation for the discipline of the sacraments.

Altaris Wine (1Ltr.)
€ 110 per case

Twelve Apostles (.75cl)
€ 110 per case

ANGELA 7 DAY SANCTUARY CANDLES
all for **€165!**

Buy 3, get a 4th Box Free

Look at our new webiste at **www.desmondwisley.com**

OUR ALTAR BREADS ARE PRODUCED IN ACCORDANCE WITH THE CANON LAW

• **BEST PRICES IN IRELAND** •

St. Finbarr's Altar Breads Supplies Ltd.

Altarbreads, votive candles, sanctuary candles, incense, charcoal, mass cards, and religious books.

Farranferris Education and Training Campus,
Redemption Road, Cork
Tel: 021 4300227 *Fax:* 021 4228199
Email: altarbreads@nce.ie

OFFICE HOURS: 9.00AM - 5.00PM
AFTER HOURS TELEPHONE ANSWERING SERVICE AVAILABLE
COLLECTION AND POSTAL SERVICE AVAILABLE

VERITAS

NOW OPEN IN LOURDES

BOOKS • GIFTS • ART

Veritas Lourdes
13 Rue du Bourg
65100 Lourdes
France
Tel: +33 5624 222794
lourdesshop@veritas.ie

www.veritas.ie

**Live Video Streaming of Church Services on the Internet,
Parish Radio Link Service to Housebound Parishioners-WPAS**

BELLS & CLOCKS
- Bells – Automation, Restoration & Re-hanging
- Survey, Maintenance and Replacement of Bell Support Structures
- Digital Electronic Bells & Carillons via speakers – (1000 hymns/peals)
- Tower Clocks – Hour Ringing – Westminster Chime
- Liturgical Calendar Event Programming

COMMUNICATIONS
- The Parish Radio Link System
- Live Streaming Video of Church Services on the Internet
- Sound & PA Amplification, Radio Microphones etc
- Audio Induction Loops for the Deaf
- Church Music Systems & Radio Remote Control

ENGINEERING & BUILDING MAINTENANCE
- Bell Support Structure installation and restoration
- Water ingress protection. Guttering & drains – cleaning – repair
- Pointing and sealing of stone. Roofing slates, tiles & flashing repairs
- Stone surface cleaning & restoration
- Lightening Protection: Dynasphere 3000 & Traditional systems
- Automation – Control of Heating, Lighting, Door opening etc
- Height Access for Survey's & Engineering reports

Installations by our Experienced, Highly Qualified and
Fully Insured Technical Team
Full Guarantees & After Sales Support
Contact Jim Doyle

Head Office: Dunleary House
83 Dublin Road, Sutton, Dublin 13
Tel/Fax 01-8392220 • Mobile 087-2538916
Email info@belltron.ie • Website www.belltron.ie

VERITAS IS PROUD TO OFFER OUR
CUSTOMERS THE FINEST SELECTION OF BIBLES

*From children's and teens' Bibles,
to family, study and gift editions,
Veritas has a bible to suit
all ages and needs.*

Order now online at www.veritas.ie
or email *derek.byrne@veritas.ie* to request
a copy of our new Bible catalogue.

The Irish Catholic

Ireland's biggest and best-selling religious newspaper offering news, comment, indepth analysis, and features showcasing the life of Catholics in parishes and communities across the country and from throughout the world.

Your invaluable source.
If you would like to promote The *Irish Catholic* in your area or community please call 01-6874020.

The Irish Catholic
St Mary's
Bloomfield Avenue
Donnybrook
Dublin 4

www.irishcatholic.ie
news@irishcatholic.ie

Visit Veritas Online

Check out our great website,
with hundreds of books and gifts
available for purchase online.

Free delivery in Ireland.

www.veritas.ie

www.veritas.ie

SOUND

AUDIOVISUAL

CCTV

LOOP SYSTEMS

ACOUSTICS

CONFERENCING

Established 1990

grainger
COMMUNICATION LTD

specialists in sound

Providing the complete communication solution, from acoustic and consultancy services through to installation and commissioning of systems

All acoustic work is carried out by our in-house certified acoustic engineer

- Acoustic Analysis & Simulation
- System Design & Specification
- Installation & Commissioning
- System Upgrade & Maintenance Service

0044 (0)28 8224 4800
sales@graingercommunication.com
www.graingercommunication.com

EMMAUS

Emmaus Retreat & Conference Centre, Dublin, Ireland

*The Emmaus Centre provides
an excellent location for Seminars, Workshops, Chapters
and Parish Renewal Day Programmes.
Our facilities include:*

- *Wide Selection of Meeting/Conference Rooms Available*
- *62 Ensuite Bedrooms*
- *2 Prayer Rooms*
- *Private Chapel – (Available for Small Private Weddings)*
- *Extensive Grounds for quiet reflection*
- *Free Car Parking*
- *Wheel Chair Accessible Rooms*
- *Massage and Therapy Room*

*For information on our excellent all inclusive conference
packages, starting from €25.00 per person.
For a complete programme of our in-house Retreat and
Workshops being held at Emmaus in 2011
call us on Dublin 8700050
Or Log onto our website www.emmauscentre.ie
Email niall@emmauscentre.ie*

Emmaus Retreat and Conference Centre,
Ennis Lane, Lissenhall, Swords, Co. Dublin

O'Donovan Pipe Organs

Tuning & Maintenance, Restoration, Installations.

A selection of Quality Instruments from the UK is currently offered for sale, both 1 and 2 manuals.

A refurbished Pipe Organ provides the cost effective solution to obtaining a superior quality instrument , for the same price as an electronic!

Harmonium restorations.

Call Pádraig on, 023-8838802 or 086-1550033

Address: Gurranes, Ballineen, Co. Cork

Email: odonovanorgans@gmail.com

www.odonovanorgans.com

KN☘C K

OUR LADY'S SHRINE, CO. MAYO

Phone: (094) 93 88100 • Fax: (094) 93 88295
www.knock-shrine.ie • Email: info@knock-shrine.ie

Programme of Ceremonies and Devotions April 28th - Oct 13th, 2013
6 Public Masses each day. Confessions from 11.00 am onwards
Public Devotions: Weekdays 2.00 pm Sundays 2.30 pm
National Public Novena (14 - 22 Aug. incl.) 3.00 pm & 8.30 pm

The Apparition Chapel – Knock Shrine

KNOCK MUSEUM

Knock Museum captures the compelling story of the Knock
Apparition of 1879 and the fifteen ordinary people who witnessed
this extraordinary event. Open Daily: 10.00 am – 6.00 pm
Tel: 094 9375034   **Email:** museum@knock-shrine.ie

CAFÉ LE CHÉILE

Great Food All Day ♦ Groups Welcome
Open Daily: 10.00 am – 6.00 pm
Tel: 094 9375350   **Email:** cafelecheile@knock-shrine.ie

**FOR RELIGIOUS BOOKS AND SOUVENIRS YOU CAN
NOW SHOP ONLINE AT www.knock-shrine.ie/shop**

THE CHURCH FURNITURE SPECIALISTS

*For your Church Furniture requirements
Traditional or Modern contact the experts*

IRISH CONTRACT SEATING

**DROMOD, CARRICK-ON-SHANNON, CO. LEITRIM
TEL: (071) 9638230 • FAX: (071) 9638290
Email: info@icsfurniture.com • Website www.icsfurniture.com**

*Irish Contract Seating
are Ireland's most experienced manufacturers of*

CHURCH PEWS • KNEELER PADDING
SANCTURAY FURNITURE
STACKING CHAIRS IN WOOD AND STEEL

• DISTANCE OF DELIVERY IS NO PROBLEM! •

We can supply
IRELAND, ENGLAND, SCOTLAND & WALES

All overseas orders delivered by our own transport direct via Car Ferry

ST KIERAN'S COLLEGE, KILKENNY
(founded 1782)

St Kieran's is a Catholic Diocesan College under the patronage of the Bishop of Ossory

It has two objectives:
To provide a well-rounded education at second level and to furtherongoing formation and education for mature students.

The College has four departments on one campus:

1 **A secondary day school for boys** which offers a complete programme at second level to 700 pupils, with a wide range of sporting and extracurricular activities.

2 **Theological Studies** which aims to provide general theological education and formation in the main aspects of faith and provide the theological background needed for lay involvement and leadership roles at parish and diocesan level.

3 **The National University of Ireland, Maynooth** which offers an off campus degree course (BA in Local and Community Studies) and a range of other initiatives for mature students.

The Kilkenny Research & Innovation Centre for research teams from Telecommunication Software and Systems Group in WIT and Carlow IT.

The College also provides office facilities for the the Co-ordinator of the Ossory Diocesan Pastoral Council, the Director of Vocations and the Director of Ossory Adult Faith Development.

**For further information apply to:
The President, St Kieran's College, Kilkenny
Telephone 056-7721086 • Fax 056-7770001
Email skc1782@iol.ie • Web www.stkieranscollege.ie**

CHURCH GOODS

CHURCH VESTMENTS • TABERNACLES
CHALICES • MASS KITS • ALTAR LINENS

UNIQUE RELIGIOUS ART PIECES FOR HOMES

BANNERS MADE TO ORDER
STATUARY AND CRIBS

Liturgical Centre

pddm

8 Castle Street, Athlone
Tel (090) 6492278 • Fax (090) 6492649

Newtownpark Avenue, White Cross,
Blackrock, Dublin
Tel (01) 288 6414 • Fax (01) 283 6935
Email pddmdublin@eircom.net
Website www.pddm.org/ireland

Spirit Radio is a registered charity
and while it will carry some amount of
sponsorship & advertising,
we are largely dependent on
donations to carry out our mission.

To support Spirit Radio please visit us online
www.spiritradio.ie

Your support will make a difference.

With a nationwide service, Dectek
Offers maintenance and support contracts
Keeping your business IT costs low and
Performance high. We are here to let
You get on with your core business.

26 Redleaf Bus Park
Roseville
Turvey Avenue
Donabate
Co. Dublin
Tel +353 (1) 8219002
Fax +353 (1) 8219004
www.dectek.ie

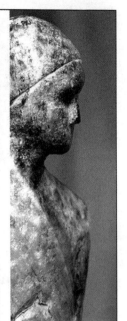

FROM VERITAS

ART FOR CHURCHES, PARISH CENTRES, PARISH GROUPS AND SCHOOLS

Contact: Mary Kelly Flynn
Veritas, 16–18 Park Street, Monaghan
Ph: (+353 47) 84077
monaghanshop@veritas.ie
www.veritas.ie

 VERITAS

Founded in 1944

The Abbey Stained Glass Studios

Specialists in Ecclesiastical Work
Designers and Manufacturers of Stained Glass
Restoration of Old and Damaged Stained Glass
Stormglazing
Glass Etching and Sandblasting
Dalle de Verre
Opus Sectile
Stations of the Cross
Bronze Ventilators

***Contact:* WILLIE MALONE**
KEN RYAN

**18 Old Kilmainham
Kilmainham, Dublin 8, Ireland
TELEPHONE: 01-677 7285
Mobile: 087-738 9749
Website www.abbeystainedglassstudios.ie
Email enquiries@asgs.ie**

VERITAS

NOW OPEN
IN NEWRY

BOOKS • GIFTS • ART

Veritas Newry
40-41 The Mall
Newry
Co. Down
BT34 1AN
Tel: +44 28 302 50321
newryshop@veritas.ie

www.veritas.ie

Index of Advertisers

Abbey Stained Glass	203
Allianz	174
All Hallows College	178
Art Glass	185
Aungier Print	177
Belltron	187
CBC	206
churchservices.tv	182
Dectek	201
Emmaus	193
Grainger Communications	192
Hudson Killeen	173
Intercom Magazine	176
Irish Catholic, The	190
Irish Contract Seating	196
Kevin Kearney	188
Knock Shrine	195
Liturgical Centre	199
Mason Hayes & Curran	175
National Bible Society	179
O'Donovan Pipe Organs	194
Paceprint Ltd	197
Priory Institute, The	181
Rollebon Press	Inside Front Cover
RPD Limited	173
St Finbarr's Altar Bread Supplies Ltd	184
St Kieran's College	198
Shanley, Michael J.	179
Sheridan Stained Glass Creations Ltd	Inside Back Cover
Spirit Radio	200
Veritas	180, 186, 189, 191, 202, 204
Wisley Ecclesiastical Supplies	183

Comprehensive Selection of Church Furnishings and Supplies.

Church Candles | Altar Wine | Incense & Charcoal
Mass Kits | Priest's Sick Call Sets | Indoor & Outdoor Statuary Vestments
Stations of the Cross | Lecterns | Priedieux
Tabernacles | Papal Blessings | Chalices | Ciboria

 CBC DISTRIBUTORS
Greenbank, Newry, Co. Down BT34 2JP
Tel: (028) 3026 5216 **Fax:** (028) 3026 3927
If dialling from the Irish Republic: **Tel:** (042) 93 32321/2 **Fax:** (042) 93 37248
www.cbcdistributors.co.uk E.Mail: sales@cbcdistributors.co.uk